IN LIGHT AND IN SHADE

The Inspirational Story Of A Love That Refused To Die,
Even After Death

PATRICIA IRVINE

For permission, serialization, condensation, adaptions, or for our catalog of other publications, write to Ozark Mountain Publishing, Inc., P.O. Box 754, Huntsville, AR 72740, ATTN: Permissions Department.

Library of Congress Cataloging-in-Publication Data

Irvine, Patricia − 1950 -
In Light and In Shade by Patricia Irvine

A story anyone seeking answers to the big questions about life and death should read.

1. Spiritual   2. Healing   3. Death/Afterlife 4. Metaphysical
I. Irvine, Patricia, 1950 - II. Metaphysical   III. Healing   IV. Title

Library of Congress Catalog Card Number:2019938317
ISBN: 9781940265735

Cover Art and Layout: Victoria Cooper Art
Book set in: Calafornia FB, Footlight MT Light
Book Design: Tab Pillar
Published by:

OZARK
MOUNTAIN
PUBLISHING

PO Box 754, Huntsville, AR 72740
800-935-0045 or 479-738-2348; fax 479-738-2448
WWW.OZARKMT.COM

Printed in the United States of America

'Even if you are a minority of one, the truth is the truth'
~ Mahatma Gandhi

<u>The Healing Power of Words</u>

The following are comments and endorsements received from beta readers:

"Thank you for asking me to check your manuscript, I read it straight through as it grasped my attention immediately." ~ Julie Francis

"What a magnificent, spiritual story!" ~ D Graham

"How comforting it was to read your enthralling and fascinating book." ~ J Edwards

"...your words mean so much to us and we have found them to be both interesting and reassuring." ~ Julie Francis

"Thank you for your wonderful words I shall keep your writings in my mind." ~J Edwards

"Knowing you to be straight, frank and honest, your 'revelations' are even more compelling." ~ Julie Francis

Dedication

This book is dedicated to the memory of my beloved husband,

Malcolm Campbell Irvine

And also
To the memory of

Frederick Stephen Aldridge and Mary Elizabeth Aldridge,

My beloved parents

Acknowledgements

In addition to my sons and all those mentioned in
the book who travelled this journey with me,
I wish to thank my UK editor, Kim Kimber
(www.kimkimber.co.uk).

Her quiet encouragement and clear and obvious
knowledge was inspirational and greatly assisted in
the successful production of this book.

Prologue

Our lives changed on 1 March 1996. Prior to that date, life with Malcolm Campbell Irvine had been like living in a golden bubble, where we were treasured and protected. My sons and I were the centre of Malcolm's universe, surrounded by his love. We knew it and felt it, always.

Early that day Malcolm had set off from Mulberry Down, our Surrey home, to board his yacht *Mulberry*, moored at Port Solent, Portsmouth. He was smiling broadly and was armed with a fresh batch of his favourite homemade cakes, joyfully anticipating the weekend ahead. Malcolm was always a very private person and normally undemonstrative in public, so I was pleasantly surprised when he doubled-back to the doorway and kissed me firmly goodbye before leaving.

Malcolm was planning to step back a little from the arduous hours that he worked in the family business and he hoped to spend some of his newly anticipated free time giving sailing lessons on board the *Mulberry*, to young people less fortunate than his own children.

He had already passed his Yachtmaster's Certificate but had chosen to repeat it this particular weekend with Clare and Bryan, two of his regular young crew. He wanted to ensure that his qualifications were first class and totally up to the mark if he was to be responsible for youngsters.

It was a warm spring day. I remained in Surrey and was out for several hours with friends enjoying it fully before returning home in good time to collect our youngest son, Duncan, from school. Golden rays of sun poured through the conservatory windows, lighting the blooms I was arranging in a vase. As I placed the final piece of greenery, the doorbell rang ...

Moments later, our protective bubble burst and our glorious family life was shattered. Clare, Malcolm's sailing companion, was at the door. Intuitively, I knew that something was very, very wrong and that she had come to give me dreadful news. My initial fear was that Malcolm had drowned.

But he hadn't drowned. While still full of anticipation for the weekend ahead, Malcolm had suffered an aortic heart aneurysm and died that morning on board his beloved yacht. Clare explained that Malcolm, the instructor and the crew had been enjoying coffee and cakes, chatting together, while sailing through the Portsmouth Harbour entrance. Never one to make a fuss or complain, Malcolm had suddenly said, very quietly, "I have a pain in my chest. It really is quite severe." He then slumped to the cockpit floor.

The instructor leapt into action and within minutes a helicopter and crew from Royal Hospital Haslar, Gosport, were in attendance. Malcolm had the very best possible attention but nothing could be done. He was dead. From that moment and yet, completely unknown to us at the time, the colour of our lives was being washed from gold ... to grey.

Brave young Clare had insisted on telling me herself; she couldn't bear the thought of me receiving such news from police strangers. She had driven past Mulberry Down several times that day waiting for my car to reappear in the driveway. Finally it had.

Inexplicably, there were no tears from me. A deep, deep sadness filled me from the very core of my being but there were no tears. There was an immense feeling of calm, of logic, and most definitely, being 'in charge'. A great, long list of things to do was clicking into place in my brain. It was as though I was being told 'not to waste time on tears but to get on with the job in hand'. I was being pushed, gently, from behind ...

I couldn't understand it at all but was powerless to do anything else but follow the calm, quiet orders I was receiving. It made sense to do exactly as directed at that time. I immediately rang Malcolm's brother, Ian, at the office. Clare stayed with me. I ensured that Ian was alone and asked him to close the door and sit down before I told him the news.

The next priority was Duncan. He was twelve years old, still at school, and needed to be collected. Clare offered to do this for me and brought him home. Then I took him into the lounge and told him, as gently as I could, the devastating news. "My father? Not my *father*?" he repeated several times as the awful reality sank in.

Knowing that I must travel to Charles and Alastair, at school in Canterbury, I rang my stepdaughter Karen's mother and explained what had happened. She was distraught but I asked her to speak to Karen on my behalf, as I couldn't possibly be in two places at once.

By this time, Bryan, the other crew member, having returned from re-berthing the *Mulberry*, had joined Clare, Duncan and I in Surrey. I telephoned the housemaster at King's Canterbury saying that I needed to visit in order to speak urgently to my sons that evening.

We hastily packed overnight bags and set off for Kent. Bryan drove my car. Clare sat in the front and I remained in the back with Duncan. The shocked silence was tangible and the awful enormity of the situation threatened to chip away at my calm façade. I knew I had to remain resolute. I could not dissolve. My sons needed me to remain strong, dependable, and reliable. Breaking down was a luxury I couldn't afford.

On arrival, Duncan and I were taken to the matron's office and shortly joined by my two bewildered-looking sons, Alastair and Charlie. Telling my sons that day of their father's death was one of the most difficult and horrendous tasks of my life. The colour drained from their faces. They were stunned but they too kept calm, as we all silently clasped one another in a much-needed family hug.

They returned to their dorms to pack and then, with Clare and Bryan, we travelled to Mulberry Cottage, our home in Kent, where we spent that night.

I arranged for my brother, Stephen, to call the next morning. There was still this inexplicable influence filling my mind with calm and logic but there was also a crushing sadness that reached every part of me. It was as though I had 'stepped outside' my own body and was watching my actions from a different perspective. I felt like a puppet with an invisible puppet master.

Stephen arrived and explaining what had happened to him was a daunting task as he was a very close friend of Malcolm. Together, he and I drove the short distance to my parents' home where I repeated the awful news once more. Watching my beloved parents' faces crumple as I repeated the events of the previous day was heartbreaking. They loved Malcolm like a son and bringing this pain to them equalled my own despicable sadness.

Little did I know at the time that I had only just taken the first steps of what would prove to be an incredible journey of realisation and proof that life continues after death. And, as we later discovered, we would not only have to deal with Malcolm's death, but also cope with a long court battle with his brother over the family business.

'I flourish in light and in shade' is the Irvine family motto. That is what we, Malcolm Campbell Irvine's family, tried hard to do. Love can be glorious, wonderful and enthralling. It can be deeply painful too. But, as I was about to learn, love can be stronger, *far* stronger, than anything else seen or unseen.

The names and identifying details of some individuals have been changed to protect their privacy.

Chapter 1
As Black and White as a Zebra!

February 1999

I was still reeling from Malcolm's tragic death, when I was approached by Derrick, a friend and member of our local operatic society, who said quietly, "Patricia, I can see your distress. I belong to the Belgravia branch of the Spiritual Association of Great Britain and if you ever need my help, please, just ask."

I had been a member of Betchworth Operatic & Dramatic Society (BODS) for many years and had remained involved following Malcolm's death as I had been made chairwoman and did not want to let down my friends and fellow members halfway through a production.

Derrick was in his sixties and had known Malcolm and me for around seventeen years. The subject of 'spiritualism' had never before been mentioned. I had no real knowledge of the subject and had always felt that it was rather irreverent. I wasn't remotely interested in pursuing a spiritualist path at all. My Christian upbringing made me fear that it could possibly be downright dangerous.

My reply was fairly typical of my character at that time. I was shocked, sceptical and a little afraid. Jokingly, I replied, "Oh Lord, Derrick, I couldn't bear the thought of Malcolm telling me that I'm doing everything wrong and my not being able to answer him back." I dismissed the entire subject from my mind. In those days, my views on spiritualism were totally black and white.

Feeling terribly alone, and with three sons to care for, I had more than enough to deal with. I certainly had no wish to dabble in things which felt completely foreign to me. I battled on, trying to cope with wearing both mother and father hats for my young sons;

organising our lives and homes, desperately trying to keep all our heads above water. No more was said and life ground on much as before.

But by the winter of 1998–99 I had reached an all-time low. I found I could not stem the frequent flow of tears when I was alone. Friends, who realised that I was not the person I once was, began insisting that I go to the doctor. But I feared the suggested solution would be Prozac or similar, which I did not want. I did not want a suppressant. What I needed was reassurance.

I longed for the promise of my Christian childhood upbringing that death is not an end, but a new beginning. This was something I had been taught since birth, that there is a safe haven where life continues after death on earth. If ever there was a time when I needed proof, it was now. I needed to know that the man I married still cared for me, still loved me and would continue to guide me after his death.

I was forty-five years old. I had been loved, cherished and protected by my wonderful husband. Now, in my depths of despair, I needed solid reassurance. I wanted absolute proof in order to help me accept and continue forward in this game called life. Somewhere, in the depths of my mind from all those many months previously, I remembered Derrick's words. One evening, when the children were in bed I decided to ring him.

His response was immediate. He and his wife, Diane, invited me to accompany them to Belgravia the following Tuesday so that they, in a safe environment, could introduce me to the spiritualist experience. It was their generosity of spirit which enabled me to explore the possibility that spiritualism might offer a way to soothe my deeply troubled soul.

We spoke little on the journey. Derrick and Diane responded to any questions I had, but there were few. They knew me very well. No attempt was made to convince me of anything. They were simply allowing me to go with them in the hope that it would help me in some way.

What I recall most clearly is that, within those walls, I felt an immense peace. It calmed my soul. It was virtually tangible. My experience that evening, quite simply, broke any taboo I'd previously harboured in my mind about the concept of spiritualism and, more importantly, I knew I had felt the first stirrings of healing.

Yet, alone again the next day, I once more felt desolate. With my sons and an extended family, it was my duty to pull myself together somehow. My despair was accentuated by the fact that I knew the reassurance I required was from Malcolm, no one else. As I recalled the experiences of the previous evening, I felt more confident that I would find a way forward. I knew now that there was hope.

I had recently read about mediums in Rita Rogers's autobiography, *From One World to Another*, following the death of Princess Diana, whom, it was reported, had been a client of hers. This was the first book I had read on the subject and then, only with a mild curiosity, simply because her book had been featured in a newspaper.

According to Rita, she had also helped people via the telephone. I was so desperate at that time that I had gone as far as finding her number from directory enquiries but my courage had failed me and I didn't pursue it any further.

However, on that day in February 1999 I was so totally desolate and in despair, I summoned my courage. I felt that there was little to lose by trying. After all, how much worse could I feel than I did already?

I tried Rita's number but it was constantly engaged. Since the death of the Princess, she had become extremely busy. I explored the local *Yellow Pages* where there were four or five clairvoyants listed. One, Nina, was based in Brighton and stated in her advertisement, 'also by telephone'.

Nervous and uncertain, I dialled. I knew from reading Rita's book that I should give no information about myself and, when Nina answered, I asked her for her confirmation. "You don't need to," was the reply.

An appointment was made for the next afternoon. I was anxious while waiting. However, I decided that hope, no matter how tenuous, was better than the desolation I had been living through.

This took place prior to my visiting our home in the West Country alone. Malcolm had bought Westfield in Devon two months before he died. It was his dream home for us and I didn't have the heart to sell the property after his death. I let it instead, which would allow me breathing space before making any big decisions. I let it for short-term holidays so the boys and I could use it occasionally, while I made up my mind what to do.

Several months earlier, I had begun discussing plans with an architect about a proposed extension to Westfield. However, I was unhappy with his attitude, his initial plans and his inability to listen to me. He seemed to forget that I was the client and his misogynistic attitude towards me was one which my husband would most definitely not have approved of. It was as though he was designing the extension in order to win an award, or for his own personal ego, rather than my needs.

I discussed this with three architect friends and a quantity surveyor who knew of my concerns. They had studied the proposed plans and were appalled at their lack of detail. They were also astonished at the fees I had paid to date and I was advised by them to sack him and find a more suitable Devon architect. I was grateful for their input but still nervous of what I had to do.

I was without my husband's influence and support. There was no one with whom to share and resolve the complications or to enjoy the project with. I was not looking forward to facing this particular problem, which seemed to stretch out before me like a swathe of quicksand. I felt sick with apprehension.

However, I had spoken to Stephen, my brother, about the situation. His reply was profound, "If you find the courage to do this, you will probably find people thank you for it in the future." He was right, of course. We were brought up to have the courage of our convictions and my intuition regarding this particular matter was very strong. I decided I would take action and end the business relationship when I next went to Devon.

All this was playing heavily on my mind, which is why I contacted Nina. At the agreed time, I telephoned her. Apart from my Christian name and telephone number she knew absolutely nothing about me. No questions were asked by her. Replies only were made by me. I merely listened and noted down her gentle monologue, with pauses occasionally for her silent meditation.

"*I have here a grandmother figure,*" said Nina. "*Several long-haired animals surround her; they could be cats or dogs. Definitely they have long hair. This lady loves animals.*"

"My paternal grandmother had seven long-haired cats," I replied.

"*Her message to you is clear. Indeed, she is a strong spirit and is very definite in her views. She knows there is an event you are not looking forward to. You are full of anxiety and don't want to make a decision. You are to stick up for yourself and say your piece. Live for yourself rather than anyone else. Ask the angels for help. You must have faith in yourself.*"

This shocked me. Nina was describing my grandmother's character exactly. It was remarkable. This was precisely the way my grandmother would have spoken to me. I was anxious, of course, about the architect's planned visit and also, by this time, about the family company, Campbell Irvine Limited (CIL), and the profit share concerns which had recently arisen.

"*I have another person here,*" Nina continued. "*There is a soft, mild-mannered man here now. He is a gentleman. He waited and stood back to allow Granny to finish. Is there something wrong with his voice? No, he has a quiet voice, an exceptionally quiet voice. He is strong but not forceful. He also has a gentle soul. He has tender, romantic, but also protective, feelings towards you. He is a very spiritual person.*"

She was describing my husband perfectly. Malcolm had a very soft and gentle speaking voice. It was one of the things I found most attractive about him. And he was most certainly always a gentleman towards me.

She continued, "*You are full of grief. He knows this. You are intent on protecting your young and he says you are making a great job of this, well done. This shy, gentle man has his head in his hands. He says he is so sorry to have left you with all this responsibility. He is adamant, you must stick up for yourself, do what you think is right. He realises it is hard but you must do it. It is right for you and for your children. He knows you have a lot of integrity. He knows you are right and true. You are to face your fear. The other side will back down. You will get help from above.*

"He is laughing now, and saying that you are stronger than he is. He is also saying, 'Well done,' he is so very proud of you." My eyes welled with tears. I desperately tried to swallow a lump which had risen in my throat.

"Wait!" There was urgency in her voice. *"There is a daughter figure. Do you have a daughter?"*

This was the only question asked. "My husband's daughter from a previous marriage," I said.

Nina continued, *"There is a daughter who has clairvoyant gifts. Question her. She has both heard and seen her father but has said nothing. She doesn't want to upset you. You also have the power to hear. If you learn to listen for his voice, you will hear him also."*

The session was over. I was absolutely astonished. Nina had clearly accessed a route which was open between Malcolm and me. She had spoken with reassurance, yes, but it was more than that. She had spoken with a *knowing*.

I was drained. She had correctly identified Malcolm and had tapped into something that supplied knowledge in order to give me an accurate description of my husband and this resonated so very deeply within me. I felt emotionally exhausted and tearful. However, this time, they were tears of joy, realisation and, above all, hope.

My niece was expected that afternoon and was to spend the weekend with me. The poor girl arrived shortly after my call to Nina. She was dismayed to find me in such a state and I had to try and explain to her, as sensibly as I could, the reason why.

I had taken notes during the telephone reading to aid my memory. I have since learned that some mediums allow sessions to be taped but I knew nothing of this at the time.

Following a good night's sleep, I woke refreshed. I felt as though a great weight had been lifted from me and, once more, a glorious feeling of peace protected me. It was quite wonderful. The healing had indeed begun. The survival evidence I had received helped me incredibly and I began to recover from the deep depression I'd been feeling and I was so very grateful for the reintroduction of hope into my life.

Obviously, I realised that this was not something to discuss over the telephone with my sons. In fact, at that time, I was not sure I would be discussing it with them at all. However, when the Easter holidays came and they all seemed just as deeply sad as I had been, I decided that if Nina's words had helped me, then they could help them too. I kept vigilant and hoped for suitable private moments to occur but I didn't hold out much hope as they were constantly together.

Amazingly, by the end of the weekend, I found that I had indeed found opportunities to speak to Alastair, Charles and Duncan alone. I showed them, independently, the notes I had made during the phone call with Nina in Brighton. They were equally amazed and quietly receptive.

My middle son, Charlie, was very close to his half-sister, Karen. Immediately, he insisted that I should speak to her as soon as possible. He didn't tell me why but he was adamant. My eldest son, Alastair, also asked me to speak to their sister. I was puzzled and explained that I had every intention of speaking to Karen but, naturally, I had wanted to speak to the three of them first.

Because of their insistence, that same weekend, I rang and made plans to visit Karen and her husband, Paul, on the following Wednesday. I arrived at their home in the early evening. Naturally, they were very curious as to why I had asked to see them with such urgency.

I knew that Paul had to go to work and, therefore, decided to read my notes to them aloud, simultaneously to save time. They instantly recognised Malcolm's character and were equally moved. Paul said, "My God, that's Malcolm!"

Soon afterwards, Paul had to leave for work and I stayed longer with Karen. She said, "Tricia, of all the people in my life I had no idea that it would be you who could help me with this problem."

I was puzzled. "What problem, Karen? What do you mean?" I asked.

It was then that she told me she had recently visited a medium herself. Her need was not for reassurance like my own, but to confirm the feelings that she'd experienced first hand. Karen explained that she had been conversant with knowing the future for years, since being a child, and had accurately predicted people's deaths. Many technical developments such as the CD player had also been visualised by her, long before they were developed.

She had tried to discuss such things with her family in the past to no avail. Karen told me that she had recently seen her father in an upstairs mirror, which had frightened her. She'd had no one to turn to, to speak about such things, and it was troubling her a great deal. Karen said that her experiences had become more frequent and stronger since Malcolm's death.

In fact, two weeks prior to her father's death she had told her mother that someone in the family was going to die. She also said that the death would be to do with water and boats. Naturally, I was astonished, as Malcolm had died while sailing.

Karen said that before I arrived, she knew that I was coming to say two particular things. One, that I had had spoken with a medium. Two, that the medium had told me that she is also gifted in this way and I should question her about it. She was right. I was there, unexpectedly, in her lounge, doing exactly that, although the subject had never been discussed by the two of us before.

Karen had been ill, on and off, for years with minor, inexplicable and often unnamed illnesses. She was in hospital more than once and the doctors were at a loss to name either the cause or a cure for her problems. Karen's health had only improved since she began going to a natural healer just over a year previously. I had read that if psychic gifts are not used, and the messages received not passed on, this could result in illness to the medium. Retained information, I understood, could cause harm. This was a possible explanation and I knew that I must try to help.

I spoke to Derrick again, explaining Karen's plight, and said that I wished to help her if I could and to put my own mind at rest. He organised a meeting for Karen and me with the past president of The College of Psychic Studies in Queensberry Place, London.

Clare accompanied us. She had read the notes from Nina's reading as she had always been interested in the subject. Clare had studied several aspects of healing and in the light of recent events was equally keen to explore the subject of spiritualism. As we were stepping into totally uncharted waters, Karen and I were glad of her company.

The only logical explanation I could think of was that Malcolm, distressed to see the enormity of the responsibility Karen has been keeping to herself for years, devised a way for Clare and me to assist her.

Malcolm would never have chosen to leave unfinished business, particularly if it related to one of his children, and I knew that if he found that he was still able to influence things on their behalf, he would do so. It seemed that he drew Clare and me together in order to give relief to me and assistance to Karen. It was as though he had engineered a situation for us to work together, in order to achieve this.

Chapter 2
Exploration and Education

April 1999

Karen, Clare and I visited The College of Psychic Studies as arranged. Prior to our appointment, we waited together for twenty minutes or so in the library. It was a beautiful room, with wall-to-wall, floor-to-ceiling, books on a wide assortment of theological subjects and spiritualism. We were amazed by the fascinating choice of ancient and modern books and we began to delve into one or two. We came to the conclusion, later confirmed during our meeting, that spiritualism is universally tolerant of all religions. The books in the library covered Hinduism, Buddhism, Islam, Catholicism, Christian and Jewish philosophies, etc. Spiritualism is like an umbrella encompassing all, without the constant world-weary, ethnic battles which are sadly so prevalent today.

Clare stayed in the library, while I took Karen into the meeting. We were greeted by a graceful, elderly lady who impressed us both. She was intelligent, sharp-witted and very matter-of-fact about the whole subject. She treated psychic phenomena as though it was commonplace and normal to everyone. I explained that, as her stepmother, I was concerned about Karen. My recent discovery of her ability, coupled with the fact that she had been alone with the knowledge for so many years, troubled me. We were hoping someone could explain the subject more fully to help her.

I took a seat in the corner of the room and listened as Karen discussed her previous experiences. She grew more positive, assertive and stronger in voice and manner than I had realised was possible. She quite literally blossomed. So glad was Karen to be discussing all her worries and fears with someone who believed and understood her that she seemed to be like a flower bud opening before my eyes.

More importantly, Karen began to understand the entire concept and not to think of herself as 'different'. She came away feeling a good deal better and much more confident than ever before.

Karen had lived for years with knowledge that she had neither invited nor wanted. She had been frightened and uncertain of what to do about it. After this experience, however, she was made aware that if she receives information, she can get in touch with the college to unburden herself. Satisfied, and grateful that Karen was on the road to recovery, we said thanks and joined Clare in the library. We later returned home brimming over with our new-found knowledge, totally in awe of all that we had witnessed and learned that day.

After our meeting in London I attended BODS. It was the first time since giving up the chair in order to spend more time in Devon. Earlier in the year I realised that I should get my health in order. Having already attended a medical check-up, I decided that, perhaps, my spiritual health was equally important. So I spoke to a friend at the rehearsal who I knew was involved in alternative therapies and healing remedies. I asked her to suggest a spiritual healer and she gave me Betty Blackburn's details. I telephoned the next day to make an appointment.

Reading: 29 April - Betty Blackburn

Betty was warm and welcoming. Her fabulous smile made me feel instantly at home. The room was light, airy and pretty. There were two chairs and a treatment bed. That was all.

I explained that I needed her help because I was still feeling particularly low after the death of my husband in 1996. I said that she had been recommended as a possible way forward. I gave no further details. It wasn't necessary. I was simply there for healing. There was little time for conversation anyway, for Betty spoke almost immediately.

"Patricia, you are very lucky. I don't normally allow survival evidence from spirit to be channelled through me. I specialise in

healing, not mediumship. But I am being asked by a man, a really lovely man, if I will allow him to come through. He loves you very much and the message is very strong, will you allow it?"

"Yes!" I said, shocked.

"His name begins with M ... Michael? No, it's Malcolm. He wants you to know he is aware that you are about to go to Devon for two weeks on your own.

"He says that you will feel his presence most strongly there. It will be a happy occasion. He is asking if you remember how wonderful it was, the one time you were there together."

I did. Malcolm and I had only had one weekend together visiting Westfield after its purchase. This was before the house was properly furnished. He had bought beds but they were still covered in plastic and we had to stay in a local B&B. Malcolm died before he'd had the opportunity to sleep in his beloved Westfield.

"He wants you to know that he is always with you, he never leaves you and is constantly guiding you." Betty paused, before adding, *"I don't understand this. He is saying how greatly you are loved and yet he is holding a blue flower. Just a minute ..."* She concentrated again. *"Yes, it is a blue flower. I would expect it to be a red rose but it is definitely blue. Does this have any significance at all?"*

I answered immediately, "Yes, it makes complete sense. Blue is my favourite colour and our homes in Kent and Devon have blue flowers everywhere. Malcolm once bought me a blue porcelain rose, which I treasure."

Betty continued, *"This place you are going to in Devon he loves. He says it was meant for the two of you together, but now it is for you. He is adamant that it is to be yours once the children have left home. It is right for you and the family.*

"He has very strong opinions your husband, doesn't he?" Betty smiled. *"You are to trust your instincts. He adores this place and so will you. You are to wait before extending; you will know when the time is right.*

"You are to learn to meditate, which will open a channel between you, for him to come to you. It will happen at Westfield; it did once before but you were frightened."

This was true. Previously, I *had* experienced something extraordinary there. Normally, I sleep well, even when alone in the house. However, one particular night I simply could not sleep at all. Unusually, I was not frustrated or angry, I just accepted it, and the night was punctuated with me reading a book, making a few notes and fetching glasses of water.

Early in the morning, between three and four, I was lying completely still when I realised that I was quite unable to move. I was totally leaden and had no ability to get up from the bed. Initially, I was unafraid, simply hoping that, perhaps, this was an unusual onset for sleep at last. I was perfectly comfortable. But then I heard strange noises in my head.

To even try to describe these is almost impossible. The closest I can come to it really is remembering the old black-and-white films, where the scene is set below deck on a submarine. The sounds were exactly like the indecipherable instructions barked into a speaking tube and piped below. I became scared. I remember thinking, *Malcolm, please don't frighten me.* No sooner had I thought these words, the voices ceased and I could move again.

Betty continued, *"It will be stronger next time. But you asked him to go previously, so you will have to ask him back, it is the Universal Law. He cannot return unless you ask him to.*

"Well!" Betty exclaimed, *"I have never had to do this before. He is instructing me to heal you in the chair, not on the bed."* Betty got up and moved the bed to one side and repositioned my chair centrally. She continued, *"He is aware that you are a very private person and that you will feel vulnerable lying down and will not concentrate. He is laughing now and saying, 'If you can get her to sit down for five minutes you are a better man than I.' He is also saying, 'She worries too much and tries too hard. She must learn to relax to open the channel between us.'*

"I don't understand this, Patricia, but I am being shown a pair of braces. He is trying to cheer you up, my dear, it's a joke. He says he knew how much you hated him wearing them particularly if he insisted on putting them on to go out."

This shocked me again, as it was absolutely true and was, indeed, a private joke between Malcolm and me. He would put on these awful red braces and jokingly threaten to wear them out of the house. Not even our sons knew about this.

"Your relationship with Malcolm was very strong. You had a wonderful marriage, family and life together. You still have your family and life. You still have Malcolm, but in a different form, and you are just beginning to realise this.

"Malcolm wants you to know that he is fine, he is home. You will meet again and he is waiting for you but you have much to do before that time. There is a pathway unfolding before you. You will help others by talking to them. Not by counselling nor by platform performances, that is not your way. But you will help others by talking to them in one form or another. You will heal with words.

"A strong bond is developing between you and a young woman. There is a triangle, three of you." A thought went through my mind, *Karen, Clare and myself? "You will be drawn closer together. This is developing rapidly now. Do nothing until you are ready. You will be told when the time is right. You are greatly loved!"*

The reading ended there.

With these words ringing in my ears, some two and half hours after arriving, I left Betty. I was astonished and decided that, regardless of the things I had to do elsewhere, I would return home and write everything down as I remembered it.

Later that afternoon, I drove into Reigate to collect my eldest son's suit from the cleaners. A woman I knew only vaguely served me. She looked thin, drawn and very unhappy. After the usual greetings she told me that her husband had died two years previously. Suddenly, her desolate look made complete sense. I said, "I know exactly how you feel."

She replied, "I hate the house, the garden, everything. I feel as though I am not living but simply existing. Tell me, Patricia, does it ever end? Will it ever get any better?"

I felt rather awkward. Following my visit to Betty earlier that day, I felt as though my life had been changed forever. I was almost upbeat and, in front of me, there was this lady I barely knew, staring at me with dead eyes, completely without hope. There was a notion inside my head. *Well, what will you do? Walk out of the door and leave her to suffer? Or will you find the courage to speak?*

One more look at the desolate face in front of me made the action required obvious. After a few moments of awkward silence I spoke. "You might think what I am about to say is a bit odd but I think I can help you."

"Anything, Patricia, any help at all will be better than how I am feeling at the moment."

So, with a deep breath, I told her how, until February, I had felt as though I was only existing myself. I explained how the desolation and sense of hopelessness I had felt at that time had caused me to open the *Yellow Pages* and by doing so, I had found the number in Brighton, which had helped me to begin my own path of recovery. I believe she could see my sincerity because she asked for the number. I found it for her and, as we said goodbye, I was comforted to see there was a renewed spark of hope in her eyes.

Chapter 3
The Witches of Westfield!

May 1999

Life continued. I was to spend a week at Mulberry Cottage prior to going to Devon and I wanted to find a mutually convenient time to discuss my notes with my parents before my brother and sister, which I did. I was very nervous about this. Spiritualism was not something that I could ever recall discussing but my family matter greatly to me and I wanted to be completely honest with them.

Stephen was very busy that week; therefore, the opportunity to speak to him didn't arise. I knew that it warranted more than a quick chat over coffee so I decided to wait. However, I met my sister, Carol, for supper in a quiet marshland pub, away from both our routines so that we could talk without interruption. I asked her to read the first few pages of the notes I had made of the spiritual happenings and synchronicities during the previous weeks. I said that I was nervous about her response and I think she was a little hurt, which was not my intention. She said that anything that helped to alleviate the obvious pain I was living through was all right by her, adding, "Anyway, we have all had the odd spiritual experience, haven't we?" I was quite surprised by this but let the comment go until later, after she had finished reading my notes, then I asked her what she had meant.

Carol explained that at 2.30 p.m. on 1 July 1970, the day our grandmother passed away, she had turned to a friend in the playground at school and said, "My grandmother has just died."

I was astounded. Carol is seven years my junior and, on that same day, I had begun a new job and was working for the first time for Malcolm Irvine, a new boss. At exactly 2.30 p.m., I had glanced at my watch and experienced an overwhelming desire to go home. I could feel that something was not right but I could not walk out on my first day, just because of a whim. So I ploughed on through the rest of the afternoon, all the while longing for 5 p.m.

Arriving home later, my father greeted me. "Tricia, I have something to tell you," he said.

"Don't worry, Dad," I replied, "I already know. It's Granny, isn't it? She has died?"

"How do you know that?" he asked in surprise.

"I just do. Was it at 2.30 this afternoon?"

"Yes, my dear, that's right. How on earth did you know?" He looked very puzzled.

"I felt it, Dad. I just felt it," I said. We walked indoors together but did not discuss it further.

Amazingly, if the events of the past few weeks had not happened, I would still be unaware that my sister and I had simultaneously *felt* the death of our grandmother, at exactly the same time.

I received a call from Karen, which surprised me. She had a very strong urge to visit Westfield and asked if she could go to Devon with me. I was surprised because in her previous twenty-eight years, Karen and I had never really spent quality time together alone. I said that I would be delighted and we planned to travel down together.

We settled in and my housekeeper called as arranged. I had already learned that she was a spiritual healer and the sole purpose for her joining us was for her to meet Karen. We were together from 10.30 a.m. until 3.30 p.m., lunching at the local garden centre. Afterwards both Karen and I felt enlightened but exhausted.

That evening we rang Clare at her office. Her voice sounded dull, heavy and lifeless. We knew that her boyfriend was away sailing that weekend so I said, "Get on a train and come down for a break!"

The response was immediate, "I'm coming!"

Karen arranged to stay a little longer and Clare bought a ticket. We were to collect her from Plymouth station on Friday evening. The girls would return to London together on Sunday afternoon.

The next day was Friday. I suggested to Karen that we should avoid talking about spiritualism. Regardless of how fascinating we found it, we both needed a break. It was too much, too fast. Karen agreed and we went shopping, ending up at the Dartington Cider Press shops near Totnes.

I was planning to visit a friend who lived locally and had recently been diagnosed with cancer. I saw a bookshop and hoped that I might find something to take as a gift. Karen and I could not believe our eyes. This tiny bookshop held the largest selection of books on natural and spiritual healing that either of us had ever seen. It seemed that even when we made a conscious decision to leave the subject alone, we were still drawn towards it—or it towards us.

I bought tapes on fighting cancer and medicine and miracles, hoping my friend would find them useful. I also bought a small book on meditation and Karen bought one on crystal healing.

That evening we collected Clare from the station and returned to Westfield for a late dinner. We had a wonderful time, sharing in-depth discussions; reading aloud passages from books; burning scented candles; consuming wine and delicious Devonshire cheeses well into the night.

On Saturday, we resolved again to give the subject a rest. Both girls needed time to relax and unwind. They bought face packs and hair colour intent on enjoying a girlie Sunday morning without having to rush. I'm not quite sure where I would have fitted into this scenario!

On Sunday morning, Karen and Clare decided to try meditation. In the lounge the curtains were already drawn, candles lit and relaxing music was playing, and they began putting their new-found skills to the test. They were practising meditating, channelling and finding the auras.

Karen said, "Tricia, have you seen the film *The Witches of Eastwick*? Well, we're the 'Witches of Westfield!'"

"Goodness," I replied. "What a horrifying thought." Howls of laughter followed.

I went to bed knowing that Karen still needed significant proof of her abilities. I knew she had questions and this was on my mind. Overnight, I remembered that when Clare and I had previously visited Plymouth we had noticed a clairvoyant's premises. I reminded Clare of this and instantly all thoughts of a girlie morning were shelved. They hurriedly packed their bags and within forty minutes we were Plymouth bound.

The shop was empty. No clients were waiting. But it didn't suit me at all. I felt claustrophobic and sick and I simply had to get out. Quite frankly, it was as though I was being shown the door. I felt distinctly uncomfortable and went for a walk. Also, I had no wish to offend whoever or whatever the energy was that had given me the gift of reassurance of life after death. I had already received very powerful help which I had needed in order to get on with my life and was truly grateful.

While waiting for the girls, in a different shop, I picked up a sodalite crystal. I held it in my hand for a while and thought of Karen. There were four crystals she was particularly interested in and this was one of them. But she had clearly stated she would concentrate on one at a time, so I put it back, not wishing to interfere or make her choice for her.

First to come out was Karen who looked lighter and was smiling. She said, "Tricia, within thirty seconds that woman told me that I am psychic and will be healing with crystals!" Karen had bought a book on crystal healing three days earlier. Later, Clare too, was thrilled with the reading she had received and announced that it had all made perfect sense to her and had given her fresh hope.

Karen, who had shopped while I waited for Clare, rummaged in her bag and said, "I found some crystals in a shop." She had wondered if I had bought one for her already but as it wasn't expensive she had decided to get it. Karen opened the package. It was *exactly the same crystal* that I had held in my hand earlier that afternoon.

Both girls returned to London more positive, relaxed and with greater confidence and assertiveness than I thought possible in such a small space of time. I remained at Westfield and missed them dreadfully at first. Then, on the following Wednesday, I received the most beautiful bouquet of blue and yellow flowers from 'The Witches of Westfield' which made me smile.

The following Thursday, I went to visit my friend, Trudi, who had been diagnosed with cancer, and took a small gift bag with the tapes I had bought her; the book on spiritual healing; plus a notebook and notelets in the Westfield colours of blue and yellow.

After chatting for a while, Trudi asked me to tell her what had been going on in my life recently, as she could hear such a change in my voice on the telephone and could now see that I was looking so much better. It was the moment of truth.

Initially, I sidestepped the issue and said that it would keep for another time. However, she stressed that she was really interested. "Since your recent phone call asking for my permission to include me on the absent healing list at the Harry Edwards Centre you visited recently, I have been intrigued. Also, Gloria, my neighbour, wants to meet you. When I told her about it, she owned up to being a spiritual healer herself."

So there it was. The path was set. Gloria and I were both trying to help Trudi and she, in turn, had also helped Gloria. Previously, Gloria had kept her healing books with their spines turned to the wall, so no one really knew what type of books they were. Now she was willing to invite us both up to see them. Gloria had been empowered.

I handed my notes to Trudi and she began reading. I was more than a little nervous but needn't have worried, for she was completely open-minded about the subject. She also said that she knew me well enough to know that if I had written it, it would only be the truth. And she was right!

Trudi then asked if I knew where she could buy relaxation tapes. I delved into my gift bag and presented her with the one I had found for her. She smiled her surprise. She also said she would like to read for herself about healing. Another delve into the bag and I retrieved the book I had also bought for her. Trudi gave me another delighted smile.

Much later, Trudi told me that Gloria had said that healing colours were blue and yellow. A final rummage into the bag and I brought out the yellow and blue notebook and notelets. It was the final surprise. *All in all, three pretty amazing synchronicities,* I thought.

*****

Later that month, following a busy day with friends, I found the evening rather lonely. I sat there, feeling sorry for myself, when suddenly my aunt Muriel came to mind. My aunt lived in Sussex, was blind, and also a widow. She was aware of my recent experiences and my growing notes. I felt quite ashamed that I was being miserable, yet am sighted. I can read, go for a walk or drive and watch TV. My aunt could do none of these things. It prompted me to call her.

"Tricia, how lovely," she said. "I have had rather a miserable day and have been longing to talk to someone."

We had a long chat and both felt better afterwards. Surprisingly, during our conversation, I discovered that not only had Aunt Muriel and my uncle holidayed for several years in a house next door to Westfield but that she is also godmother to my Devon housekeeper! We were equally astonished. Two further synchronicities, neither of which I would have known had I not telephoned my aunt, when it felt right to do so. This showed me that I was right to take intuition seriously.

Chapter 4
The First Words

I woke at 4.23 a.m., fetched a drink and returned to bed. I didn't go back to sleep immediately but lay there thinking about rising early to get my paperwork done and make the most of the day ahead.

Suddenly, this incredible feeling began rippling from the base of my spine, moving upward before seemingly exploding around my shoulders and head. It was so powerful that it encompassed the entire top half of my body, happening repeatedly, becoming stronger and stronger. Although I could not control it, I was totally in command of my thoughts, which were, quite simply, *this is wonderful!*

There was no physical movement of my body but, surprisingly, I felt no fear. There was just this glorious, warm, deep rippling feeling. It was like an electrical surge throughout my entire torso. Then the most amazing thing happened. I could *hear* a metallic-sounding voice inside my head. I could not discern the words but the pattern of sounds was repeated several times.

The surges became even stronger and then I clearly heard the words, "Do you remember what we said about ... ?" But, irritatingly, I could not decipher the last two words. This was repeated twice more, each time accompanied by this deep, glorious tingling feeling of power within my body. I could not understand the experience, yet I welcomed it because it made me feel so incredible.

I wondered if this was Malcolm trying to contact me. I was afraid that if I thought too deeply, it would end. I could not believe that I could clearly hear words and yet I was entirely alone in the house. I had tried to remain relaxed so as not to upset the vibration or whatever it was creating such a glorious feeling.

My knowledge of such things was very limited. All I knew at the time was that I wanted the amazing sensation of peace to continue. I was entirely without fear. This calming, powerful, surging continued rising and exploding around my head. And then, I heard another voice, still 'metallic' but undoubtedly different.

I did not recognise any of the voices, or even begin to think who they might be, other than Malcolm, but there were two very distinctive tones. The incredible, uncontrollable, rippling feeling continued throughout. It was indescribably wonderful and I was filled with joy.

The only word I could discern from the second voice sounded like 'exterminator', which I heard several times while trying so hard to decipher the rest of the sounds. This concerned me because this was not a word that I would normally use.

I was amazed that I could hear, with such clarity, voices inside my own head. I was also bemused because, although I was completely awake, my body continued to be delirious with joy as the surges of power continued rippling through me. They were absolutely beyond my control and, because it felt so wonderful, I simply didn't want it to end.

I knew that I must remain in control of my thoughts and relayed this inside my head but the electrical power surges, which had been rippling through my body, consuming it almost, began to fade. I desperately wanted it to continue and wished I could understand exactly what it meant. How on earth was this feeling created?

Realising that my own thoughts had interfered with the process, my mind was full of apologies, as though I had let someone down; someone who was trying to communicate with me. I felt that I had failed them by being unable to recognise the two words at the end of the sentence which had been spoken to me. I felt a total failure. When I accepted, at last, that the rippling had ended, I reluctantly raised myself up in bed, turned on the light and checked the time. The experience had lasted for twenty-one minutes without interruption.

I noted that it was when I began to *think* that the surges had started to fade. Quite definitely, it was when questions formed in my mind that the sensation began reducing. My body remained intensely hot. I was literally dripping with perspiration. It was an extraordinary, indescribable feeling.

I was puzzled and delighted by the experience but absolutely unafraid. How could anything that felt so fabulous be wrong? I felt safe, secure and filled with a calm gentleness. I was full of hope. It was not an excited feeling but a quiet, gentle, positivity totally welcome, and yet, beyond my control. It was the most all-encompassing feeling that I have ever experienced. If asked to describe it, I would use the words 'emotional ecstasy'.

Nonetheless, whatever power chose to course through me has to understand that my mind must remain my own! I will happily *hear* and pass on messages if that is what is required, when I am able to decipher them properly, but nothing must be allowed to control my thoughts. *I will not accept that.*

Journal entry: Tuesday, 8 June

I spoke to Karen and Clare earlier today. I thought it would be a good idea if we were to meet up again following my recent experiences.

I visited Betty Blackburn to ask if she could explain exactly what had occurred. I was warmly greeted once more and I gave Betty my most recent notes. Incredibly, after the first two paragraphs she put my notes aside and began to tell me what else they contained without reading them, describing the content most accurately.

Betty explained that the powerful feeling I had experienced was the cleansing of my chakra system. The rippling was the flushing, or cleansing, of my energy centres. She went on to say that it denoted the beginning of my psychic work, that I had been chosen and was considered ready.

She explained that the initial feeling is unlikely to be repeated in such a strong way but I would recognise it in a gentler form, prior to any future psychic work sessions. I was told not to seek such contact, for it would come to me naturally. I was warned to protect myself daily from spirits of the lower realms, which frankly scared me a little. I guess common sense dictates that where there is good, evil is usually just around the corner. But we don't have to choose it!

Betty told me to envisage daily being surrounded by a white light, 'the Christ light' and to picture an egg shape of this light which encompasses me entirely including my feet. Psychic energy is evidently encouraged by water and cleansing. Betty suggested I do this daily during my morning shower.

She went on to explain that cosmic law states that no spirit can deny a fact three times. It is imperative that when either an intuitive or actual voice comes through, I ask it three times, "Are you from the highest spiritual realms ... the kindest, the greatest, and the good?"

They may choose to lie twice but will not do so a third time. They will simply go away. This is the Universal Law, she explained. On Sunday, I'd had a gut feeling that the first voice was good and well-meaning but the second voice definitely made me uncomfortable. It is at times such as these that I should use this.

Betty told me that I am in control. If I ever feel uncomfortable with any messages I must block them by simply telling the spirit voice to 'go away' firmly. It will obey immediately. Also, if concerned, I should recite 'The Lord's Prayer'.

Then Betty said, *"Your husband's here again, look!"* Her left arm was covered in goosebumps. *"He says that he sanctioned your involvement and agrees with your new path. This role will fill the space in your life which was left by his departure.*

"You will live a fulfilling life, helping others. You are ready now and spirits will begin working through you; after they have supplied you with the necessary proof."

Betty went on to say that in her recent awareness class, where people go to open up their own psychic channels, one student had told her that she would soon have a visitor to her healing room. She told Betty that this visitor is one who has been 'chosen' and healing would be unnecessary. *"It is you, Patricia,"* Betty said, *"you no longer need my healing, and certainly not my classes; it would be a complete waste of your time.*

"Your healing and teaching will now come from a higher level. By now you will have a guide of your own, who will take over teaching when you are ready to continue. They will be the judges

of that.

"You must remember that you are two people now, with quite separate roles to play. You are both a mother and a healer. You have to learn to differentiate; you will instinctively know whom you may trust with this knowledge and whom you are free to discuss this subject with. You will be told."

She stressed that I could call her any time of the day or night if I was concerned but that I was not to be alarmed, adding that I was embarking on an exciting new era in my life. She also explained that psychic power was often activated by emotional trauma and Malcolm's death had obviously made me more spiritually aware and receptive.

As I was leaving, Betty called out, *"Just a minute, I have the word 'book' coming through. Yes, 'book'. Perhaps I have got to lend you a book, or maybe you will write one. I don't know yet ..."*

Journal entry: Friday, 11 June

Following my visit to Betty, I returned home to write up my notes. I didn't know what it was that compelled me to write everything down but it was almost as though I had no choice. I found that, unless I did, I could not rest or settle to doing anything else. If asked, I would say that I did it for the sake of my own sanity.

On the evening of 10 June, I met Karen and Clare at the Sevenoaks Posthouse. I took along the new section of, what was now, my journal. It included details of my experiences the previous Sunday night. It was a great relief to get together with them. I felt totally safe and free to discuss everything without any fear of recriminations.

During the course of that same evening, Karen said that she could see me writing a book on the subject. I accepted this comment with a huge smile and a great deal of doubt.

The previous day, I'd had problems with my computer. I could simply not get the machine to word-wrap. It was taking me far longer than necessary to finish my task and I was becoming increasingly frustrated. Ever the technical zero, I rang Jane, my computer studies tutor, for help. She could not understand what the problem could be so we agreed to meet with my laptop and together try to sort out the problem.

When I arrived, Jane apologised for the state of one of her toes. She was wearing sandals and her large toe was covered in Iodine and looked painful. She told me it had been troublesome for several weeks and that she was unhappy with the treatment she had been receiving. Nothing seemed to be curing it. I gathered my nerve and suggested the alternative therapy route.

To my amazement she said, "My daughter, Suzanne, is a spiritual healer. Lately, because medical treatment has been no help, she has begun working on my foot and only now is it finally beginning to recover." More and more, I was beginning to realise that if you are brave enough to voice the previously frowned-upon subject of spiritual healing, you frequently discover that many people have had their own experiences.

Jane looked at my computer and when we turned it on, to my intense irritation, she could find nothing wrong with it. Nor could I, which was even more frustrating. I simply could not believe it. The blessed machine, which the previous few days had seemed to have a life of its own, now chose to do everything expected of it. It felt to me as though it had been an annoying ruse to get me into her office to discuss healing!

I felt totally comfortable in Jane's company. With the computer now working properly and her next client not due, we had time for coffee and a chat. She asked me how I had learned about spiritual healing. I began telling her my story of Malcolm's tragic death and the quagmire of events I had been, and continued to be, struggling through. At one point she was in tears. At another she laughed and said, "Look at my arm," which I did and, at the same time looked at my own, for we were both covered in goosebumps and stone cold.

I said, "Malcolm's here." We remained cold for a further thirty seconds or so. It felt like a confirmation of my words.

When Jane's next client arrived, we were both disappointed to have to return to our normal day and, regardless of the fact there was seemingly nothing wrong with my computer, we agreed that the morning had been far from wasted. She gave me Suzanne's telephone number and I left.

As her stepmother, I continued to feel a great deal of responsibility towards Karen. I wanted not only to help her, but also, if I could, to protect her while we were stumbling along on the path opening before us. She was keen to visit the Dorking Spiritualist Centre, which I had been told about. Karen still had a lot of questions which needed answering. She particularly wished to know the name of her personal guide.

I made an appointment and rang Clare to tell her of our plans. I asked her where she was going to be on that same Saturday.

"Dorking," she replied. This was before I had the chance to tell her of Karen's and my proposed visit. Amazed that we were both going to be in the same town, let alone the same county for once, we made plans to meet at Mulberry Down later on Saturday.

Journal entry: Friday, 11 June -7.30 p.m.

I have just spoken to Suzanne, the computer teacher's daughter. What she had to say was surprising. She has also only recently been involved with spiritual healing but her introduction was not as gentle as mine was. Suzanne has experienced seeing and hearing spirit, astral travelling, automatic drawing ... The list seemed endless and, quite frankly, I understood little and found it all rather frightening.

I have no wish to be *frightened* by spiritualism. What's the point of that? If I am willing to assist spirit in getting its messages known, that should be good enough without being scared. I asked aloud, "Please, don't frighten me." I record this here because I feel it is necessary. As I understand it, if I make my position clear then my request should not be denied.

Suzanne and I have agreed to meet in the near future. I will speak to Karen and Clare and, no doubt, we will visit Suzanne together. She is happy for us to do this. I may be wrong, but I feel there is safety in numbers.

Journal entry: Saturday, 12 June - 11.15 p.m.

I was very late going to bed last night. I visited a close friend and didn't leave her home until gone midnight. She'd asked me to visit her because she had noticed such a dramatic change for the better in me and wanted to ask what had happened in my life to bring this about.

As she is a staunch High Anglican, I was a little afraid for, just as with my own family, I wanted to be totally honest about what had been going on but I was concerned as to what her reaction might be. However, in my opinion, honesty is always the best policy and I was rewarded, for during the course of my explanation that evening, I was happy to learn that she had a totally open mind on the subject. This was a relief and a surprise. Once home, I eventually went to bed hoping to have a good night's sleep. I didn't.

Eventually, at around twenty past three, I sat up in bed with words coursing around in my head. Because I so desperately needed to sleep, I reached for the pen and pad beside my bed and wrote, what was to become, the first of many channelled poems and prayers that I felt compelled by some unknown force to write:

A Medium's Prayer for Protection

Lord God in Heaven above, I am a willing channel
For thy healing, light and love.

Teach me to seek and learn, how to heal with simple words
Spoken with my voice and written through my hand.

The Holy, Great and Almighty spirit is welcome
As are the healing spirits from the highest realms
The kindest, the greatest and the good.

But the forces of darkness, evil, negativity, fear and disease
Have no place in my being and I bid them GO!
Back to the light, from whence they came
All their thought forms and intentions.

I call upon my guardians and my guides
To cherish and protect my mind, body and soul
Fill and surround me with the white, protective
Christ Light of God's power
And grant me thy peace.

May the star of the Christ Light stand between me and my enemies
And a spherical mirror be placed around me, my protection
And the people and places that I love.

May I remain in the centre of this protection
And be calm, balanced and centred, decent, honourable and true
May I always show kindness, compassion and forgiveness.

Father of all things seen and unseen
Teach me faith, patience and trust - that I may live without fear.

Speak and I will listen
Lead and I will follow
Inspire me—and I will lead.

Help me to live my life and demonstrate with it
All you would have us to be.
Amen

I still didn't sleep but luxuriated in a blissfully deep feeling of peace and I was no longer angry or fearful. At 8.30 a.m., I got up. Before beginning my day with Karen, I felt compelled, once again, to write up the experience of the previous night. The journal is growing longer. I have no explanation as to why I continue to do this other than for my own sake.

Karen arrived at 11 a.m. and we drove to Dorking to keep our appointment with medium Diana Summer at noon. We enjoyed browsing in the shopfront, studying the crystals, music, books, and so on, all of which was strange and new to us. However, our minds were full of anticipation.

We were asked to go to the private consulting room, which was a converted cellar beneath the shop. It was comfortable and

"When you step onto this path and embrace this, you will meet challenges. Experiences and miracles will begin to happen. There will be small, very subtle things, which are miraculous in their way. Also, as our light grows stronger, and your light is beginning to burn brightly, you will be approached by dark things, for as much light as we give out, attracts equal darkness. This is the polarity. This is the truth. You must recognise that you need to appreciate the balance. We do need to look at the dark sides within us. Our polarity is in us and around us, so we always have to seek our own truth, our own way forward as to who we are.

"You were the healer, the wise woman. The knowledge and wisdom within you will be rekindled to come forward in this life also. This is what healing is about. As you go forward now you need to seek a good teacher. You need one who is well versed in knowledge and wisdom who can bring you forward on this path and who can keep you safe. He will show you how to expand your own awareness, wisdom and knowledge. From him you will also grow, blossom and experience all kinds of wonderful things ahead. Remain aware of the dark. Where there is light there is also darkness but there is no real evil. Evil is manmade. It is brought about and manifested by man.

"You are being encouraged now. You are being brought forward to the fullness of your potential and being made aware, within your heart, of these truths. Take this gently, take it slowly, there is no need to rush. You are currently aware of the urgency for spirit to see that you acknowledge who you are."

At this point Karen interrupted, "Excuse me, can you stop for a moment? I am not feeling well. I feel very faint."

"Sorry, it is probably the energy," said Diana.

Karen went upstairs to recover and Diana continued, *"This is a fear process. There is fear."*

"Yes, we are both fearful," I replied.

"Sickness is the gut feeling of disempowerment and fear. There is also a feeling of not wanting to embrace this particular path at this moment because of the questions it raises. She is thinking 'what exactly is this and where is this taking us?' It is the fear of being not sure, not ready. It needs to be very carefully brought forward."

"We both feel that way. This is why we came together," I said.

"Yes, but there is a definite message for you. Although you might, on one level, be quite nervous and fearful of it, you have such strength. The messages here are coming through for you strongly but at the same time, saying, 'Take your own time. One step at a time.'

"This is what is here for you. This is who you really are but you do have free will. You don't have to accept any of this. It is up to you to say whether you want to take it or leave it. If you don't feel you are able to accept it at this moment then let it go. It is really important that you embrace it only when you are ready, perhaps at a much later time."

I said, "I find I am not sleeping because I am waiting for something to happen."

"You need to close down at night. You see, your daughter is very open. She needs to close down too. She is taking in everything and it is affecting her emotionally. I see her aura as being very fragile so I will show her how to close down. Whether she still wishes to come down and see me is another matter now."

"I am sure she will," I replied.

"But for you, this is the way forward. If I were you I would just step back, think about everything. Take as long as you like."

"Could it be a result of my husband's death that I have become more spiritually aware?" I asked.

"It could be that it was the trigger. Your husband's passing was probably preordained. It would have been decided that he would be with you until that point. His leaving would be your trigger and your time to accept your place in the order of things. It is your awakening. The millennium shift is around us and there is a more spiritual time coming."

"I am more than happy to be part of this," I said, "but I am anxious also. I don't want to lie in bed at night wondering what's going to happen next. I don't want that, I can't handle it."

"No, nobody wants that," said Diana. "If we feel anxious, we are feeding the energy of fear, therefore, we are inviting it. From tonight, ask your guardian angel to come close to keep you safe. Put yourself in a deep violet bubble with gold around it. It will clear the energy and you will feel at peace."

"Do we have a way of knowing who our guides are?" I asked.

"We all have guardian angels that are with us from birth right through every incarnation, until we don't need to come back to earth again. They support us until we are re-joined to the higher levels of consciousness and then go back to the heart of God. Our guides are there and they can change through our evolvement. There may be guides that come to us and stay with us to help us a certain way along the path. Then, as we reach the next point of awareness, a new guide may come in. I will try to link in and see if your guides will come forward and make themselves known."

A few moments passed ...

"There is a Tibetan monk around you; he is resonating with sound. He is peaceful and gentle and is bringing peace to you. He may well communicate with you himself. He is the only one who is coming forward at present. If you wish confirmation, ask him to present some evidence. It could be that someone will speak to you about Tibet, someone could present you with a book or Tibetan music ..."

I broke in, "My fifteen-year-old son has said that he wants to go to a Tibetan monastery when he finishes university." We both laughed.

I continued, "I am doing a lot of writing. Is this a natural thing to do at this time? I am literally writing everything down as it occurs for my own sanity."

"This is very much a part of the spiritual path because it is, indeed, important to keep a spiritual journal. It can contain your everyday events, your experiences, feelings, and your dreams. Dreams are very important."

"I never dream."

"You do. You just don't remember them," said Diana. *"At night, we often go to the halls of learning in the spiritual realms and come back. Most of us have no knowledge or recollection of this but it is how wisdom begins to come through."*

"I have also found some of the most unlikely people are receptive. I get a very strong feeling of who I can discuss this with and whom I should not."

"This is the teacher in you. You will find that as you go forward, your friends will change. You will encounter those who are more like-minded. Other friends will fall away. It will not be a conscious thing but it will slowly change. You will find that you will associate with those who will help you to blossom and grow."

At this point my session ended and Karen returned.

I asked, "How can you tell that I am a medium? How could you just look at me and know?"

Diana replied, *"It is within you, it has always been there. I can see the energy in your eyes. I can sense your energy and feel it. It is simply a part of you. When I tune in I see a moving picture show. I can see what you could be doing but you have choices. I feel that you and Karen are both at a doorway. Take your time about making your decision as to whether you wish to walk this path. Once you make the commitment to spirit, your spiritual path will take off. But don't rush into it. They need to know that you are ready to do that."*

Chapter 5
A Deep and Glorious Secret

Journal entry: 13 June - Dymchurch, Kent

I am at my parents' home. I sat typing all last evening, finally finishing at midnight. At about 11.30 p.m. my father was asleep but my mother, who had been waiting patiently for me to go in and say goodnight, came into the conservatory where I was still working. I apologised for unwittingly keeping her up so late.

Earlier in the day, Mother and I had spent some time together travelling around the Romney Marsh while I took photographs. She had read the most recent parts of my journal during this time and also listened to Diana's tape, which I had only received the day before. I knew I could discuss the matter with her without causing concern. My mother has very firm beliefs of her own and often we find that we share thoughts.

Before we said goodnight, my mother hugged me tightly and said the following, which I found so moving: "Just believe in yourself, my dear, because in the future there might be many other people who need to believe in you too."

"This is a tough one, Mum," I said.

She replied, "I know, my dear, but I have every faith in you." Then she went to bed. My love for her was then, and remains still, overwhelming.

Journal entry: 15 June - Surrey

If asked at this precise moment how I feel regarding all of this, my reply would be that I am fascinated, yet fearful; honoured, yet humble; curious and filled with a quiet wonder. I feel as though I am carrying a deep and glorious secret but with it, also, a responsibility of unfathomable depth.

I have been trying to focus on photography at college today but I am finding it difficult to concentrate. I feel almost compelled to discuss everything with my friend, Carol O, and another mutual friend there. Why? I have absolutely no idea. Carol plainly admits to being agnostic. I don't really know her friend well enough to form an opinion regarding a possible reaction. Yet, we have agreed to meet next week.

During the early part of the evening I telephoned Suzanne. I have arranged for Karen and myself to visit her on Friday. We are curious to speak to someone who is already living with this experience before we make our own decision as whether or not to commit, as we were advised to do by Diana Summer.

Journal entry: 16 June

I have been feeling strange today. I tried 'cleansing' the house yesterday but I didn't really have the confidence and frankly couldn't get rid of the feeling that I was behaving like a complete idiot. The night was uneventful but the heat woke me a few times.

Each night now I take the tape recorder upstairs and put on Charlotte Church's album, *Voice of an Angel*, to listen to while in bed. And, each night also, when I am gently slumbering and about to fall asleep, the tape ends with such a loud 'click' that I am rocketed back to consciousness, which completely defeats the object. I must find a continuous play recorder! The final words of Sir Cecil Spring-Rice's poem 'I Vow to Thee My Country' have taken on an entirely new meaning:

And there's another country, I've heard of long ago,
Most dear to them that love her, most great to them that know;
We may not count her armies; we may not see her King;
Her fortress is a faithful heart, her pride is suffering;
And soul by soul and silently her shining bounds increase,
And her ways are ways of gentleness and all her paths are peace.

One thing I never forget to do is to repeat 'A Medium's Prayer'. This calms me and makes me feel safe.

After lunch I was still feeling odd. It is difficult to describe; I felt abandoned but I had no idea why. Yesterday, I boasted to my friend Carol that I had not had one headache or migraine since the beginning of these events. This is quite a record for me, who was used to suffering them on a regular basis. However, I was beginning to sense that one could materialise now.

I rang Diana Summer. Realising that I was clearly needing help, she kindly agreed to come to the house next Wednesday, to assist in cleansing the negativity from the family home. It is naturally full of sadness following Malcolm's death. I do sometimes feel as though it is closing in on me. Karen and Clare have since told me that they had often discussed, without my knowledge, the heavy atmosphere here at Mulberry Down.

I explained to Diana how I was feeling. She said this was perfectly normal considering it was only a week ago that events had begun to unfold rather rapidly. Also, it was only five days since I was declared a medium and this would be a shock to anyone!

Journal entry: 18 June

The headache finally came. It woke me at 6 a.m. yesterday and lasted twelve hours. It has been exceedingly hot and that could be the reason for the migraine. Alternatively, I think I am spending too much time thinking about spiritualism and my recent experiences. What was it I was told recently? "She worries too much and tries too hard." Perhaps it was simply a warning.

I was in bed by around 10.30 p.m., said my (now regular) prayer and visualised the protection ritual as suggested. For three hours I lay luxuriating in an overwhelming feeling of peace.

On the peripheries of my senses I could feel a very mild form of the rippling. This time, it was gentle and pleasant, sufficient to make me expect something to happen. That is my problem, of course; 'expecting something to happen' and being a little fearful of what course my 'initiation' may take next.

Eventually, at 1.30 a.m., I decided to take a sleeping pill. I simply *had* to get some rest. My last full night of sleep was Saturday in the sanctuary of my parents' home. I cannot continue like this if I am to remain strong enough to cope with regular everyday life, let alone make a considered decision about this new path which has opened up to me.

I woke at 8.30 a.m., roused by my alarm. I felt refreshed and no sense of a migraine was left. This afternoon Karen, Clare and I are going to visit Suzanne, to discuss the subject with someone who has more experience than we do. Hopefully, we will come away with a greater understanding.

*****

We were kept entertained with details of Suzanne's 'initiation', some of which was a little alarming. She confirmed that she had been to a development group to get back in control and that things were much quieter for her now and had levelled out. I could see Karen and Clare's faces echoing my own relief.

Earlier the same day I had begun my third notebook. The first contains notes of my personal experiences. The second, quotations which I feel might be useful. Now there is a third notebook, listing all the people that I feel could use healing, either physical or mental. This was the first thing that I did on that Friday morning. I listed the names, together with the problems I knew each person was experiencing at that time.

We spoke about this and I said that, as I had been told that I have the necessary powers, it seemed only right to make an effort, even if I didn't quite understand how to go about things yet. I explained too that the list was so long that I couldn't envisage how I would be able to deal with it properly.

Suzanne said, "That's okay. All you have to do is put your hand on the book and send your energies to all contained within it. You are not expected to repeat every name individually." I was really *very* glad to hear that.

She then said, "I keep seeing flashing lights. Can any of you see them?" We looked blankly at her. Suzanne had, I'd noticed, shielded her eyes several times during the course of the evening. I had wondered if she suffered with migraines. She then went on to say to Clare and me, "There is someone sitting between you, I can sense him. Is anyone else as cold as I am?" We all confirmed that we had goose pimples. "That is one way of spirit confirming we are on the right track," she declared.

Karen made us all laugh by saying, "Poor old Dad, I am amazed he hasn't given up on us. We are so thick at getting the hang of all of this." More goose pimples followed, accompanied by a ripple of laughter.

Suzanne recommended that we explore a development group run by Valerie Kirkham, who lives nearby, in Sussex. We were again warned of the need to use only reputable and highly recommended teachers.

We had all found our visit to Suzanne enlightening and reassuring. To meet someone who has been living with these phenomena for the last two years was really helpful. Clare and Karen stayed the night with me, which gave us time to talk and ponder. It was wonderful to have company in the house at night for a change, especially with the boys still away at school.

The following day, I returned to my parents' home to celebrate Father's Day. I feel so secure and at peace there. It is also the only place where I get a good night's sleep. I decided to leave the computer at home in Surrey and enjoy a weekend without thinking about spiritual matters.

On the Sunday evening, I finished a book Karen had lent to me, *Channelling for Everyone* by Tony Neate. I am due to see Karen next Friday and want to return it to her. I made several useful notes.

Thankfully, things have been quiet for a while following my request for 'time out' but I sense this is beginning to change. Who was it who said, "Prayer is talking to God, meditation is listening?" I am wondering if I will ever get the hang of it.

*****

Back in Surrey, I woke, deeply saddened. I never dream, or perhaps I should say I never *remember* my dreams. But this particular morning I woke *knowing* I had been in Malcolm's company. But when I woke, it was as though I had left him behind somewhere. It wasn't that I expected to find him beside me; I simply woke with a great sense of loss. I felt alone and wanted to get back to my dream. I wanted to reunite with him, desperately, but I didn't know how. I lay pondering and feeling sorry for myself. My eyes were closed.

Suddenly, behind my closed eyelids, I saw outlined what looked like masses of tiny hands, no arms, just hands. Then, clearly amidst the outlines there was one pair slightly larger than the others. The fingers were pointing downwards and they were white, completely contrasting with the rest of the image, which was dull brown. One of Malcolm's most attractive features was his strong, well-shaped hands. His voice and his hands had always been admired by me. So, it was as though this vision was reassurance to me that he was nearby. Immediately, as this positive thought entered my head, I was filled once again with an *immense* peace. The negative thoughts which were present on waking dissolved totally.

*****

I went to visit the art mistress from my old school, at her home in Kent, and we spoke about spiritualism. She has had her own experiences and I have completely taken her into my confidence. I left one of the copies of my journal, which she has read, and I subsequently received a letter from her, an excerpt of which follows:

"One must be careful not to be drawn in too quickly into spiritualism, or too closely to the doctrine. One must consider carefully the full aspect of it all. Be grateful for the peace and rest it has given you and nurture the strength of spirit to shield yourself from sudden misfortune. Be at peace with God, whatever you conceive him to be and whatever your labours and aspirations. In the noisy confusion of life keep peace with yourself, your soul. Don't let things consume you. Keep your mind and spirit free, exercise caution and keep your faith in a loving God.

"Each day and each night I think of you, I pray for guidance to help you in the best way forward. There are things which one is meant to do and from that source of God come comfort and courage. I don't want to dissuade you from spiritualism. Study it, work it out, and don't let it overtake and envelop you. You are forever special in the sight of God. You have wonderful gifts, which bring joy to many. You have great sensitivity and talent. Keep your interests going they will be of great strength to you. You will find your path. God is with you and you will receive strength and comfort. Remember, I am always ready to help if I can, you are very dear to me ..."

I was so moved by the depth and sincerity of her letter, particularly from one for whom I have such great respect.

I also wrote to old friends of Malcolm's, Philip and Joy. I knew that they were staunch Baptists. However, because they were curious, I felt I should be honest and tell them exactly what had brought about such a change to my life. The letter I received back from them told me that I would be "better to pick up my *Bible* than use the services of a clairvoyant."

Not wishing to destroy a friendship of over twenty years, I replied gently, asking if they had actually read anything about the subject. Obviously, they had no wish to fall out either and agreed that they had not. I decided to visit them and took *My Life as a Medium* by Betty Shine, a well-known medium who lived in their home town, as a gift. We agreed to meet again after they had read the book.

I have since heard from them saying that they found the book impossible to put down and had attended a signing of her new book and bought it. But the most surprising news was that Joy had also recently sought help from a local spiritual healer and that the rheumatism in her hands has improved so much that she is once again able to enjoy gardening.

Another example that proves one simply has to find the courage to 'stand and be counted' if we wish to make a real difference in the world.

*****

I recently visited a homeopath as suggested by Karen, who was also using his services. I was utterly fascinated to watch him at work with his dowsing crystal. After studying my palms, fingernails and handwriting, plus the results he gleaned with the crystal and iridology chart, he said: *"You are a fighter. Not a noisy fighter but silently strong. There is inner conflict and a course opening to you, which you are reticent about. You are holding back but your strength will see you through in the end."*

I found my trip to the homeopath fascinating and was grateful to Karen for suggesting it. I had also spoken again with Betty Blackburn about the subject of spiritualism and the possible conflict with my previous religious upbringing.

She said: *"God, by any name, is like a tree with many branches joined to the main trunk and can be traced back to the same root, The Source, the very heart of God."*

That made perfect sense to me. If people worldwide would only accept such common sense it would save so much heartache. After years of lapsing, I now pray every night without exception. I find it easier to accept things that previously I had never quite understood.

I am beginning to see clearer pictures when I close my eyes at night. The frantic shade changes from brown, to ochre, to white, are becoming more varied and a little clearer. Early morning on 15 July, I was trying, fruitlessly, to sleep when amidst the evolving patterns I clearly saw a tiny baby. This wasn't ochre or white but coloured like a beautiful, faded, old print. I saw a man's face, head and shoulders. He looked like the elderly Gandhi with his spectacles. It only lasted a moment. I had no fear. I think I am learning acceptance.

I feel I must stress, I am still *me*! I have not lost my mind or my own personality. It is simply that a wider aspect of life seems to be unfolding around me.

Chapter 6
The Committal

Journal entry: Thursday, 15 July 1999 ~ 23.38 p.m.

I think someone is playing a joke at my expense! I lay down in bed but within minutes of closing my eyes there was a blinding white flash like lightning, accompanied by a loud crack like a whip. This made every nerve in my body jump. I really was frightened! Immediately, I began thinking the words of 'The Lord's Prayer'. I repeated these many times like a mantra, until I felt my fear receding.

I have made it clear that I will not co-operate with any forces that frighten me. That is no way for a useful partnership to work and if that is how it will be then I want no part of it!

Journal entry: Friday, 16 July ~ 1.30 a.m.

I have not yet been to sleep following the above-mentioned shock. However, it has been better than sleep. Once again, as I tried to settle in my bed, an immense feeling of love and peace overtook me. I was fully conscious but the only part of my body I could actually *feel* was my head where it touched the pillow and I was also aware of my breathing. The rest of me seemed to lack substance. It was as though I was luxuriating in a sea of love, as if, physically, I didn't exist and, mentally, I was only aware of delight. I didn't want to try and reclaim my body. I didn't want to break the spell and cease the wonderful feeling. So I gave myself up to it entirely. I lay there, basking in joy.

Of course, I knew it would end. Usually, as I am learning, these experiences end when normal thinking, worrying and, in particular, wanting to hold on to it, takes over. It simply begins to fade away.

This remained positive for longer than previously. When the state finally receded I could again, albeit reluctantly, feel my entire body. It was as though the tide had gone out and all I could do was patiently wait for it to return.

Throughout this experience I had a very strong image of Malcolm. If asked to describe this sensation, I would say that I had been 'made love to ... mentally'.

As it seems that I have to write these experiences down, I now keep a notebook and pen by the bed. It has to be documented. I know what is expected. I was excessively hot, presumably from the energies, and it was with great reluctance that I hauled myself upright to begin writing.

Journal entry: 20 July

Last night, I made my decision. I committed myself fully to The Source and whatever this chosen path is for me. There is no turning back. I am willing to work for the purpose of good, absolutely ...

I read until 11.30 p.m. I was totally absorbed, noting many passages. During prayers I totally committed myself to the work and the pathway ahead. I have made it absolutely plain that I am 'a willing channel only for the forces of light and good'. I then tried to sleep.

I lay there and, initially, I felt my entire nervous system rocket into awareness, but there was no light flash this time. It startled me but I accepted it. I banished all forces of 'darkness and negativity' from my being and accepted this experience as part of my learning. Within minutes, an overwhelming feeling of peace and love enveloped me. I could actually *feel* the heightened, rippling of vibrations. It was as though this was an acknowledgement of my commitment. It was glorious. Again, I was incredibly hot.

I had been dreaming about trance mediumship and I was the medium in trance. I can remember little except that the work I was doing was received positively. When I woke, the memories of this dream scared me. Then I remembered my promise and, convinced that I am now to be hand in hand with The Source, my fears vanished. I was so at peace that I didn't feel like waking fully to begin to write.

But there is no real choice; it seems to be part of the deal. I know I am required to write these notes. I don't know why. But I do it, because it *feels* right.

Journal entry: 21 July

I telephoned Betty Blackburn and arranged to see her before her appointments began. I had questions and wanted to show her my latest notes. Betty read the pages confirming that my path is unfolding far more rapidly now. She explained that the frightening 'nerve-jumping' and flashes of light is spirit's way of making me realise that messages will not always come through in a gentle manner. I need to prepare myself for this and learn how to cope with the various ways of communication. The gentle sessions which followed the light flashes are reassurances for me, so that I am aware that my path is always guided.

Betty told me that I need to meditate deeper. As an impatient Aries, I know that I am really not good at this. She feels strongly that my first firm experience of being a medium, whereby I am able to provide evidence, will be by writing. When I meditate I must make sure that I have pen and paper to hand. Slowly, people will begin to come to me for my opinion. Soon I will be able to enter the necessary meditative state with ease and my productive work will begin. Betty clearly sees my notes being transformed into a book and is positive that this is being guided by spirit.

Journal entry: Monday, 26 July

I went to bed at midnight. It was incredibly hot and sleep would not come but I wasn't worried; I had slept earlier. I lay resting in bed, occasionally drifting into meditation. Whenever I felt myself *altering* I said 'The Lord's Prayer' for protection. This happened four or five times, each time after the prayer I *returned*. I was still awake at 3 a.m.

When next I felt myself drifting I decided to allow it. Within seconds I heard a deep voice. I couldn't understand what it was saying; it was as though the voice was being stretched somehow. I felt no fear because I was in a state of *oneness* where there is none. Then I realised, I was not alone in my bed! I could feel an arm beneath me and it felt as though I was communicating with Malcolm. I cannot recall the words but there was a telepathic conversation between us of a loving nature. We also kissed. But something was wrong! I lifted the bedcovers to see his face. When I did this, I was terrified, it was not him. I didn't recognise the face at all. It vanished. I felt very odd. Then I realised that this person had been lying to the right of me. Malcolm had always lain to my left. I was furious. I felt saddened, cheated and angry. I could still sense the arm beneath me. I left my bed, unwilling to return. It upset me for the entire day.

Later, I remembered what I'd been told; "Check things three times, spirit can only lie twice, it is cosmic law." I had forgotten to implement this. Because I was so needy, I simply accepted the first assumption which I had made. This was a very hard lesson.

Journal entry: 28 July

Duncan and I had an arduous journey to Devon in the Morgan, the car that Malcolm bought for his fiftieth birthday, but, upon arrival, we felt instantly at home. Westfield has such a good feeling.

Journal entry: Friday, 30 July - 12.33 a.m.

The night is warm and there is a glorious moon. Listening to the grasshoppers outside my open window, it sounds very tropical. We had a marvellous day. I visited Trudi and found her looking very well; the combined efforts of traditional and alternative medicine appear to be working.

Journal entry: Friday, 30 July - 11 p.m.

A very productive day in the garden, I am enjoying myself entirely. Duncan lit the garden candles and we watched the moon rise together from the veranda.

Journal entry: Friday, 6 August

I have been allowed something of a holiday from spirit, for which I am grateful. It has been restful and good things have happened.

I thought I would try listening to an automatic writing tape. When the music started, I began to drift. A feeling of great peace came over me in surges. I wish I'd had the ability to retain it constantly. My hands felt separate; it was as though they were searching ... floating ... dancing. I did not have a pen and paper easily to hand, as previously instructed, so clearly no writing could materialise but my hands certainly seemed to be operating on a different level. Perhaps next time I should try doing as I am told and have a little more faith in what I am trying to achieve.

Journal entry: 9 August

An amazing thing has happened. A few days ago, when I had finished reading *The Beginner's Guide to Mediumship* by Tony Neate, I noted that one of those thanked for help with writing the book was Dilys Guildford, a medium who lives in Devon a few miles from Westfield. I telephoned her and left a message on her answerphone to say how much the book had interested me.

This evening Dilys returned my call. I explained that I'd read the book and wanted to say thanks for the help it contained. She told me that she'd noted my name on a pad and every time she looked at it she felt a man's presence around her.

"This man is very nice, my dear, he really loves you," Dilys said. *"He keeps repeating, 'Tell her I love her.' He is holding the most enormous bunch of yellow roses and is insisting that I tell you to put them in a blue vase. Does this mean anything to you, my dear?"*

I was astonished. Dilys knew nothing of me, nothing of Westfield, and certainly not its colour scheme. Yet, here I was again, being given explicit detail of the colours most significant to me at Westfield.

She continued, *"He is repeating the same name to me, he keeps saying, 'Tell her Robert.' Does this mean anything to you at all?"* I recalled that earlier in the afternoon on the quay at the bottom of the garden,

I'd been speaking to a young man. He was cleaning his sailing craft ready for sale. We'd never met before so I introduced myself. His name was Robert.

Dilys went on, *"Your husband is with you at Westfield. He wants you to realise the significance of the name Robert; it is his way of proving to you that he was with you this afternoon. He is also saying the name 'James'; does that mean anything?"*

It did. Earlier the same evening, Carol and I had been enjoying a glass of wine on the veranda watching activity on the creek. We were discussing someone we knew called James, whom we could see in his boat out on the water enjoying the evening with friends.

"There is so much coming through for you!" Dilys said, *"He really loves you this man."*

I asked her to pass a message to Malcolm; "Please tell my husband how much he is loved by me and all who knew him."

She replied, *"He knows that, my dear, and the reason he gave you the name Robert is so that you realise how recently he has been with you."* She laughed, "He is going nowhere without you."

Dilys continued, describing to me a yellow *fleur-de-lis* design on a background of blue. She said that ducks were also significant. This shocked me totally. I was standing in the hall at Westfield where the wallpaper had a blue background with an embossed *fleur-de-lis* in pale gold. There was a frieze above the dado rail of black and white Loons. Dilys had never been there and this was the first time we had spoken.

There will be twelve of us gathered at Westfield for the eclipse and, thanks to the call from Dilys, we shall be aware of Malcolm's presence. I am full of gratitude for these messages and the healing they bring, not only to me but to our entire family.

Chapter 7
Astral Travel and the Eclipse

Journal entry: 11 August 1999 - The Eclipse

After I went to sleep last night, I experienced something new. I was fully awake. Yet, my whole body appeared to be whisked at tremendous speed, horizontally, upward. There was a variety of mirages before my eyes; patterns, lights, a coastal scene of cottages on a waterfront. There were a few white plastic chairs and a veranda. The images were not frightening and I remembered to ask three times for protection. I was so enjoying it that, of course, I wanted it to continue but, again, as soon as I began to think the images faded. *"She tries too hard, worries too much ..."* sprang to mind once more. Will I ever learn?

We witnessed the eclipse in the garden. Clare, Karen and I were alone together on the front lawn, encircled by garden candles. Gentle conversation drifted across from the veranda but it was in the background and didn't encroach or spoil the experience for us.

We felt the enormity of the occasion. Sounds faded, darkness overtook us, and the candles flickered gently. Clare and I made eye contact, which seemed to lock for a moment in recognition. My entire body was in tune with the moment. My flesh was alive and tingling as the seconds passed.

During the peak of the experience I recognised the scene from the night before. There was the coastline of Noss Mayo, the Westfield veranda and even the white plastic chairs which we had put out only moments before. All was exactly as I had visualised the previous night. The eclipse for me was a moment of unification, recognition and, above all, acceptance of the path before me.

Journal entry: 3 September

Things have continued to be quiet. It is as though I am being
given space and time to 'get my house in order'. I have been feeling
rather depressed with the accumulation of paperwork and the
heavy responsibility of Malcolm's estate and the questions that are
beginning to arise regarding the family company and the children's
trust fund. This morning, I woke with words in my head, resulting
in the following poem:

On Waking

You are my first thought on waking
And the last before I sleep
I often feel your presence
And welcome the loving eye you keep
When everything seems hopeless
And I feel terribly alone ...
Something wonderful then happens
To remind me that's not so
You know how deeply I miss your smile
Your touch and words we used to share
I am so grateful for the knowledge
That you are, in fact ... still there.

Reading: 2 October - Dilys Guilford

Dilys Guildford visited Westfield for the first time. I had been
curious and excited to meet her and was pleased to find I felt
completely at ease with her.

Dilys began: *"This morning I received lots of information
regarding your welfare and what you need to do. When I arrived you
said to me, 'It's a shame Malcolm never got to sleep here,' but I think
it was supposed to be. It's been bought for you. He knows where you
are and Westfield is in his heart.*

*"Before arriving, he took me on a visit around the village. I was
taken to the harbour and generally shown the area. So, before I*

even met you, it was an adventure. As a medium, I don't know what is going to happen. I don't know who will come and take part. From the moment I woke this morning I was told, 'don't rush, be casual, be relaxed.'

"It is Malcolm's wish that you live here and he hopes that you don't mind him saying this. Malcolm is making it very clear. He wants you to have a fresh start.

"Godalming is mentioned. This has some specific importance to both of you. Maybe it is a memory which he's giving me? 'She'll remember,' he keeps saying, 'let it go, she'll remember.' I did remember. It was Godalming where we began our first narrowboat holiday.

"Is the letter 'C' significant? He is sending his love to this person."

"We have a son, Charles," I replied, "whom I have just taken to Exeter University."

"He mentions December as an important time and is showing me that it is definitely not Christmas."

"Charles' birthday is 23 December."

"He says, 'You must tell him that I won't miss it. I'll be there. Wherever you are, he will be with Charles for his birthday. Malcolm is very pleased about Exeter. There is someone called David linking with Charles. This could be someone he might meet in future." [Later in life, Charles' father-in-law was called David.]

"Malcolm is saying, 'Charles is doing well and he is very proud of him ... and you,' he says, 'Tell her she is doing well. My heart aches. I need you to tell her, she is doing well.'

"The month of June is significant. Can we go back to when Malcolm was here? He is showing me something that was important to him in June. When I link to him I pick up something in the base chakra which is painful, something to do with him or you? There is a great heaviness there. Do you know what this would relate to? Is there someone else in spirit besides him who had a condition where they have passed, maybe with cancer? This is not him and it is not you, so there is somebody I am receiving at the moment who had this condition?" [Malcolm's mother's birthday was in June. She died of cancer.]

"Malcolm says, 'I don't want her being upset. I want to answer her questions.'"

"Can I ask questions?"

"Of course, as many as you like, it doesn't interfere. It helps to confirm things. Malcolm tells me that his heart caused his death." Dilys snapped her fingers. *"Just like that!"* She snapped them again. *"No warning, nothing at all."*

"Yes ... that's right. A heart aneurism."

"He says, 'I was very hot and my feet were throbbing. I didn't have the chance to say goodbye.' He loves you." [It was difficult for me to control my tears at this point but I forced myself to as I didn't want it to end.]

"I see an upright vase, it's crystal, with just a mass of red roses, stood on one side of a windowsill. To me, strangely enough, it is a kitchen windowsill that looks straight out onto the garden. It's a very odd place to put flowers but can you think about that please, because he is saying, 'She'll know exactly what I mean.'"

"I do know. It is our kitchen windowsill in Surrey. I place flowers there and I recognise the vase he is speaking of. It belonged to his mother."

"This is a gift for you. Malcolm is showing me and saying, 'There are twelve roses one for each month, I love her each month of the year.'"

"Can I ask another question?" I enquired. "I want to know if he completely trusts his brother, Ian."

"'Well, you don't,' he says."

"I'm not sure."

"You don't, you have made up your mind, and he is telling me so. There is something not fair that has gone on. This is a younger brother?"

"No, it's his older brother."

"Does Malcolm have a younger brother?"

"Yes."

"Well, there is some confusion here. It feels like the younger brother has nothing? Which one do you want to talk about? Malcolm would like to talk about his younger brother."

"It's true the younger brother has very little comparatively but that is not what I need to know. I want to talk about the older brother, Ian."

"Malcolm is concerned about the younger one because he has so little and this worries him. He doesn't feel Ian will take care of this situation whereas, if Malcolm was here, he would. He would have clemency and understanding and would help, because that was how he was. But, the older brother ... be cautious.

"Is there a further question about that because there is a lot here about finance and money? 'Strange, shady,' he keeps saying to me. He wishes he had given the 'golden share' to his younger brother because it would have given him something. 'It would not have allowed Ian to be so bumptious,' he says. 'It puts everybody in jeopardy.' You have to be cautious and do what you know Malcolm would have done. For him that is important.

"Malcolm is saying, 'Dad met me,' and he is thrilled about that. He also has a lady with him. It is his mother. I can see her.

"Don't be frightened to ask questions, he wants to give you guidance. The name Robin is also around his older brother to do with the business, you may not know him?"

"That is the name of the company accountant," I said.

"This needs to be sorted out. I am hearing Malcolm very clearly. He is being backed up by his parents. It feels as though his father passed away a long time ago because he is now a glowing light beside Malcolm. His mother was not so long ago." I nodded that this was the case.

"Father is giving energy to his son and both are there for the love of him. He says, 'I am giving you evidence. Now, can we talk about R?'"

I said, "This is the accountant drawing up figures for my future."

"You are not sure about him and Malcolm isn't either. 'As with my brother, you must be cautious; R knows too much background. You must have an objective viewpoint. You might still go with what R wants but,' Malcolm is adamant, 'you must have independent advice.'

"He gives me the name Saul; he gave me this name earlier and he would like to talk about him now."

"Saul is a quantity surveyor," I said, "who is assisting me with a project in Devon."

"Malcolm took me over to that picture earlier [she indicated to a framed photocopy of Westfield's initial architect plan, given to me by the former owners of the house] *and he said, 'We must talk about this.'"*

"I would like to make the house larger."

"'Yes, please,' he says. Saul feels a little younger than Malcolm, somebody in his forties? Malcolm thinks he is a good man, who will give you sound advice to help you move forward. You must go to him with your ideas. Malcolm will help you."

"Could you take, please, the name Frederick?"

"Frederick is my father."

"Malcolm liked him and you need him, he says. Malcolm is explaining that he had a special closeness with Frederick.

"I am now being shown Land Rovers, Aston Martins, MGs and things more hand-built where motor cars are concerned. He is saying to me, 'Just talk about it, laugh and talk about it, tell her I am laughing.'"

"Malcolm bought himself a Morgan."

"'Hand-built,' he tells me."

"Malcolm loved cars. I think he approves of my bringing the Morgan to Devon. You haven't seen it but it is stored in the garage."

"Absolutely he does. It is now 'home'. Later on, when the boys are older, they can share it. Don't give it to either one and don't give it to them straight away, because they will crash it.

"There might come a time when you want to change the Mercedes. Malcolm is saying, 'Feel that you can, when you are ready to do so. We spent a lot of hours in it together but just know that you can change it. Whatever you drive, I will be with you. I want you to know that I am around. Rest assured I am with you. There will be a time when I go for peaceful relaxation but it won't be until we have worked through things.'"

"Meaning that Malcolm is helping me?" I asked.

"Yes, he is working with you. That is his decision. He wants to help."

"I don't want to hold him back," I said.

"You won't. He wants to be here until things are sorted. He knows what he wants. He has made his choice, just as he could in the physical plane."

"He is giving me the letter 'S' from spirit. He shows me the sea, with 'S', for some reason; do you understand? Now I am seeing a golf course and then I am looking out to sea."

"My brother Stephen, he is the children's guardian. He lives near a golf course and Romney Bay."

"He says, 'Stephen is an "alright chap".' You must let him know that Malcolm has spoken about him from spirit.

"Malcolm says, 'He is more reliable than my own brother. He has been there for you and the boys.'

"Malcolm is giving me the name Peter ..."

"Charlie's best friend at Exeter is called Peter."

"This Peter feels older. Malcolm is showing me Peter Sellers from the film Being There *and he is giving me the month January."* [This meant nothing to me at the time but was to become relevant later on. I didn't realise then just how significant the name 'Peter' would be.]

The session ended there. My mind was in turmoil. That Dilys could touch on so much acutely personal, accurate information at a first meeting was mind-blowing and tremendously reassuring.

*****

Having seen an advertisement for a spiritual artist in *Psychic News*, I decided that this is something I would like to do. The artist, Rose, offered to draw a person's guide and forward any information channelled to her while she drew and I received a pastel drawing of a Native American in full headdress with the following information:

"My child, it is a pleasure to be able to show myself to you and to work with you. We, in this world of spirit, have for some time been working with you, trying to make you aware of your talents. You have many abilities, my child, not least the one of communicating directly with the spirit world through the power of mediumship. Do not doubt what I say, for it is so. You have much work to do; you must, for now though, go where you are led. Follow your heart and your

instincts, for these are your own spirit which knows the correct path for you. The pathways you will be led to will give you opportunities to learn and advance in confidence and knowledge of the works of the great spirit. Do not, however, take all that you see and hear as the truth. Learn to discriminate between what you feel is right and what I will term 'rubbish'. For there is much nonsense out there in your world, including people who preach that they alone know the truth.

"The only real truth is what you 'feel' is right. Trust your instincts, for they will never let you down. It is necessary for you to hear and see many different views on life and the spirit, for this is the only way you will learn your own truth. For we would not know what pain is if we had not experienced life without it, we would not know what sunshine and fine weather is unless we had experienced rain and cloud. I hope you understand what I am trying to say to you, my child.

"You are intelligent, trust in yourself and your own abilities and go and find opportunities for learning. I also ask you to sit with my picture, sit in the quiet and think about me, write down your thoughts as they come and you will see that you can indeed communicate with the world of the spirit. My name is Eagle Eye, and I am within you and part of you. Sit with me, my child, and allow me to come close to you. The power and the love of the great and almighty spirit is with you always."

I rang the artist and we spoke for several minutes. Rose has been involved with spiritualism since birth but has been drawing for only the past ten years. She fully admits she has no artistic abilities personally and can only draw at all when guided.

Chapter 8
Deep, Penetrating Fear

Journal entry: 13 November 1999 - Devon

Something really odd happened tonight. I am constantly worrying about the children's trust fund and our financial future, which I had always understood to be watertight by Malcolm. My fear is out of control and I am comfort eating; I gorged myself on cake and biscuits and cheese. I felt so ashamed that I went to bed early. I felt about the lowest I had ever been.

I woke just after midnight feeling terribly sick; this is an uncommon experience for me. I don't remember being physically sick since childhood. However, I was so sure that I was going to be that I went to the kitchen and sat by the sink armed with a glass of water. Angry and frustrated with my self-inflicted state and my lack of control I waited, shamefacedly, for the inevitable. Nothing happened. Sometime later, I dragged myself back to bed and lay down feeling absolutely dreadful.

Shortly after two, I felt an awakening within my body. There were deep power surges which I had learned were the onset of a fresh spiritual experience. I could see clearly the same pair of hands as before being shown to me. In addition, there was a face wearing spectacles like Malcolm did. I did not recognise the face but welcomed it. It *felt* as if it was him. The accompanying feelings were reminiscent of mine for him, which still flourish very strongly. It was an inner *knowing*. There was no fear; in fact, I welcomed the experience. After weeks of little spiritual activity or contact, it was reassuring to know that I had not been abandoned.

Then the sound came. There was a tremendous increase of power within my body and there was a rapid voice speaking. I strained to hear it. It came a second time repeating the first indecipherable sentence pattern, recognisable by the syllables and tones. Finally, it came a third time and built to a crescendo.

I could hear clearly, approximately two-thirds of the way throughout the pattern of words, "Making yourself miserable again!" These words were perfectly clear and accompanying them was a strong impression that I was being severely reprimanded. The power then depleted, continuing momentarily at a reduced rate then it passed. Simultaneously, the dreadful, self-inflicted discomfort disappeared. The intensity of the sickness had gone and I felt *purged.* It was an incredible relief and I was so grateful.

Why do I put myself through this? All I can conclude from the experience is that we sometimes need to reach the very depths of misery in order to be given positive assistance. I am now fully convinced that I am being cared for. A great deal of energy was extended in my direction earlier and it would be morally wrong to waste it.

Someone does care. He is interested in my mental and physical welfare and it is my place to address my behaviour. There is no doubt that I have the ability to hear spirit messages, albeit unclearly. No doubt it takes practice and meditation and I am wasting valuable time and risking my health with my appalling habits. I must change so that I can get on with the job I am here to do. Help is at hand and I have not been abandoned. I have to get on with my life and accept that I have my own destiny to fulfil. I am humbled and ashamed but feel that I have been given a fresh start. Most importantly of all, I feel greatly loved.

This brings to mind a quotation I noted earlier from *The Power and the Glory.* "The first understanding you must have when embarking upon the reading of this book is ... that I had spiritual help in writing this."

It is equally necessary for me to make it clear that spiritual help is present in the writing of this journal. Without all the various happenings there would be little for me to write about.

Journal entry: 7 December

Financial problems continue to cause me concern. I am deeply worried about our position regarding the family company. I am hoping and praying for fairness and justice and that our financial future, so hard won by Malcolm, will be assured. I made an appointment with my solicitor to discuss matters. I was nervous, afraid even, of the outcome. I was in need of reassurance and wished to have all possible assistance available to me, including that of my husband, so I rang Diana Summer.

Reading: Diana Summer

The first thing I mentioned was the period of spiritual quiet I had entered; it was puzzling me.

"You mean like being disconnected?" asked Diana. *"Being isolated, where things are happening around you but not to you, a fear of losing the connection, of not being able to tap into the energy?*

"What is happening when we go into this stillness is that we are on a pivot which is about to turn. It is the point of transformation, a still point before rebirth, before going into the next stage. Often this stillness makes people wonder, 'what am I not doing?'"

"Or, what have I done wrong?" I added.

"But really, it is a time of rest and once we begin to accept this, it will all start to flow again. Over the next ten years or so there will be many changes. This is why you are stepping onto this path. You will be put in the place you need to be, in order for your work to begin. Changes will affect individuals, globally and universally. The earth changes are here; they are happening; the earthquakes and the floods. Some of this will get worse, some of it will get better. These changes are documented, prophesied from years ago. We have chosen to be here, working at this time in order to hold the energy and take it forward into this new millennium.

"This is a time when others are going to be fearful and doubting. There are going to be souls needing guidance. We are all students; we are all learning, preparing for what we are really here for. When

these souls come to us, we will be able to give them guidance, compassion, healing and help to put them on the right path. That is what I feel you will be doing.

"You are a natural medium," she laughed. *"I know, I keep telling you this but it will just flow. The wisdom that is yours will begin to filter through because you are connecting to your higher self, your soul.*

"Our soul has sent us down to learn. It wants to expand its consciousness. Every time we reincarnate, we are teaching more than just ourselves. I feel you are now connected to your soul. This wisdom will begin to filter down to you. You must meditate on linking to your soul; it is a very positive thing to do and this will bring down wisdom and knowledge to help you. This is there to be accessed. Sometimes, guides are given and they appear. These are often aspects of our higher selves who come to help us access our inner wisdom.

"You'll be able to reach out and fill yourself with this knowledge. The right words will flow; the right feelings will come through. Your inner knowing will expand. Most important of all is for you to understand about inner knowing because that is more important than clairvoyance, clairsentience ... or any of that. Just knowing, simply knowing what is right. Use this gut feeling.

"You will find that you connect to certain people. This is soul recognition. You have come together to connect again on this level, in order to work alongside one another and offer support. Distance makes no difference. There is no such thing as 'far away' in reality.

"In the next few years, people are going to be changing. The emotional and the mental planes are going to come together. There will be a lot of confusion. The changing energies around us at present are a shift of consciousness. There will be many who are lost. This is why we are on this path to give them a push in the right direction. Even if we cannot fully awaken them, we can sow a seed of light and then they can find their way. Just as we have a guardian angel, we have a guardian demon too. Polarity is a mixture of light and dark. We have to learn through discernment how to harness the power of each and walk a balanced pathway. This is what we are working towards. It is important to always honour your own truth.

"Do you want to ask questions?" Diana enquired.

"I am afraid," I said. "My husband and his brother trusted each other completely but I am not a blood relative. I think he has treated me well so far but I have doubts. I am faced with a very big decision [whether or not to take him to court] which not only concerns me, but also my children. Either way, I don't see that there is a great deal I can do.

"All I want is for someone to be on my side, to give me a hand when I need it. I guess I am asking this of my husband, which is, perhaps, an unreasonable thing to do?"

"You have a meeting tomorrow and you want to know whether this is a positive step?"

I nodded.

"Malcolm wishes this meeting to be carried out with legal representatives. You need to look at your position and establish the financial situation and all that it entails. You need to be completely at peace with it because there is something here that is not quite as it should be. You should be cautious.

"I feel that there is trickster energy here, something might be tried. Call on the wisdom to give you guidance. Tomorrow, tune into the energy of it, keep alert and ensure that nothing is hidden. Ask the right questions.

"I keep seeing lots of water around you."

"Our house in the West Country is on a creek."

"There is a beautiful energy around you as if you are preparing to fly, spreading your wings and embracing all that is rightfully yours. This is on a spiritual level, mental and emotional.

"Your work will be connected with the higher realms, the masters and the angels. Go straight to that level. If you feel you are not linking with your higher self and you need help, go to the finite source.

"I am being shown that there is a situation around you where mischief abounds. There is temptation for a male but there is also stability, justice and discernment. You will access the necessary wisdom to put everything on an even keel. While you are going through this your husband will support you. You will feel the very essence of him around you.

"It is time for you to acknowledge your own awareness and to link with your light and your true essence of being. This is an expansion of your consciousness. I feel it is very important for you to accept that you are a light worker.

"There is doubt here. The experience you need will be drawn to you. As you go forward, all the people you meet and the connections you make will be an experience in itself. Your accessing of knowledge, of words that need to be spoken, will become natural to you and wisdom will flow. It will come!

"You are reaching a circle of completion where things come to a final full stop. Everything is changing. There is a big release, a big letting go. These changes will be quite catastrophic. It is time for rebirth and renewal.

"Everything that you tap into will spring forth with energy. Everything is going to start manifesting for you. The phase you have come through up until now has put you where you need to be. Soon you will be completely free in order to do the work that you were born to do. This is your big transformation.

"I see the threefold flame. It is like the fleur-de-lis. This has connections in France. It is representative of the Trinity but also discernment and you must use your head.

"In the New Year there may be conflict with someone who is trying to make their presence felt. There is stubbornness here but I see you resolving this. What you do is for the good of all. It could be that you are going to meet some resistance and this brings up emotional responses from those closest to you.

"You are in a period of big changes. There is a rolling wave of energy, which will push you forward and put you where you need to be. You have the free will to discern when it is right for you. If you feel that it is right then go with that, use your discernment and things will blossom and grow."

Journal entry: 8 December

I went to bed at 11 p.m., praying for guidance in representing myself the following day at the solicitor's office. My brother-in-law wants to sell the family business and the thought terrifies me.

I want to be scrupulously fair to all parties. However, these things are difficult for me to judge as I am far removed from the world of business. Malcolm had been my champion in that. My role was as a supportive wife and mother. My loyalty towards my husband and his life's work is paramount and I am deeply concerned about protecting my children's trust fund and our way of life. We have already lost Malcolm and now our financial future seems uncertain. I don't know Ian well; he and Malcolm made a good working team but we rarely socialised.

I woke at 5 a.m. and prayed again for guidance from the masters, angels and, of course, Malcolm himself. Nervous tension consumed me; I was constantly churning inside. After a few moments I felt a deep peace rise, calming my physical body, my nerves and my thinking. My hands were pulsating, throbbing with energy. My eyes were closed but I could clearly see pictures. A greater clarity was present than with any other previous visionary experience. I saw the face of a Native American. I saw two tiny, angelic-looking forms which looked as if they were made of cream-coloured porcelain. They were utterly flawless and slowly they turned and as they did so, huge 'wings' appeared on their backs. I could only think of angels. Also, miniature, fairy-like creatures flitted across my vision. I saw many faces come and go all looking very tranquil, which brought to mind *The Light of the World* painting of Jesus, by William Holman Hunt.

It was as though I was being reassured that I am far from alone. The deep, tremendous peace remained with me all the while the reassurance was taking place.

When I rose, the turmoil began to creep back rapidly. Yet when I sat to record these events in my notebook, the exact, same feeling of peace returned. I believe this spiritual subject is far greater than I will ever fully understand. I feel very privileged to have been allowed a glimpse of some of the possibilities. I must learn to trust myself, listen to my inner self, and follow my own spirit. It alone knows the true destiny and pathway for me.

Chapter 9
One God, Many Names

December 1999

During the long meeting at the solicitors I held myself together and took in all the information that I could. I spoke up when I felt the need to and listened intently. However, once outside away from the suited men and the office itself, I was an emotional wreck. My mind was in utter turmoil. Fear of losses, lack of loyalty, incomprehension, suspicion, grief and yet more fear were all completely mixed and indistinguishable.

In the meeting, serious concerns had been raised about the treatment of both me and the children's trust fund, regarding the questionable past sharing of the company's profits. That, plus the proposed unequal figures, should the offer to buy the company go ahead were causes of grave concern. The offer brought to the table, which my brother-in-law, Ian, was proposing, filled me with suspicion and confirmed the concerns which had been festering within me for months.

It was cold, raining and dark when I left the office in Westminster. I decided I needed air and I began to walk in the direction of Victoria Station, displaying a confidence that I did not feel. With tell-tale tears coursing down my cheeks, only partially disguised by raindrops, I felt isolated and totally alone. Trudging along the pavement with sobs wracking my body, I longed for help from someone who knew far, far more than I about such matters.

When I reached the Roman Catholic Cathedral near the station, I entered. In the state I was in I could not go and buy a coffee anywhere, nor did I want to board a train. I needed to calm down.

It was by now late afternoon and dark outside. I sat as silently as I could on a chair beside a pillar, towards the back of the building, struggling desperately to control my emotions. I made a point of sitting beside the pillar, because in a strange way, I knew it would comfort me. In time, I quietened. After fifteen minutes or so I realised that Mass was about to commence. I am not a Roman Catholic but fiercely believe that all religions come from the same source, so I decided to take part. I needed the comfort and support, which I knew taking part in the service would offer.

When it was over, I felt more composed. I lit a candle in memory of Malcolm and enjoyed the solace of the building for a while longer before leaving. Outside, I gazed up at the cathedral's magnificent tower and mentally expressed my thanks. A silent prayer later, I resumed my journey.

Journal entry: Thursday, 9 December - Exeter

The next day it rained hard. I made an exhausting trip to Exeter in order to collect Charlie from University for the Christmas holiday.

This journey cumulated in my collapsing in a heap on the bed in a guesthouse that Charlie had arranged for me. The weather had been foul the entire time and I was totally worn out. I lay there, remembering the days when Malcolm and I would enjoy driving together to collect the boys from school. Remembering too the lovely hotels he would seek out, in order to surprise and spoil us all at these times. I looked around the room and was hit by a tsunami of self-pity.

The ringing of my mobile phone interrupted my thoughts. It was a friend, Peter Darby, whom I had not heard from for at least a year. His wife, Susan, a close friend of mine, had died in the year following Malcolm's death. Because it was the Christmas season, he had telephoned to catch up. We chatted generally for a while and after a few moments he asked, "Is there something wrong?" I was so shocked that he was able to tell, over the telephone, the deep sadness that I was feeling; it took me by surprise.

Initially, because I was so exhausted, I tried to change the subject by saying, "Oh! It's a long, complicated story, Peter, don't worry now."

"I can hear by your voice that there is something worrying you, Patricia," he said. "Perhaps I can help?"

Peter's concern sounded absolutely genuine and sincere. So I proceeded to explain to him my fears regarding my brother-in-law, the past profit sharing and the proposed sale of the family company.

His reply astonished me; "Patricia, don't you *know* what I do for a living?" I mumbled something to the effect that Susan and I had never really discussed his or Malcolm's business.

He replied, "Well, my field is accountancy and I deal with the buying and selling of businesses every day of my life. I am sure I can help you if you would like me to. I must still be here for some reason and what better one than to help a friend of Susan's?"

I was amazed that on this dreadful, lonely, miserable evening, I was being offered help of such great magnitude. Out of the blue a friend had called, offering professional help with a situation which was way above my head and causing me an enormous amount of fear. I was so very thankful.

We made arrangements to meet during January to discuss the matter properly. What an enormous relief. I believe absolutely that my desperate need for guidance was acknowledged spiritually and help, so badly needed, came in the form of Peter's call.

I later realised that *this* must be the 'Peter' who was mentioned in Dilys' reading. She said he was older than my son's friend and that he wore glasses. Exactly so! She had also said that January would be significant. That night I slept more soundly than I dared hope for.

*****

A friend has introduced me to Friday Ng, an acupuncturist and healer. Although my health has improved greatly over the ten months since my spiritual experiences began, I know that I still need help.

I was very impressed by Mr Ng's quiet gentleness, his obvious interest in another's problems, his kindness and above all, his honesty. I was told at the outset that he would not know whether he could help me until after our first meeting. Also, he said he would not give treatments continually for, in his opinion, if I required more than eight or ten, then it wasn't working. I admired his frankness.

When we began the acupuncture session, Friday quietly explained as he worked what it was he was doing and why. I kept silent and simply listened.

Two and a half hours later the treatment was complete. Friday asked me to go and look in the mirror. "All I notice is that I am finding it a great deal easier to smile," I told him.

Friday looked at me and said, "Exactly, Patricia!"

He went on to say that the grief of the past years has remained blocked and was stopping the natural flow of energy around my body, causing it to be out of balance. Later, I left the consulting room feeling totally relaxed and quietly confident, that with one or two more treatments, this gentleman would be capable of helping me through the trauma, which I sensed was ahead.

Journal entry: 21 December - 3 a.m. - Dymchurch, Kent

Last night I had what can only be described as an 'electrical' experience. I went early to bed as I was feeling unwell. I couldn't sleep but numerous times I felt that I was 'falling inside myself, spiralling inwards'. An amazing number of mirages and visions were before my closed eyes. There were Native Americans, tiny, flitting fairy-like creatures, both large and small. There were incredible patterns, rolling over and over, ever-changing and with such speed. I could only just discern one shape before it was switched to another. This cumulated in my hearing a now-familiar loud 'rushing' sound in my ears. There were two very fierce flashes of light, which alarmed me.

Then I recalled Friday's words, "Are you aware that you are opening spiritually? You must not open too quickly or you will be shocked. It is necessary to open slowly, then stand back to survey the whole view."

I calmed down, remembering the need to take it slowly. The sensations were still there, minus the flashes of light. Having always been told that we can stop such experiences by changing our thinking, I decided to try. I didn't want the experience to end but I wanted to see if I had any control over it. By this time, the rushing sound had now developed into a 'voice at speed'. I couldn't make out the words, only sound patterns. I envisaged *squashing* the sensation with my mind. To my great surprise it had an effect! It was as though I was squashing an enormous balloon between my hands—but telepathically.

It is so difficult to find words to adequately describe these happenings. But words are all I can offer. Both the sounds and sights altered. I even found that I could change the volume. And I could actually *feel* the pressure that I had created with my mind. There was another really violent flash. At this point, I was afraid. So I decided to stop experimenting and immediately switched my thoughts. There were incredible electrical surges just once more. My hands pulsated; the rolling waves of shocks affected every nerve in my body and even clearer pictures began to evolve. My desire to 'search inside myself' seems to be the key. I am beginning to understand about 'connecting to one's higher self' but it is almost impossible to describe.

Before moving, I noted that my hands were at completely different angles, not opposite each other in a pushing position at all. In fact, one was beneath the covers and the other above. There was nothing physical about this.

I don't really know what is going on. I don't understand. I am simply experiencing. All I know for sure is that I am meant to write down the details as they happen and that my conviction remains as strong as ever.

Journal entry: 23 December - Littlestone, Kent

I contacted Gloria today. She told me excitedly that she had begun to make essences; not only with flowers but also with crystals and that they were already in use with some success. Yesterday, she made one to send to me and she is anxious that I should receive it soon.

Gloria is convinced that we are of the same soul group and that this is what so strongly binds us. Listening to her made me feel very privileged indeed. I told her of the spiritual experiences that I'd had which had been hindering my sleep. She said I was lucky to have received such strong confirmation. Gloria is also sending me a tape of channelled music, which will help to soothe me. She really is a most amazing person. We have only met once, yet have spoken innumerable times. I am immensely fond of her. I think she is right about our being of the same soul group. It *feels* right.

Journal entry: 27 December

A decision made earlier in the month, for me to go ahead of the family and prepare Mulberry Cottage for Christmas, was a good one. Everyone, when they arrived, could see that it is possible to create a good, welcoming atmosphere if determined enough. I used a large amount of wild ivy and innumerable candles. The house looked beautiful. The meals went well and everyone seemed as happy as we could be—without Malcolm.

Clare was with us for the duration of Christmas and Karen and her family joined us on Boxing Day. Clare and I took Karen's two young boys for a walk along the sea wall at night. It was absolutely magical. The boys were so impressed by the clear sky and the stars that they thought they were in space. We could see the lights of Le Touquet and Calais across the English Channel.

I settled into bed rather late that night and was immediately filled with the now-familiar electrical surges and the pulsating in my hands. It was very pleasant and reassuring. Even when I heard the rushing in my ears and knew words would follow, I felt no fear. A very brief few words were spoken, which of course, I failed to understand the first time. It happened a second time and I could tell that the pattern of sound was the same but I still could not decipher it. The third time, I clearly heard the words, "I love you." Then, just as quickly, it vanished. I felt absolutely wonderful. It was as though Malcolm was giving his approval for our family Christmas on Romney Marsh. It was the best possible gift I received that year!

Journal entry: 30 December

Relaxing alone in the house this afternoon I decided to watch the film *Gandhi*. I was so moved by some of his known words that I have included them here:

The words, 'Love thy neighbour as thyself' are found in all the major religious books.

If you are a minority of one—the truth is still the truth.

If you really want to change things, there are better ways of doing it than slashing someone with a sword.

The way of truth and love will always win.

It matters not which book is being read—as long as God is being worshipped.

Sometimes, it is when you are quite without hope and in utter darkness that God comes to the rescue.

This one man's effort on behalf of humankind really moved me. What a very great pity such philosophy as Gandhi's is not taught regularly and honoured globally in all schools.

Chapter 10
Everywhere We Go!

Journal entry: 1 January 2000 ~ Kent

Clare and I shared a magical millennium New Year's Eve with friends. After a splendid candlelit meal, we stepped outside before midnight into the crisp air and walked fifty yards to the beach. Everyone was waving and smiling, being cheerful and determined to mark the occasion with panache.

We were armed with glasses, tall garden candles, helium balloons and champagne. We walked onto the sand where the surf rolled gently onto the shore. The sky wasn't totally clear but that couldn't spoil the occasion. Everyone was muffled to keep warm and the atmosphere was one of excitement and anticipation. We lit our candles and on the stroke of midnight, the champagne cork was released. We heard a distant, muffled roar of voices and fireworks echoed along the coast from Romney Bay to Dungeness. It was a fabulous moment.

Pen and paper now always to hand, early the next morning I was prompted to write the following poem.

Millennium Night 2000

In a windless coastal curve we stood
On the beach at Romney Bay
With giant candles in our hands
Waiting to herald a special day
Close to midnight was the hour
Mist around us swirled
Helium balloons flew high aloft

Their ribbons round us curled
The Champagne cork was gently eased
Glasses poised in easy reach
Mysterious silence deepened now
To those scattered on the beach
Breathing in the stillness
Soft silence, waiting The Millennium Hour
Distant lights traced the horizon
From Dover Cliffs to Dungeness Power
Then, suddenly it was over
The year of ninety-nine
2000 then leapt forward
And all began to shine
The Champagne cork flew in the sky
Balloons begged their release
We filled our glasses, raised them high
In our circle of light on the beach
Fireworks leapt and swirled and showered
Collective wishes running wild
A coloured myriad of joy
Was shared by you and I
And at that precious moment
Love burst and raced across the sky
And the most amazing thing that night?
United in thought—the whole world smiled.

Journal entry: 5 January - Surrey

I went early to bed at 10 p.m. Still awake, I glanced at the clock at 11.23 p.m. and felt the electrical stirrings which rapidly became stronger. Mentally, I asked, "Is that you, Malcolm?" Instantly, the electrical surge intensified and my entire being was engulfed by the most glorious feeling of love. What fantastic confirmation! When it was over, I was too lazy to look at the clock again, although I was conscious that I should have timed the experience. But I simply wanted to revel in the peace. I wanted to hold on to the feeling for as long as I possibly could. Eventually, reluctantly, I forced myself to sit up, grasp pen and note pad and write this at 2.20 a.m. It is, after all, part of the deal.

Journal entry: Tuesday, 11 January

Again, I lay awake and clearly heard the clock strike two, three, four, five and six. In a semi-dreamlike state I was picturing myself present at a board meeting with accountants and solicitors and I had taken along Dilys Guildford. On rising, I felt compelled to call her and left a message on her answerphone.

When we finally spoke I explained the scenario to her and how, at the time, I could not get it out of my head. She told me that there was obviously a strong and important message that needed to be channelled and this dream experience was guiding me to speak to her.

Journal entry: Friday, 14 January

Yet another night has passed with little sleep. I woke at two and heard the clock strike each hour. It is now 5.19 a.m. It is so frustrating. My head has been full of insecurities and worries about the company and our future. I have been longing for proof that Malcolm is aware of my difficulties, my confusion and my fears. I am far too needy, always searching for reassurance, and it troubles me. It is as though my world is in absolute turmoil, except at these special times during the night when the various spiritual connections take place.

Since 2 a.m. I have had the electrical stirrings once more. Most affected are my hands, arms, the top part of my torso and my crown. And I feel it throughout the entire 'chakra' energy system. It is pleasant and comforting with no fear attached. At least eight to ten times the sensation began and diminished. Then, suddenly, an *incredibly* forceful surge of power rocketed throughout my entire body, cumulating in such a loud rushing sound in my ears, that I simply knew I was about to *hear* again. Two words were spoken. Once again, I heard the pattern of sound but could not decipher the words. This was *so* frustrating!

Then, when I calmed down, I heard two precise words, "I'm here." This was accompanied with the deepest, all-encompassing feeling of peace.

I was left with a renewed confidence. I have no doubt now that my husband is clearly aware of my present circumstances and is continuing to assist me in every way available to him. The love I feel for him grows stronger each time I experience these proofs. He is, I am certain now, totally aware of all that is going on.

I feel very privileged to have this new understanding of life. I used to be as 'black and white as a zebra', refuting the idea of spiritual happenings, but now my entire thinking has been changed. My emotional state has been dramatically altered in the past months. Despite all that is happening, I now have a new state of well-being. I only hope that I prove to be a capable student and can use this information wisely.

Telephone reading: 14 January - Dilys Guildford

I telephoned Dilys as we'd arranged and listened in amazement as she passed on messages from Malcolm.

"*All I feel, when I think of you,*" said Dilys, "*is confusion and frustration although I do not know what it is about. There is a boardroom situation; is there somebody 'Tony' involved?*"

"There is someone called Tony who was here yesterday helping me with a problem." [Tony is an architect friend who is trying to help me.]

"*Malcolm is showing me different aspects to get us chatting in the right direction. It feels as though you have got to release something, to let go of it. He is showing me portions, like a compass, one part has to be let go of. It is like a marketing pie and a section of it will be released. It feels out of balance here. This is where the frustration and confusion comes from.*

"*Someone with the initials 'PD' is helping you. Malcolm is depicting that the piece 'ousted' is you leaving to get on with your life but he is saying it is not fair to lump everybody together. PD has picked up on this.*" [Where did Dilys get these initials? It must be

Peter Darby. I have never discussed this with her.]

"Malcolm is referring to a sum where the children are concerned, individually. He says you have got to put your Boadicea armour on. There are four of you to be provided for and it is unfair what is going on. I think it will be difficult for you to receive half of what is due but it has to be more than what has been offered. All the expenses to do with this should be taken out of the portion that is not yours. PD will help. Stick out for what is yours, it is very important. Malcolm gave his life to the family business and this must not be forgotten.

"Malcolm feels calmer now that he has got the message to us. He is showing me that all these issues must be written down. You must be prepared. Independent advice is needed for you. He is pleased that PD has turned up. You definitely need someone on your side.

"He is saying that you are doing a very good job. He is trying to raise your spirits. He is still so shocked, still in limbo. Until this is settled Malcolm cannot move on, cannot rest."

"Malcolm would never purposely leave unresolved issues," I said.

"He wants you to understand that he knows where you are and how things are for you. He is now telling me that you will soon be sitting at your long table that overlooks the estuary."

"Yes, at Westfield."

"There are questions about this house that have to be solved. When he talked to me about Tony, he also showed me the house in the west. He is putting the two together. He is saying you should think about Tony for the house in Devon also. Do you have any questions regarding the house in the West Country?"

"Does he still think it is a good idea to make it larger?"

"Yes! He has shown me exactly what it was going to look like. But in order to do this you must stick up for what is yours.

"I keep being shown large fees being paid to an accountant, a solicitor and a consultant to the company. Something is not right here. It is a fee-paying issue."

"I think I know what this is. My brother-in-law, Ian, is used to taking, not only a good salary, but also enormous director's fees."

" 'Yes,' Malcolm says, 'the fees; that is what I am talking about.' "

I replied, "Ian says that these fees will have to come out of my share of any sale of the company, because if he sells out, then once they have bought me out, he will only get a salary and no longer any director's fees."

"So you understand what Malcolm is talking about. 'Go for the half,' he says '… and don't take any nonsense.'"

"I would like to ask Malcolm a question; how important is his own blood family in all this?"

"'Not a lot,' he's replied, 'Ian was always out for his own ends.'"

"So true!" I said, "His mother once said to me, 'Patricia, it is always Ian first, Ian second and Ian last of all.'"

"Well, it won't be this time, Malcolm says, 'Go for half. And tell Patricia to keep in mind that truth always prevails.'"

*****

A friend lent me *Principles of Reiki* by Kasja Krishni Borang, which I began reading and was immediately consumed with interest. I rang Betty Blackburn the next day to ask about the possibility of learning Reiki. Before I could even ask the question, she said, *"Yes, Patricia, you are meant to learn about Reiki."*

We discussed how to go about this. I am unable to take weekly courses because I am often away but this was not a problem as the initiation is only a two-day course. I rang Clare and Karen and they were both keen to join in. I confirmed the dates with Betty, who was completely unsurprised as usual!

Journal entry: 20 January

I travelled to Scotland for four days with my friend, Linda, who worked for CIL. This trip had been arranged almost a year beforehand. On arrival, I telephoned old friends, Audrey and Geoff, whom I had not seen for thirty years. They had left Romney Marsh with their family in 1968 for the Isle of Mull. It seemed crazy to be staying so close and not call on them. We made arrangements to visit them on the following Sunday.

On arrival, we were welcomed into a warm farmhouse kitchen. After a while Audrey asked me, "What do you think of Geoff? He had a stroke just before Christmas." I said I was astonished because he seemed great to me, exactly as I remembered him.

Audrey then said quietly, "That's because I have been working on him daily since the moment it began. I am a healer." And then she looked at me and added, "And so are you, you just don't realise it yet."

My poor, long-suffering friend Linda rolled her eyes skywards and said, "I don't believe this. We cannot escape. Everywhere we go, she [me] finds something, or someone connected with this subject!"

I was overjoyed. It was more than a coincidence to discover that Audrey, whom I had known so long ago and had not seen for so many years, was involved in this same subject, which had become so very important to me.

Geoff said with a smile, "These past two days we have been asking each other, why is Trish visiting us after all this time? And why on earth would she choose to come to Mull in January of all times? It was really puzzling us. Now we know. You have been led here. It couldn't be simpler really. You are a reassurance to us as we are to you."

We chatted for four hours. They told us of the experiences they have had and their successes with particular, difficult illnesses. One lady was wheelchair bound when they met her and has now given it away.

Something really wonderful has come out of that trip to Scotland. We were also blessed with incredibly good weather, which meant I was able to take some excellent, atmospheric photographs. Good weather in January is almost unheard of there we were told. So that was a real bonus.

Journal entry: Tuesday, 25 January - 2.22 a.m. - Surrey

The stirrings began after 1 a.m. It was more like a dream than anything I had experienced before. Yet I was fully awake because I looked to see what the time was.

There was a scene, a parlour or lounge. I was with a middle-aged lady with greying hair. I immediately thought of Betty Blackburn. I didn't recognise where I was but felt very at ease in her company. She was standing and appeared to be completely at home. There was conversation between us yet I can't remember any of the words and I certainly did not physically hear any. It was not a work situation but a social one.

All the while the scene was being set, the electrical surges within me had increased to such a crescendo that I expected words to come. They didn't! What did happen was, in silhouette, my own hands appeared close up to my eyes. The left hand was growing alarmingly large and was trying to link with the fingers on the right hand. It really frightened me. In fact, so much that it shifted my thinking. It ended.

The scene remained but the hands had gone. Then, I was watching the same woman papering over some cracks in the walls. It was in only one corner of the room. I remained unmoving, in the same position, just looking on. The two hands returned. The same thing happened. The left hand grew larger before my eyes and strained to link with the right one. This time the power was so great that I allowed the hands to link. The fingers became entwined. They were as if clasped in prayer before my eyes. In an instant they reduced in size and the colour became normal. The power subsided. The lady continued her papering, oblivious to my experience. I *returned*.

In reality, my hands were far apart, one inside and one outside of the bedclothes. I drew them together and linked them exactly as shown in the scene. I did it to acknowledge the experience, which instantly ended.

I didn't know what to make of this. The romantic in me thought that my husband was reassuring me of his love. However, I began to wonder if it was an indication that I am meant to be attending Betty Blackburn's course to learn Reiki and how to heal with my hands? Perhaps I am meant to be working with her in some way? Or it could, of course, not be Betty at all but Audrey, from Mull. She could have simply been trying to link with me; it was all very puzzling.

ᥲ

Journal entry: Wednesday, 26 January

Earlier this evening Joy rang, the staunch Baptist friend who had initially reprimanded me. It appears she has two extra days holiday, which she had not realised, so I invited her to come and stay with me so I can introduce her to Betty Blackburn. If Betty is in agreement, she will join Karen, Clare and I on the Reiki course.

Journal entry: 7 March

I have to be honest; the Reiki course was not for me. I think it was my job to get the others on it. I seem to be the facilitator. Clare and Joy certainly benefited from the experience and gained confidence from it. However, even though I was desperate to learn and make myself useful, I came away with the definite impression that Reiki is not part of my path.

However, while I was trying to heal others, Betty told me that the overhead mobile in the room went berserk when I stood beneath it. When I touched someone, I was told it sent shock waves through them. I managed to give Clare an enormous headache which disappeared the moment I removed my hands. I didn't see the mobile turning, feel the shock waves or experience Clare's headache, of course, but the others certainly confirmed it all. I'm confused. I have every confidence in a force that heals. *It is in me that I lack confidence.*

On 23 February when I went to bed, I found it impossible to sleep again and was constantly looking at the clock, tossing and turning. It was nearly midnight when I felt the incredible pulsating in my hands and arms. It was the strongest I have ever experienced it. A glorious feeling of warmth and gentle electrical sensations bathed my torso in waves.

Then it came. I was not expecting the amazing strength of this experience. There was not the usual build-up that I have come to expect. The rushing sound in my ears and the voice were simultaneous, and again accompanied by a feeling of all-encompassing love. There was a gentle childlike voice and it was singing. At one time I was singing with it. The voice was gently la-

la-ing to the tune of 'Strawberry Fair'. I could feel myself squirming in the bed in time with the music, which we were making together. I was bathed in absolute delight.

Then all too soon it ended, at which point, wide awake, I picked up my pen and paper and began to write. What an incredible reassurance this was. It was like the human equivalent of the Internet. I was clearly receiving electrical power and an accompanying message from elsewhere. Are our brains not supposed to be the greatest computers ever devised?

It always amazes me that, although many of our religions clearly state that we are right to believe in life after death, when those who receive proof and reassurances dare speak they are shunned and treated as oddities. Just how many messengers of God have been burned at the stake or locked away in lunatic asylums, like Conan Doyle's father, I wonder, because of a refusal to deny what they *knew*? How many have been killed through the intolerance, ignorance and fear of others simply because of the unknown? How very brave they were for, in an effort to share their enlightenment with a then closed society, these poor people were treated appallingly and their messages fell on stony ground indeed. Perhaps my factual recording of these experiences may one day help to give a voice to them all.

*****

Joy rang me and told me about Paula, another healer, whom she thought I might benefit from meeting. Paula runs Bodyguide in Sussex and practices Reiki. Joy sounded so serious about my contacting her that I phoned and made an appointment. Again, I wasn't sure why, I simply knew that it *felt* right. I have been told to go where I am led during my period of learning so I am doing just that.

My appointment was one day after the fourth anniversary of Malcolm's death. We spoke for a short while, during which I outlined briefly the past year's happenings and my interest in all that had begun unfolding. Paula suggested that a Reiki treatment would both calm me and give her an insight into what is going on. I lay on the bed fully clothed with a blanket over me. No words were spoken and I kept my eyes closed.

Once I had settled, I saw the usual swathes of violet before my eyes, but nothing else. After Paula had been working for quite a long while I could suddenly feel her hands on my upper torso. They felt incredibly cold.

After half an hour or so, she asked me to turn over. Again, there were swathes of violet. My legs began tingling and Paula's hands again became very cold and I could no longer feel where she placed them. I was wide awake the entire time. I really don't relax well. At the end she placed her hands on my shoulder and I sat up almost immediately.

Paula said, *"Patricia, you are a very powerful person! What did you feel?"*

"Do you mind if I ask you what you experienced first?" I replied.

"Not at all, it was an interesting experience. While working on your upper body, in my mind's eye, I could see the most incredible pyramid of purple; it extended as far as I could visualise. It was there solidly all the time, and remained so throughout the first part of the treatment. However, I was a little concerned because when I got to your legs and began work, you began levitating off the bed and I was having great difficulty in keeping you grounded. Did you feel any of this?"

I explained that I always see purple swathes and that I did indeed feel a significant difference while she was working in the area of my legs.

"Are you a teacher?" Paula asked, "Only when I turned you over and began working again, I saw you surrounded by young children. There was also a young Native American with you."

I said that I was not a teacher but have been told that I had been in a past life and that I would also teach in the future. I explained that I had been given the name of one of my guides, a Native American, Eagle Eye.

"You have a great power, a gift, and there is something within you that is desperate to get out and be used, and at the moment this is being wasted. You began levitating once more when I turned you over. I don't think you realise the strength of this power that you

have. Do you attend an awareness class or a development group where they can help you?"

"No, although it has been suggested to me."

"What you have, Patricia, is quite wonderful but you have a long way to go and you have barely stepped onto the pathway. However, I don't think your way is healing with your hands. Your healing will be done with words. I am quite sure you are going to be a very capable medium, you have great power and ability within you. You must use it!"

Paula and I had never met before. She knew nothing of what Diana Summer, Betty Blackburn and Dilys Guildford had said to me previously. I had not even told her I had met them let alone what their opinions were.

Perhaps it is time to listen and to do as I have been told, even though I never seem to be very good at it.

Chapter 11
Feeling the Fear

Journal entry: 23 March 2000

Clare wanted to visit Paula and, while waiting for her, I visited my aunt Muriel. She was eager to learn how I had got on with Paula earlier in the week. When I told her about the pyramid, she was interested. The previous evening she had been listening to a radio programme. During this, the author of a book had been discussing the significance of the Pyramids of Giza in the year 2000 and the prophecies recorded in them. She could not remember the title of the book but knew the author's name was Gilbert.

Later the following afternoon, Clare and I drove into Dorking hoping to find information about possible development courses. There were none on offer at the time, so we decided to go into a mainstream bookshop and there I found the book described by my aunt. The title is *Signs in the Sky: The Astrological & Archaeological Evidence for the Birth of a New Age* by Adrian Gilbert. The book cover was *purple* and the backdrop to the printed title was a giant pyramid. Incredible, as my aunt is blind!

Last June, Suzanne had recommended a development group run by Valerie Kirkham. We later met Valerie and, although I was not ready to become part of any group at that time, I was impressed by her honest approach to spiritualism. In view of what Paula had suggested to me, I felt it was time to join such a group.

I asked Valerie if she could recommend someone in my area. She said she would try and find out but, at present, people from the Horsham, Farnham and Guildford areas seemed to join her group at East Grinstead. In view of this, it seemed sensible to ask Valerie if she and I could meet to discuss things.

We met at my home on 19 March and she stayed for several hours. We had a fascinating evening and I felt totally at ease with her and very encouraged. I didn't request a spiritual reading. I simply wanted to speak to someone about the entire concept, but it had to be someone in whom I had complete trust. All I can say is, again, it *felt right,* talking to her.

Valerie passed on survival evidence as it occurred ... and it seemed that an old aunt and uncle of mine whom my brother, sister and I had referred to as 'Titch and Lionel' were present. Valerie said that the names given to her were Beatrice and Lionel. My aunt's correct full name was indeed Beatrice. There were other snippets of information, which provided further reassurance to me that this was indeed genuine survival evidence.

Valerie explained that I was surrounded by an egg-shaped aura of white light and my understanding is that this is the Christ Light. She also told me that I have great strength emitting from me, together with healing powers but that these were not the conventional forms. I would be healing through words. Valerie laughed and said, *"Can I come to your book signing, Patricia? It looks as though it is going to be quite an event with a great deal of publicity!"*

I felt confused. "Sorry?" I said.

"Your book signing. You are going to write a book, perhaps you already are?" [Valerie had not been told about my journal at this point.]

"This book will be of great comfort to those who have been bereaved."

As she had broached the subject without any help from me, I told Valerie about my journal and how it had grown over the last months.

She continued, *"You will make an area in your home to do spiritual work but it is not here. You will be writing in a conservatory, overlooking a harbour or a river."*

At this point I explained about Westfield. She asked to see a picture and said, *"Yes ... I could see all this greenery in the picture but it is not quite right. There will be a conservatory here ..."*

She indicated a conservatory would be built on the right-hand side of the property, which is exactly as it appears on the plans that have been drawn up recently but Valerie would have no knowledge of that.

She went on, *"Also, I can see you having garden parties but the land will not be like this, it will be flatter somehow."*

I then told her of my intention to terrace the garden so that we could place tables and chairs on it and create a more useful space. I am interested in helping the Royal National Lifeboat Institution (RNLI) by opening my garden to the public in the future. I had discussed holding such events in the garden at Westfield with a friend, only the previous year.

As Valerie was leaving I asked if I could attend the healing circle that she runs on Monday evenings. She said I would be welcome but noticed that I looked a little hesitant. I explained that I felt it morally wrong of me to have taken Reiki One and then make no effort to use it. I felt that I should, at least, give it one more try.

The following day I attended the class. I was made very welcome but knew, almost from the moment I sat down, that this did not feel right. I joined in wholeheartedly but had to be completely honest when asked about what my experiences had been during the class. I simply cannot nod like a donkey and pretend to see what I have not seen or heard things I have not heard. The fact was that I experienced very little and, although I could follow the leader of the meditation's thinking, I could not pretend experiences which I had not had. I left the group feeling disappointed with myself.

The next day, Valerie rang me. I told her the truth about the class. She said she was not the least surprised as she feels such groups are not for me; it is not my particular path.

"The fact is, Patricia, you are far more advanced than those who sit in the circle. This is a waste for you," she said. *"But I do feel that you would benefit from the mediumship circle, held on alternate Mondays. You will definitely be healing but with words. Listening to you speaking last Sunday was electrifying and of enormous benefit to me; I learned a great deal that evening, you have no idea of the power within you and how you come across to others.*

"You are unconscious of the knowledge you hold, which is precisely why people both now and in the future will be drawn to listen to you, to learn from what you have to say. Your gift will come

soon and it will be strong. I feel that you and I have been connected for a reason and it is not so you will be sitting in my classes, far from it, you are beyond these really. However, you are very welcome to join us if the support will be of use to you at this time."

I accepted her invitation to attend the class on the following Monday evening.

Journal entry: 28 March

Last night I attended Valerie's mediumship class. I was made welcome and looked forward to it. However, at the end, I felt it was simply another clarification of the point made to me some time ago by Betty Blackburn. *"Classes are a waste of your time and money. This will come naturally to you when the time is right."*

After linking jointly together in thought we were asked what had transpired. Others gave their accounts. I could give nothing. Unusually for me, I saw absolutely nothing at all when I closed my eyes, not even the colour violet. I explained to the class that I did not mean to be unhelpful but I felt that I would have to accept what I had already been told. Whatever was in mind for me, I would have to be working entirely alone. This was confirmed again, when working in pairs, trying to tune into another person. Penny, who had the misfortune to be paired with me, said that in her vision all she saw was a large door virtually being slammed in her face. She went on to say that she felt no animosity just an enormous peace which made her drowsy.

When it was my turn to say what I had experienced when trying to link with her I could only say, "I'm sorry, Penny, I seem to be useless at this!" At least it gave everyone a laugh.

I was desperate to try and accomplish something. I was in dire need of some direction. I left and am quite sure now that I need to accept that I am not meant to be attending any classes. As if I wasn't already lonely enough!

I am, however, pleased to have made contact again with Valerie and I feel sure that this was the reason for the entire exercise. I believe we are meant to keep in touch. I hope we will be helping each other.

My problems regarding the company business have escalated and I went to bed in turmoil, my head full of the business affairs. I was in tears, terribly cold, and felt dreadfully alone. I asked for reassurance. After the normal prayer routine, I slept and didn't wake until 5.30 a.m.

After a drink I decided to go back to bed and listen to the tape that Gloria had sent to me. I listened to it four times and eventually felt more relaxed. Then, I began to feel the stirrings of electricity, which are now so familiar. I was amazed at the intensity. I heard what I thought was an Elvis Presley song (I was never a fan). This faded and then I heard a noise similar to a radio being tuned in. The electrical surges continued their *squeezing* motion. Then a different rock and roll song could be heard. There was a voice speaking at the same time. I'm not sure whether it was a single voice or several; it was confusing and I could not hear the message clearly.

Into my thoughts came the story of the singer Buddy Holly, who died in a plane crash. I also heard two words, 'wing' and 'rust'. It scared me. I was worried that it was symbolic of my flight to India planned for the following Saturday and so I rang Betty Blackburn for advice. She told me it is the present uncertainty and pressures I fear which are confusing things. *"You need to get back to nature; take yourself for a walk somewhere where there are trees. Go, then phone and tell me what comes to you."*

Later that day I walked in Reigate Park. I leant against a huge horse-chestnut tree and words came to me within minutes, so I scribbled them down on my shopping list. Later these became a poem, which I read to a delighted Betty later that day:

Nature's Power

I have no wish to maim or break
Or another's sadness make.

I only wish with joy to see
Unfolding leaves upon a tree.

I have no need to rant and rave
I'm grateful for the air I breathe.

I love the horizon before my eyes
The quiet green and soothing skies.

I have no wish to cause great shame
Or hurt someone with unkind names.

May I see the beauty in each flower
And cherish every passing hour.

Away from noise and busy street
I relish the earth beneath my feet.

I only wish birdsong to hear
And that my pathway be made clear.

When darkness and despair I see
Nature's Power will strengthen me.

Journal entry: 29 March

Something uncanny and not very pleasant happened last night. I was woken abruptly at 1.30 a.m. by a deafening sound, just like an aircraft engine. After the initial roar, there was nothing but deep, penetrating silence. It terrified me. It brought back all the fears about an aircraft crashing.

I demanded, mentally, that unless the message was repeated three times I would simply refuse to believe it. It wasn't. But I was still petrified and I couldn't return to sleep. I was thinking about all the dreadful scenarios should this happen on my way to or from India. I simply couldn't rest.

It was a nightmare. I have travelled thousands of miles around the globe and flying has never worried me, but I took this very seriously indeed. Logic returned. My father is usually ultrasensitive about my trips so I decided to ring him to see how he was feeling.

Obviously, I did not tell him my fears; that would have been grossly unfair.

Dad was on top form. He was very cheerful and speaking to him reassured me. I simply wanted to assess his mood and take guidance from him. My mother confirmed that Dad was untroubled. Nonetheless I decided that later in the morning I would call the mediums I had met in the last year and ask their help.

The first person I rang was Diana Summer, then Dilys, Paula and Valerie. I left messages on all of their phones. I rang Nina in Brighton last and she kindly dowsed for me and asked specific questions of her guide about my upcoming trip to India.

"Would the outbound trip be okay?"

"Yes."

"Would the inbound trip be okay?"

"Yes."

"Would anything go wrong while I was there?"

"No."

It was such relief. We spoke for a while, and Nina told me that she felt we would meet again in the near future. She trains mediums and might be able to help me. She said I would gain, spiritually, from my trip to India and wished me well. I thanked her then got on with the day.

Still a little puzzled, I rang Betty Blackburn, who confirmed my thoughts that some mischief had been played on me. During the course of the day, Diana, Paula, and Valerie each rang, confirming that, in their opinion, all would be well on my proposed trip. I was relieved. If I had told my friend Carol that I was thinking of cancelling the trip to Goa, she would have probably slaughtered me anyway!

One thing that has occurred to me during the course of the day is that last night when I went to bed I glanced only momentarily at the picture of Eagle Eye. I knew it was sometime since I had used his picture for meditation. I felt as if I should do so but was so tired.

It is now midnight and I am going to bed once more. Tonight, tired or not, I shall use his picture for my meditation. How can you expect help and protection from your guide if you don't acknowledge The Source?

Chapter 12
Escape from 'All Things Spiritual'?

Journal entry: 19 April 2000 - Goa, India

After seventeen hours we arrived at our hotel in Goa. We were exhausted and it was very hot. During the first night I experienced the usual electrical sensations and in the morning was awake at 6.30 a.m. to write down notes, which later became the following.

Meditation

I need to learn how to reach deep inside
Into recesses, where I'm trying to hide
Truths, known only to my own soul
Which unacknowledged, will hinder my goal.

Allow me to enter my own private place
Where silence is beauty in unlimited space
May my mind wander into the unknown
Strong in the knowledge, that I'm never alone.

At times, recognitions will give me a clue
There's much more to life, to me—and to you
Buried within us there is, I believe
Incredible power which longs to be free.

There was no activity of any type whatsoever. I was truly being allowed a holiday. I was hoping to leave all the spiritual stuff behind and have a real rest.

During the course of the second week, one evening Carol and I wandered into Dawn Rose, a crystal shop in Candolim, in order for me to buy gifts for friends. Sitting in the corner behind a counter was a woman. When the only other two customers left the shop, she looked up at me and said directly, *"You're a healer, aren't you?"*

I was furious. I replied, "So everyone keeps telling me but I'm trying to leave it behind at the moment!" She laughed out loud. Her name was Kellen Hakhroo, an Englishwoman who has lived with her Indian husband in Goa for a number of years. I was instantly drawn to her. We enjoyed discussing the crystals and chatted together for a long while. Kellen was about to pack both shop and home (prior to monsoon) and return to the Bristol area of England with her husband. It transpired that she has some close friends who live only a few miles from my home.

I felt very comfortable talking to Kellen and asked if we could meet to chat on a one-to-one basis another time. We made arrangements for two days later. On discovering I was staying at the Prazeres Resort, she commented that she also lived there, in one of the flats, so it would be very convenient to meet in the hotel room. Coincidence or synchronicity?

On the day, Kellen arrived at 10 a.m. as planned. Carol had arranged to go out for the morning so we had complete privacy.

"I knew you were a healer the minute you entered my shop, Patricia," Kellen said. I was again surprised by this.

We talked at length and Kellen told me about herself and her work. In turn, I told her about some of my experiences. Kellen amazed me even further by saying, *"Patricia, you are far more advanced than I but you don't realise it yet. You need training to make it flow. I am getting clear visionary pictures as we are speaking. I am in a jungle with many people trailing behind me. I am hacking away with a machete trying to go forward but I have no idea where it is I need to go. Suddenly, you appear, you take my hand and also take over the wielding of the machete. You carve a definite pathway, pulling me behind you, and all the other people follow us.*

"You have to remember who you are. You are a very old soul, you have lived many lives, and you have advanced in your aims. You are well beyond me, Patricia, and it is time for you to accept your

role. Believe in yourself and begin the work you are here to do at this time. If you don't wake up, you will be given a kick-start to make you. Trust in your guides and the angels protecting you.

"*Time,*" she reiterated, "*is short. Many have been 'woken' and it is time for us to begin networking, pulling together in order to be in position and fully supported and operational at the right time. Why else do you think you have travelled halfway round the world only to meet me who can guide you towards a support group, which you badly need, only a few miles from your own home?*"

She read my Tarot and saw my business problems plainly. She said that it was clearly stated that unless I admit to feelings of anger, resentment and revenge I would be unable to forgive, get over them and move on. I will be blocked from claiming what is rightfully mine. At present, I am stifling feelings in order to protect others. I have to learn how to release these in order to *'ascend'*. She also warned that if I do not somehow achieve this I am likely to lose the first business battle in an effort for these feelings to be pushed forward. I will then be in a position of being unable to deny such feelings as I will be so angry and will have to acknowledge these and get over them.

Kellen gave me a long list of book titles which will help me and also the contact details of a medium in Sussex, called Shane. She said I should get in touch with people who would support me more than she is able to. I told her about Valerie Kirkham in Sussex. I felt sure they should meet when Kellen returns to the UK. Amazingly, it transpired that Valerie and Kellen have the same guide.

Before she left, Kellen said, "*Patricia, you are the most powerfully spiritual person I have had in my shop in the past eight years. I feel that you have come to help me in some way. I have been told before that my shop is to be a meeting place, a crossroads for people like us to be put in touch with others. This has made sense to me today. I feel that I am meant to meet Valerie and hopefully my introducing you to those in Sussex will also help you.*"

Following her visit I was prompted to write the following:

A Prayer for Assistance

I ask of my angels, please help me to find
A way to express all the anger inside.

I know, that unless this resentment is free
I'm unable to use the power which is me.

Teach me to trust and acknowledge myself
So this power may be channelled and be of some help.

Letting go of one's feelings is hard to do
But not if I learn to place trust in you.

I wish to accept and acknowledge my role
Some things, though unpleasant, are good for my soul.

Help me discover just who I am.
Together, let's simply get on with the plan.

Then later, lazing around the pool, I wrote:

Steps

Close your eyes, quietly enter your mind
Then step beyond your mind ...

Search the very corners of your heart
Then step beyond your heart ...

Reach inside, find your own Spirit
Then step beyond your Spirit ...

Listen to the cry from deep inside
Take confidence, in the presence of your guide

Enter the essence of your own soul
Here truth you'll find and your own special role.

Later that evening, still interested in crystals, Carol and I ambled along to Dawn Rose once more. We spent a couple of hours talking to Kellen about the various uses and asking her advice on them. Her honesty was amazing. We had a long list of crystals which we had read about and thought necessary for our well-being and personal situations. However, Kellen used her intuitive and spiritual powers and told us it was unnecessary to buy so many. She helped us to gauge which would give us the required assistance. While there, I held a piece of moldavite, which I was told aids alignment with the higher self. After a few moments Carol asked me to put it down. I asked her why.

She said, "Because I can feel it from here, an immense power which is making me feel light-headed and 'high'." (I could feel nothing, as usual!)

Carol was very hot and uncomfortable and Kellen agreed, for she could also feel it from the other side of the counter. Ever doubting, after a few moments I surreptitiously picked it up once more while they were engrossed discussing another crystal entirely.

Suddenly, Carol said, "Have you picked that up again? For heaven's sake put it down. I feel as though I am floating!" Convinced this time, I did as asked. I was less than popular!

Reading: 2 May - Dilys Guildford

Back in the UK, I returned to Devon. Deeply concerned about the business and our future, I had made arrangements to visit Dilys Guildford for a reading. I arrived in Dartmouth in good time but looked in vain for a parking place. In the end I abandoned the car on the pavement and rushed inside to tell Dilys that I had arrived. She met me on the stairs and said, *"You're having trouble parking, aren't you?"*

"Yes!" I replied, breathlessly. "What on earth do you do with cars around here?"

"Don't worry. Hand me your things then go back outside and drive just beyond the chemist. You'll find a space big enough for you there."

I looked incredulously at her. She laughed and repeated her instructions and added, *"Hurry or you'll lose it. Malcolm has told me where there is space!"*

I didn't argue. Thrusting my things at her I hurtled back out into the street, jumped into the car and turned on the engine. I drove once more around the block and past the chemist. Four car lengths beyond there was a space more than adequate for me to park in. I returned to a smiling Dilys.

"Well?" she enquired.

"You were right, just beyond the chemist. Thank you!"

"Don't thank me—thank Malcolm!"

The ever-present sceptic in me scoured the walls of the building to see if there were any windows from where Dilys could have seen the space for herself. There were none.

Once settled inside we began the session.

"I never channel Malcolm without having a good time."

Dilys began pouring us both glasses of water and started laughing, saying, *"He is telling me to say to the tape, this is not whisky! 'Go on, say it, say it,' he is saying, he is very present. He is right here."*

I told her, "Whisky was Malcolm's rare and favourite tipple." [Dilys could not have known that.]

"He is showing me one of those little beach huts beside the beach."

"That's Littlestone, in Kent, we have a home there," I said.

"I wouldn't know but he is clearly showing me this.

"Malcolm was speaking to me this morning about financial matters and you cannot just let this go. You are finding it hard, this business problem, but you are right to do as you are doing. He is telling me you hear him intuitively because you do many things he advises you to do. This is a good way for it to begin. He needs more time to build his energy resources, to learn how to do things in a different way. This is two-way, you know. Things must go very gently for both of you. Energy takes time to build. Other spirit relatives will join him to give him the necessary energy.

"Malcolm says that Ian has pushed it a bit too far, enough is enough. He has lost the respect of the family. 'It is right to fight for

our boys.'"

"I have learned two things in the course of the last year," I said, "one is that there undoubtedly is a God and the second is that my brother-in-law, most definitely, *is not it!*"

"Malcolm is saying, 'You finally have your little girl.'"

"He means Karen, his daughter. During the course of the last year, and the unfolding of the spiritual happenings, Karen and I have become very close. It is wonderful. I always hoped for a daughter; it was a joke between Malcolm and me, now it seems I have one."

"'Yes.' He is saying, 'You have your daughter, she is totally with you. Your little girl is with you.' Is there also on her side somebody called Evelyn?"

"Malcolm's mother was Ruby Evelyn."

"This lady with Malcolm is sending her love to Karen. Will you tell her? Malcom's mother, Evelyn, is coming in to help him. 'It is the right time now,' he is telling me and he can share you. Previously he has wanted to be centre stage, he couldn't."

"I wonder what his mother thinks of Ian's actions?" I said.

"Terrible. She is aghast. You must realise from this that the spiritual family is supporting you. Ian is going to discover this and, if he's not careful, he will lose everything and that is not what his mother wants."

"That isn't what anyone wants. We only want what is just recompense for my husband's years of hard work, no more, no less," I said.

"This proves that your actions are honourable. You must accept that this is your role and see this through. It is your job to see it through fairly.

"I am being shown a broken wrist. Did Malcolm have a broken wrist?"

"Yes, a weak wrist," I explained, "he broke it while in the Territorial Army (TA) parachuting."

"Well, it is a proof; he is showing me for your benefit. He keeps showing me the colour lilac, does that mean anything?"

"I see a lot of lilac and purple when my eyes are closed. I have been told many times that I am connected to St. Germain and the violet flame."

"Those colours are indicative of a higher power. You probably need grounding. I am being told to tell you this.

"Now," Dilys continued, *"I also have to explain to you that you have a guide with you. It is a gentleman who is also connected with the violet fire. He is on a higher plane."*

"I was hoping to find out the name of my guides. I know we may have several."

"We have so many helpers. We can ask for help from those who are technology based, or medically based or even legally based," Dilys said. *"Your guide is telling me that Ian is 'out of balance'. He is still suffering bereavement himself so we must look upon the situation charitably. However, you have to look at the law being correct in the truth of the matter. Ian has gone off course. Your role is to pull him back round to his rightful truth."*

Chapter 13
The Beginning of Seeing

Journal entry: Saturday, 16 May 2000 - Kent

I was incredibly hot, reminding me of the nights in Goa. I raised myself from bed and saw in the mirror my shape hauling itself upright. I threw off the dressing gown I had worn for extra warmth then watched myself lie down. I lay there thinking, *I didn't realise we had a mirror on that wall.* Still sleepily musing over the possibility that someone had moved my mirror I raised myself once more and watched my shape move backwards and forwards. In the half-light I picked out the shape of the bed, the pillows, the bedside table and lamp. Looking at the wall I could see everything in a mirror image.

It slowly occurred to me that the entire wall, from floor to ceiling, was reflecting like a mirror. I lay back down, reluctant to wake properly. As realisation dawned, I grew a little concerned as I knew there was no mirror in that position, let alone covering the entire wall. I raised myself once more, watching my movements in the mirror image. Then, slowly, just like a home video camera the image began to fade until all I could see was the blank darkness of the wall. Simultaneously, I heard, *"This is the beginning of seeing."*

I lay back down contemplating the whole experience. Then Valerie came to mind. I wondered if our new friendship, and the fact that we are being led to get to know one another, was for us to introduce our different circles of friends and to enable *the realisation* to widen. As this thought entered my head I clearly heard, in my left ear, *"Yes, that's right."*

Surprised at receiving such a direct confirmation, yet unafraid, I continued lying in bed. Then swathes of violet bathed my eyes; it was beautiful. I opened my eyes and, to my utter surprise, the violet colour was still visible; swathes of colour, gently rolling and gliding in clear sight. Intuitively, once more I heard, *"This is also the beginning of seeing."*

This seemed to add credence to the words, 'daughter of the violet fire' and 'the purity God desires', for I had heard this several times before but not understood. Unafraid, I thanked my guides for this experience, then I picked up my pen to write.

For the rest of the night I was bathed in feelings of peace and love. I could feel the vibrations of my body altering as, wave after wave, they rippled through me. I wondered if I might hear more voices but these did not materialise.

Journal entry: Saturday, 3 June - 3.10 a.m.

After weeks of inactivity regarding spiritual 'happenings', things have begun moving once more. This has given me tremendous reassurance. I went to bed at around midnight. Regardless of the late hour I did not feel particularly tired.

The electrical stirrings began straight away. I found this a tremendous comfort. Unsleeping, I continued to register these and was grateful for their return after such a long absence. They reached a tremendous crescendo, resulting in my feeling as though my entire body was being lifted from its prone position. In my mind's eye, I could once again see swathes of the colour purple. It was fantastic. I clearly heard once more the radio tuning in noises and welcomed them. I could not decipher actual words of course. The whole experience was so intense that it prompted me to remember to repeat the prayers for protection. I repeated these strongly in my mind, yet the experience continued and I was reassured. Eventually, things became less intense. When it had ceased, I looked at the clock, which registered a little after three, and wrote.

Journal entry: Friday, 9 June - 7.56 a.m.

Recently, sleep has been evading me. It is partly my own fault; I should go to bed much earlier. Last night was a prime example. Following prayers and protection, the vibrations began. However, it is a pleasant feeling, and the knowledge that I am not actually sleeping is no longer accompanied by feelings of anger, as it used to be. My body, particularly my hands and arms but, occasionally, my whole body, felt like a gently vibrating engine which moves in and out of different gear levels at its own instigation. As well as the normal swathes of rolling violet, I was also entertained by, what I can only describe as, a host of patterns. Outline drawings of objects and occasionally faces, some known, some unknown. It's a little like a miniature film playing before my eyes. There are often hands in the prayer position, several pairs. I also see spectacles and, now and again, I see a face which reminds me of Gandhi. My entire inner vision was taken up by these phenomena.

At 6 a.m. I finally accepted that sleep was not to be and began listening to a relaxation tape. I have a continuous play Walkman now and during the first and second playing my body continued to feel like a gently revving engine with the same cinemascope as entertainment. Then things changed!

An amazing inner peace seemed to click silently into position and I found I was staring at something quite different and my vision clearly focused on a shape which I could not identify. I would describe it as staring at the concave section of a bath, the surface of which had the appearance of a pitted orange skin. The colour was a muddy green/brown and there was a small lump of other matter, which I felt compelled to brush off as it was spoiling an otherwise equal surface. It looked totally solid and still. There was no movement at all and it lasted longer than other visionary experiences. I remember thinking, *I wonder if this is also to do with the beginning of seeing*. As I did so, the picture began to fade and was replaced with the usual violet/purple. I continued to listen to the tape a third time but the vibrations had stopped and my vision returned to normal. It was over. I picked up my pen.

Journal entry: Friday, 9 June - 23.21 p.m.

I drove to Bodyguide for my Reiki appointment. Stepping into Paula's healing room is like stepping into a haven, a sanctuary of peace. All is spotless, yet welcoming, and I felt totally at home in her company.

It took me a while to settle. Visions of purple appeared but little else happened. I remained edgy for a while but then a single thought penetrated my consciousness, "*Ask Paula to read the journal.*" I was puzzled and couldn't quite understand why I should do this. I asked for confirmation. The message was intuitively repeated clearly ... twice more. I accepted this and decided to mention it to Paula after the treatment.

At the end Paula said to me, "Are you thinking of moving? Where is the white house by the sea?" Clearly she had seen Westfield.

"You had several guides with you. Also, Peter." [I assumed she meant Peter Darby. He has been mentioned before but Paula knows nothing about him.]

"There was also a Raymond." [My intention, after treatment, was to collect my aunt Muriel from her home and take her to see her daughter, currently in hospital having treatment. Muriel's late husband, my uncle, was called Raymond.] 'Uncle Ray' we knew him as. I guess as I was in his hometown and being involved with his wife and daughter that very day, it is likely he would choose to be present!

"You also had a very imposing Native American guide who has confirmed he will be helping you with the next stage of your journey." [I asked his name, expecting her to say Eagle Eye.] "It is Red Wolf. He has an enormous headdress with feathers, which reach the floor. He is a very imposing figure."

Paula continued, "When I last saw you I also saw a lot of purple. Well, this time as soon as I touched you I saw a great pillar of golden light shoot up which reached as far as the eye could see. It is very interesting working with you, Patricia!" We both laughed.

I told her that I feel guilty because, although I have taken the Reiki first degree, I have not yet had the courage to use it. I do, however, attempt absent healing every night and keep a healing book. Paula said that I wasn't to worry. Hands-on healing is not my path. My path is to be a medium and help others in that manner but I am not quite ready yet.

I felt totally at home chatting to her. Like Valerie and Kellen, it is as though we've met before. I have no qualms about sending her my journal and feel I can trust her absolutely. I am constantly amazed at the number of interesting people I am being led to meet. I am grateful and feel very privileged.

Chapter 14
Synchronicities and Significant Moments

Reading: 10 June 2000 ~ Martin

I recently met with a medium named Martin. I made it clear that I was not in the least interested in any sort of 'fortune telling' and, to his credit, he made it equally clear to me that he wasn't either!

"On a creative level," Martin said, *"you are about to add to your work, or significantly make a change regarding it, possibly both. You are using the abilities inside you for this work. You are to encounter a far brighter future provided you are prepared to trust your instincts. In the next few months you need to retain your sceptic attitude. You will hear many opinions and you must act only when you feel entirely comfortable with advice given. Stick with what feels right.*

"You are a teacher and will impart knowledge to others. You are not aware, but you are doing it already. You don't necessarily constantly give your opinion but the very way that you are, and the way you that you speak, is indicative of the way you work on behalf of the spirit world. Trust your instincts; they will never let you down.

"You are rather abrupt on the surface but are working on behalf of forces who are the same; therefore, this is how you will appear to the rest of the world. Some people will back off from you, don't be concerned.

"Within the next few months there is a decision facing you, which you alone can make. It will not be simple. You'd love to do nothing and let it all fade away but that is not right. Some people will not understand the decision you make. Emotions will try to interfere and you will wish that you didn't have to do this.

"If you don't pursue your true course, you will be forced to. Pressure of the forces will be channelled to you. It will not be easy. There will be many areas to consider. Do your deliberation unselfishly. This is not about wealth, it is about principles. You will be in unison with spirit wishes. It is meant to be. Once you have faced this struggle, you will change and be free to move on. Doubt and uncertainty will be cleared; indeed it is already becoming clear to you but your mind is still a little confused. You are thinking, why am I not worried about this anymore?

"Because you are not the main beneficiary, that is why, and it is a good vehicle for you to use. We have a duty to ourselves provided we are sure of the correct intent. 'You are nobody's fool but someone is taking you for one,' is being clearly said to me. It is your duty to set the record straight; it is part of your learning and also theirs. Win, lose or draw, financially, unless your adversary feels that the evidence of this scenario directly affects him, he will learn nothing from it. It is your job, your duty, to teach this person this lesson and also to learn from it yourself, before you can progress.

"This same person treated your husband as a fool too. Your husband was a caring, considerate and gentle man. This was taken advantage of. No one should get away with unethical behaviour and it has fallen to you to teach your adversary so.

"If you say, 'forget it', you will never be able to move on. Remember, this is not about money, even if you lose some in the process; this is about a principle and you progressing along your own spiritual path. This is important!

"You will be more creative morally and ethically. You must do what you feel you can live with. This is what is right for you. You will find spiritual justice even if you do not gain legally. This will then leave you free to continue on your path once you get over this obstacle; otherwise, it will be a chain around your neck forever.

"'They will never stop using emotional blackmail to manipulate you,' is what I am being told. 'You'll cause me to have a heart attack if you pursue this,' is one line which springs to mind. Your answer must be firm. 'You should have thought about that beforehand,' will suffice. This emotional blackmail has to stop. It is just a matter of facts. You must deal ethically and with honest intentions with the

facts only.

"If you decide to go the legal way, be very sure you employ advisors with whom you feel comfortable. They need to be on your wavelength. Ensure you pick those who you settle with, trust your immediate impression.

"Have you noticed when you are with people that you don't have to speak to them or even look at them in order to be noticed? You don't have to do anything for them to feel your presence when you walk in a room?" [I thought, Yes, often, but I just assumed it was because they were looking at me critically because of my size.]

"This is spirit. People feel what generates from you. It is the energy of transmitted protection around you. Nothing can touch it. People acknowledge that you are always the same. You are true to yourself.

"There is someone behind this man who is challenging you. The person behind him is more devious and more materialistic than he is. This is a woman.

"The guide who has been here for you wishes to give you confirmation. Is there something wrong with his wrist? He keeps showing me that there is a problem with his wrist." At this point I confirmed, as I had to Dilys, that Malcolm had a weak wrist.

"When you go to bed at night remember that your guides are there to help you and simply say, 'You know my needs, please help.'"

Afterwards, I chatted to Martin about the various phenomena I had experienced. This was the first time we had discussed anything. Martin explained that the electrical surges are the spirits entering my aura. I said it was always accompanied by the most wonderful feeling of peace and love. He smiled and said, *"There are no words to describe it adequately, are there?"* I knew then that we both knew exactly what the other was talking about. What a relief!

Martin said that I could call him any time if I needed his help in the months ahead. I had now met yet another helpful person on this journey, all who help to enrich the entire experience.

Journal entry: Sunday, 9 July

It has been a month since I have had anything personal to note. During this time I have not been idle. Poetry is coming thick and fast. There is, however, one interesting story ...

We have to go back to 1994 when Malcolm was still alive. Linda and I were about to embark on a trip to Thailand, Malaysia and Singapore. Malcolm said, "While you are in Singapore, look up my cousin, Gordon, for me, my dear."

My reply was dubious, "Oh, come on, Malcolm! When did you last see your cousin?"

"When I was about fifteen," he replied, smiling.

"Then he is hardly going to want a complete stranger turning up, is he?" I said.

"Just do it, my dear, do it for me," replied Malcolm. "He will make you very welcome."

So, while in the Cameron Highlands, Malaysia, I telephoned Gordon. True to Malcolm's word, he did sound pleased that I'd called. He said, "I will send a car to the hotel for you and Linda when you arrive. I have been invited to friends that evening but I know they will welcome you."

We were, indeed, made very welcome and enjoyed a wonderful evening in the garden of Kiam Hong and Bee Choo's home. We sat beneath velvet, star-studded sky, surrounded by fabulous bamboos that swayed gently in the breeze. It remains a special memory.

Gordon and I met again, in 1999, when he returned to England to attend his mother's funeral. Chatting over dinner I discovered that he had retired from business and had decided to spend his time travelling, writing and taking photographs. It seemed we had these interests in common. We had both travelled to Mongolia and other parts of Asia so there was plenty of conversation. Gordon mentioned that he planned to return to Singapore and China but that he would be travelling to Europe in the summer with Kiam Hong and Bee Choo.

I mentioned to him the photography weekend, planned with a Canon lecturer, at Westfield in August. (Gordon had recently bought a new Canon identical to my own.) I invited him to join me at the photography weekend, if he wished to learn how to use it more efficiently. He accepted.

We corresponded by email and I learned that his intention was to return to England with Kiam Hong and Bee Choo for one week in June, before the three of them set off across France and into Switzerland. It was an ideal opportunity for us to meet again and for me to say thank you for their kindness to me in Singapore.

I suggested that I show them around during their stay and arranged for Linda and myself to collect the three of them from central London before travelling on to Surrey for a few days so they could see something of the South East, then an extra day in London before returning to France.

So, on 21 June, we set off early to Stonehenge. Only I could arrive on such a day and not realise the significance! It was midsummer's day; a most interesting day for them to visit the site and purely by chance. Kiam Hong and Bee Choo were thrilled to see such traditional activity around the stones. It was alive with Pagans and Druids and I was pleased that I had insisted on such an early start. Afterwards, we continued to Salisbury, Bosham and Bodiam Castle, ending up in Rye for dinner.

That morning, I asked Gordon about his completed novel. He said that, although it was a novel, the underlying point of the book was one of spirituality. I was amazed to be discussing this subject with him so openly on the first leg of our journey. It was only the third time we had ever met!

Strange, yet encouraging, things happened during the day. I would be looking at something, about to mention it to our guests, when suddenly Gordon would begin speaking my thoughts. This also happened in reverse. During those two days, it happened at least a dozen times. It became quite a joke.

During dinner, Bee Choo asked us how often Gordon and I had met previously. I said that this was only the third time. She found it unbelievable because we seemed to know each other so well. He also found it amazing that we were seemed to be so 'in sync' and jokingly suggested that we had been cousins in a previous lifetime.

We all stayed in Mulberry Cottage, in Kent, and enjoyed walking along the shore to buy fresh bread for breakfast. We set off to explore Dungeness, several churches on the Romney Marsh and late in the afternoon we drove through Kent to Greenwich in order to view The Millennium Dome from the exterior. Parking on the north side of the river, we walked through the tunnel beneath the Thames. After viewing the Cutty Sark and other delights of Greenwich, we found a Vietnamese restaurant in which to share our final meal together.

By this time I was pretty exhausted with leading this whistle-stop tour. When seated, we were all quietly contemplative but after a few mouthfuls of food we began to feel rejuvenated. Gordon sparked off a conversation about spirituality; religious beliefs, Buddhism, etc. Kiam Hong, Gordon and I became absolutely engrossed. It was accompanied for me by the oddest feeling. I suddenly became full of life, and while speaking, quite forthright views on the matter, I was also thinking to myself, *I didn't realise I knew that!* It was as though someone else was speaking through me. It was a most peculiar sensation but I felt completely *alive.*

Gordon and Kiam Hong seemed astonished that such strong beliefs could come from an Englishwoman. Gordon joked, "Perhaps Patricia is a Buddhist in disguise?"

Kiam Hong, though, was quite grave and after a moment, he spoke. "Yes, I think you could be right but it is deeper than that, Gordon. I think Patricia has been experiencing similar spiritual phenomena to those that you and I have witnessed. She is a very spiritual person."

It was my turn to be astonished!

Much later, I drove all of us to Kiam Hong and Bee Choo's hotel in central London. I accepted the offer of a coffee, simply to keep me awake. Kiam Hong said that he had a gift for me and gravely, and with great dignity, presented me with a small red book with Chinese writing on it in gold. We had been discussing Buddhism in the car and I then realised that this was a copy of *The Heart Mantra*, which is carried as a talisman by Buddhists.

Gordon looked as surprised as I. "Thank you," I said, "I know what this is. I also realise its importance and why you carry it but I cannot accept it, it is far too great a gift."

Undeterred Kiam Hong said, "Patricia, this evening has been very special indeed. It was not the making of you or I, it was by design. It was meant to be. I know that it is my duty to give this to you and it is also your duty to receive it."

There was nothing more to be said.

Journal entry: 10 July - Surrey

Paula wrote to me to say that she had finished reading the few pages of my journal which I had left with her. The words in her card were beautiful, so beautiful in fact that I have included them here ...

> *Dear Patricia,*
>
> *Any reader cannot fail to be moved by the tremendous love and feeling in your writing.*
>
> *While any diary is often matter-of-fact, in this, a beautiful spiral of love and warmth interleaves and entwines the reader into a heart full of vision, hope, caring for others and a huge spiritual depth.*
>
> *Throughout history we have all read of the great loves. Yet here is a love encouraged by 'both sides' to last for eternity, to be shared with like minds and show the way to an understanding of true love's power.*
>
> *To have shared your thoughts and hopes was a privilege for which I thank you. Again Patricia, you are very powerful and I am lucky to call you a friend if I may?*

Journal entry: 13 July

With the pressure of the legal battle mounting regarding CIL and all that it entails, I've been feeling worn out, negative and somewhat inadequate, concerned that I will be unable to cope as well as Malcolm would have in the same situation. I have also been feeling guilty because I have been wishing, and longing, to join him.

I was feeling desperate. I knew it was selfish, considering that I have such a lovely family and they are mine to love, care for and support but I wasn't feeling as powerful as I am continually being told that I am. Far from it!

I'm relieved to say it was only fleeting.

I booked a Reiki treatment with Paula in order to recharge my batteries. It was immensely consoling and I calmed completely.

An hour or so later I felt gentle pressure on my shoulder and heard my name being softly called. Reluctantly, I roused and said, "I saw a lot of purple!"

"Yes, you would do," said Paula, laughing. "The guides led you towards a giant golden pyramid, which opened. Inside, it was decorated in the deepest purple and there was a smartly dressed man, wearing spectacles waiting to welcome you [Malcolm]. He held the largest bouquet of flowers in his arms and their colours were beautiful. It was magnificent. The gentleman spoke only one word, 'ring'." [I had recently removed my tight-fitting wedding ring.]

"Your guides left you there and came outside the pyramid to the entrance once more. You were enfolded in the most incredible intensity of light and lost from sight. You remained there for a long time then your guides returned to collect you. You didn't want to leave this man and were reluctant to return. You kept glancing over your shoulder. Given a choice you would not have returned to the earth plane.

"The man, your husband, held up the palm of his hand indicating to you that you could not stay because you have too much work to do. Still, you continued to glance backwards, until your guides returned you to the gate. I then brought you back to the sanctuary. As soon as I touched you, Patricia, it was electrifying! You always make me feel so completely alive!"

We decided to do a very earthly thing and have lunch. Queuing to pay for our food I suggested to Paula that she find a seat while I wait in line. She agreed and moved towards a corner table for privacy but found her way barred by a very defensive elbow. Someone else obviously had the same idea! Such obvious possessiveness made us both laugh and Paula selected a more central table.

After a few moments I walked over to the table with the food and drinks and found that Paula was missing, yet her handbag was by her seat. Putting down the tray, I waited. She returned, apologising, "I'm so sorry, Patricia, but I've not seen Betty for ages and just wanted a quick word with her."

"No problem. Betty who?"

"Betty Shine."

Amazing! Only the previous week I had written a letter of thanks to Betty, saying how much her books about her mediumship work had helped me to understand things better. I had jokingly suggested that I "owed her lunch and much more!" And now, here we both were, about to eat lunch in the same little café.

"I have just written to Betty," I said to Paula. "Do you think she'd mind if I said hello?"

"Of course not, go ahead."

So I walked to the table where Betty was seated alone. I introduced myself and explained that I was with Paula. Betty invited me to sit down and we spoke for a few minutes during which time I told her that I had written to thank her for the help her books had given me. I said that I was aware that she was unlikely to have seen my letter.

Betty said that she was a little concerned as Paula had just told her that she too had recently sent her a personal letter, but Betty had not received either. As Paula was an old and dear friend this concerned her very much. Betty asked me if I had received a reply. I confirmed that I had and that she was not to worry on my account. I said that it is obvious there was no way she could be expected to deal personally with the amount of mail she receives and that people would understand.

She then said, "My dear, I am busy and I am writing what I think will be my last book for it seems to be taking a great deal out of me."

Again, I said that I had just wanted to thank her for the immense help she had given both to me and so many others through her work. I could see her daughter heading towards us with a laden tray so I excused myself and returned to Paula.

I was really pleased that I'd had the opportunity to meet Betty Shine. I was impressed by her quiet demeanour, her soft-speaking voice and her all-encompassing smile. However, I was concerned, for she looked very tired and it crossed my mind that perhaps we are all taking too much from her. How is it replenished? I wondered.

It was comical, and another synchronicity, that if another's possessive elbow hadn't prevented Paula from obtaining the corner table; we would not have seen Betty at all.

Then suddenly, Betty was standing beside us offering Paula her home telephone number. She was clearly very anxious that Paula had been unable to contact her. I loaned them pen and paper, joked about not looking over their shoulders and walked away to give them privacy. They bid each other goodbye and Betty clasped my hand warmly in passing. When I looked into her eyes, I felt that I was indeed looking at a truly remarkable woman. A short while later Paula and I parted, having arranged to meet at Martin's demonstration in Dorking the following week. Later that night I wrote the following poem.

A Gift for Betty Shine

Tonight, I have something deep in my mind
At lunchtime, with Paula, I met Betty Shine
When I realised who she was, I rose to say 'Thanks'
In mind matters, she's simply the first in the ranks.

Indeed I have much to be grateful for
She encouraged me to find my own inner core
Once a hard and fast sceptic, my thoughts black and white
She helped me discover, the true meaning of 'Light'.

Endlessly she struggles to show us the way
With her books and her tapes each selfless day
But I think it is time to award her a rest
After all, what's the point of destroying the best?

Instead of we 'taking' let's send her instead
Love, light and healing each night before bed
So here is our task, friends, both yours and mine
Together, help Betty, continue to SHINE!

After Betty's death in 2002, her daughter telephoned me and asked if she could include this poem in *Shine On: Visions of Life*, a book of her mother's work, which she was compiling. I felt very honoured and gave permission for its use.

Journal entry: 15 July - Somerset

Karen and I headed for Westbury, in Somerset, to attend a healing weekend and support Valerie Kirkham, who had been invited to take part in a demonstration.

Prior to leaving, I had visited the doctor as one of my ears had begun to trouble me. Being prone to ear infections it seemed sensible to try and prevent it getting worse. During our journey the pain increased and the antibiotic drops, tablets and anti-inflammatory pills seemed to be having little effect.

Arriving in Somerset was a relief. We ate an early pub meal and I was in bed by 9 p.m. I was in such agony that, in desperation, I drank three large shots of brandy, which I hated the taste of and was later reminded by Karen how this renders antibiotics useless! I slept fitfully until 12.40 a.m. when the pain became so intense that it woke me.

I was praying, silently *pleading* for healing.

I decided to try positive thinking and visualisation. In time to my own breathing I breathed *out* infection and *in* healing. Tears were in my eyes. I almost called out for Karen to get help!

After a while I seemed to 'click into silence'. My inner vision was bathed in deep violet. The incessant pumping in my ears receded and the violet colour before my eyes became even more intense. I felt myself being lifted from the bed until nothing surrounded me but violet-coloured space. Then, I was wrapped in a huge, soft, cream-coloured satin wrap. I was inside the wrap, like a newborn in a shawl and, looking down, I could clearly see the cream colour and the violet space. There was one huge hand and arm around my torso and the other I could feel cradling my head beneath the painful ear. I was wrapped and held in mid-air. There were no 'wings', no 'feathers', just these two enormous arms softly and compassionately cradling my agonised head and my body. I remained there, breathing in the beauty of the moment and in the silence, noticed a lessening of the pain. All the time I continued to breathe *out* infection and *in* healing. The pain had not totally gone but was greatly muted.

Gradually, I realised I was back in my bed. I had not been asleep, for all the while this was happening. I had determinedly carried on with the visualisation, steadfastly concentrating on my breathing *in* and *out* systematically. I was terrified that if I stopped, the dreadful pain would return. And return it did, *horrendously*, for about thirty seconds.

Then, the next I knew, it was 6 a.m. and my pain had vanished completely. Mind you, I couldn't hear anything. My glands, cheek and internal and external ear were still dreadfully swollen but *there was no pain*! I sent my thanks speedily to whoever it concerned and lay there, absolutely stunned. I got ready for the day with a new vigour and an enormous feeling of thanks.

Brilliant sunshine welcomed us to the event. We met Valerie and her friend. We wandered around the various marquees browsing at the stalls. It had a fairground atmosphere which made me feel ill at ease, but generally the people were pleasant and friendly.

Karen was keen to have her aura photographed by a kinetic photographer. I have to say, not being particularly adventurous, I was far from keen. It was only when I saw her disappointment at my refusal that I acquiesced.

One man was taking the shots, which involved placing one's hands on steel plates, and two women were transcribing the actual colour photographs. My photograph depicted gold centrally covering my face surrounded by an unbroken swathe of violet in a horseshoe shape, from shoulder to shoulder, which was topped by, what they called, a 'temple' of magenta in another unbroken horseshoe shape. Within this could clearly be seen seven circular 'blobs' of magenta. These, it was explained, were my strongest guides present at this time. As instructed, I handed the photograph to one of the two women transcribing. This is what she said:

"Wow! You should be sitting in my chair doing this; you are more powerful than I am! This is a perfect photograph of an aura; it is the same as a newborn child's. The purple denotes 'higher power' and these [she pointed to the seven blobs of colour] indicate that you have seven strong guides working with you.

"You have done all the learning you need to do and this is telling you to use the knowledge you have gained. You are highly intuitive and a great communicator. You have the ability to teach what you have learned and it is time for you to get on with it."

This was another very humbling experience. Why don't I understand the significance of these messages? Each time I hear it, I still greet this news with amazement, stupefaction and *total incomprehension*.

The next day I decided I would like to have a guide drawn. In the past, I have been told that my guides are my husband; Eagle Eye; a nameless Tibetan monk; a nameless, small Chinese lady; and, more recently, another Native American called Red Wolf. These only accounted for six.

I made an appointment with an artist on-site and sat with her in her tent at the given time. She explained that, while drawing, she is often given information, either from the guide being drawn, or another. She confirmed that she would pass on any received information. I was asked to sit in front of her and was unable to see her work.

She said: "I have a man here who is anxious to communicate with you. He is rubbing his wrist. He is giving this as a proof. He says he knows you are tied and helpless in a situation at present. You will get where you want to be."

The artist was silent for several minutes but continued drawing before saying, "I am sorry, I am very conscious that I am being quiet but this man here doesn't want to say any more. He is a man of few words, not a trivial speaker. He has just said, '*She knows I am here, she knows I love her, there is no more to say!*'"

I laughed out loud. This was so indicative of Malcolm's attitude towards such events, particularly under such fairground conditions, that it absolutely confirmed to me that it was he who was communicating with us.

At the end I was given the drawing. The moment I looked at it, it reminded me of a picture I had seen but I couldn't recall where. I therefore resolved to show it to my parents the next time we met, and ask if it was perhaps a family member known to them.

Journal entry: Sunday, 23 July - Surrey

This afternoon I took Mother and Clare to the Harry Edwards Healing Sanctuary at Shere. We immersed ourselves in the tranquillity and enjoyed walking in the gardens before going inside to the bookshop where we chose tapes and books.

Back at home, Clare asked to see the photograph of my aura which I had brought back from Somerset. This reminded me to ask Mother about the drawing. I had not looked at either since the previous weekend.

I unrolled the drawing and handed it to my mother to see if she could remember any such family member or friend. I asked if she could throw any light on who it might be.

"Well, yes," she replied. "It's the man from the place we visited this afternoon—look."

Mother opened the brochure which she had picked up that afternoon and pointed to a photograph of Harry Edwards. It was indeed the same man, in the same pose. We could all clearly see it.

My seventh guide it would appear is Harry Edwards, one of the most famous healers of the century. Perhaps now it really *is* time to get on with the job.

If *only* I understood exactly what it was!

Chapter 15
A Deep and All-Consuming Fear

Reading: Friday, 18 August 2000 - Shane

For a while I have allowed myself to be cowed by the issues surrounding the business and the children's trust. I have been too negative and negativity seems to breed more of the same. I am confused and unsure which way to go.

With this in mind, I decided to take Kellen's advice and contact Shane. When I rang him, it felt as if I knew him already. I explained that I had met Kellen in Goa and that I needed his help. Shane knew nothing about the business, my fears or my problems.

"There are several people waiting to come through," said Shane. *"The first is a gentleman with a heart condition. He had a clear head and would look at things logically and practically. He is holding his chest. He was a quiet person but still had a lot of things to say. He was a solid, reliable man and people shared problems with him. There were times when he wasn't heard. He comes through very gently and is saying that you are trying to do too much all at once. Slow down and you will be able to think more clearly. In the past few weeks you have been racing around which has prevented this.*

"He is now speaking about finances and says, 'Tell Patricia not to rush. You are under pressure, if you step back and slow down it will resolve itself. It needs to be done when the time is right.' You are to say how you really feel; you don't do this enough with the people around you. This gentleman is saying, 'We need to say how we feel, from the heart.'

"You feel cornered and you need to be firmer than you are and stand your ground. You don't normally like to rock the boat but you must. He is conscious that you wake during the night; you are not

119

sleeping well. He wants you to know that he is there to reassure and comfort you. He is trying to support you.

"There is a mother-in-law vibration now, someone who is quite stern and would take no nonsense while on the earth plane. She is standing next to you and wants you to know that you are to take no nonsense either, nor to be manipulated. She is not pleased and says you should not be in this situation. She also is saying that you need to say how you feel. You feel hurt and must say so. People need to know when they have upset you.

"An oriental guide is coming in now. He is blind. He is saying that he is here to teach you how to feel and sense. Spirituality is all about being real and you are to honour feelings that you have. If you upset somebody it does not mean you are not being spiritual, it is simply you being truthful. He says you battle with this, you are only human. If you accept this, people will learn from their mistakes and you will be helping them to understand and accept also.

"Your guides are surrounding you, Patricia. Don't let this person manipulate you. You need to be strong, brave and speak your truth. You have the support of spirit and they are on your side. You are heading in the right direction."

Journal entry: 26 August - London and Surrey

Diane, a close friend of mine, had been particularly unwell with a bad back and had endured a great deal of pain. Her parents had been caring for her so I drove Diane to her flat in London to give them a break. Diane and I have known each other for thirty years and, because of our long friendship, I was reluctant to discuss the spiritual direction my life had taken over the last eighteen months as we had never talked about the subject. However, I felt I should be making some effort to reduce her suffering; after all, everyone kept telling me I have healing ability. How to do this in a sensible way was the problem. Help has to be asked for.

Our trip to London was too much for Diane and over the weekend she largely slept. It was difficult for her to move, let alone go anywhere. A simple walk to the bathroom was agony. I remained with her all day on the Friday and Saturday, deciding to use the time to get my journal up to date. My thinking was, if she should ask what I was doing then it would open the subject naturally. She didn't ask; frankly, she was in too much pain to even care.

Later that evening she was still prone, still in her dressing gown and looking grim. We spent Sunday evening together and I had bought her a magazine in which there was an article on acupuncture. Diane had mentioned an interest in the subject before. While I was lying there reading the article she began to ask me about how I had become involved with natural healing.

I answered her questions, truthfully but briefly. I think she took it all with a very large pinch of salt but exclaimed, "Well, if you have these abilities it's about time you healed my b***** back!"

"You just need to ask, Diane," I told her, as she limped painfully back to bed.

That particular night my body became like a revving engine. I was astonished at the electrical surges, the vibrations, coursing through my body. After so long without any activity I welcomed the sensation for its reassurance and in my awakened state, I consciously sent all the healing pulsating through me in the direction of Diane. It lasted for just over two hours, before I drifted off to sleep.

To my astonishment the next morning Diane brought me a cup of tea in bed! She was up early, had showered, dressed and had breakfast. I couldn't believe the transformation! She was smiling, not grimacing, and commented, "Those two days in bed have certainly done me a lot of good!" *I said nothing.*

However, all the weeks previously that she had been lying about, being cared for by her parents, hadn't had quite the same result and last night she was still in agony. I *know* it was the energy that I had felt and redirected that made the incredible change in her condition and I was thankful for such undeniable proof.

Journal entry: Friday, 22 September - Surrey

Today I visited Paula. My business concerns continue to take their toll and it is helpful to have Reiki from Paula to calm me. During the treatment I was surprised to find that her hands felt unusually cold on my head, but I said nothing.

At the end of the treatment, I confirmed that all I could *see* was violet. This made her laugh. She knows how frustrated I am when I feel nothing is changing and that I am not 'progressing'.

Paula told me what she had experienced. *"During your treatment, when you turned on to your front my hands were gently edged away from your head and it was another who healed your head, not I."*

I found this incredible. Although I had experienced the icy cold hands on my head I had assumed that these belonged to Paula, even though I thought it odd that they were still so cold after thirty minutes or so. And here she was, without any mention of it at all from me, confirming and clarifying exactly what I had experienced.

Journal entry: 11 October - Surrey

I returned from Devon to a pile of letters from my solicitor. I was not feeling on top of the world and this made matters worse. I was drowning in fear.

My parents had been staying with me, trying to help and support me as I struggled with the home, family and the mire of paperwork and legalities. They were a constant still point in an ever-circling world. My beloved rocks, when all about me seemed to be sinking fast.

As they were preparing to return home, it didn't quite seem to be our day. First, the downstairs WC blocked; then Father found he could not start his car.

I rang Nina, the Brighton medium who had given me readings only twice in the previous eighteen months. Obviously, she would have no recollection of these and I only ever listened anyway.

"Your guide is here immediately. The presence is very strong. They are saying you must keep calm in a coming storm. Pursue your course even though you will be under a lot of pressure not to. Do expect a flare up of anger. Someone is going to be particularly unpleasant and quite frightening.

"The anger will be reflected back to the perpetrator and he will see himself clearly. At present he cannot. He is under pressure from a woman who is protecting her own interests. You are on the side of

right.

"There is someone in spirit who was good with business affairs [Malcolm]; *he is helping you as much as he can. He is saying you are to calm down, yet stand your ground firmly."*

Reading: 11 October - Shane

I rang Shane, asking for help. There was no discussion. I simply listened.

"Trust your instincts, what you feel within. Slowing down seems to be the key, things will make sense to you. There is a lot of pressure but some of this is coming from you. You are placing pressure on yourself, you don't need to.

"I have this feeling of confusion and doubt. What they are saying is follow your heart. There you will listen to yourself and you won't go far wrong. You must trust your feelings and yourself.

"There is a guide here, a nun, who is putting pen to paper and what she is saying is when things become confused you must write down your questions and then allow the answers to flow from writing. Don't look at what you are writing, read it at the end. This will get you in touch with your guides. Keep a journal, if you read it back you will see how things have changed and how far you have travelled.

"You must put certain people in their place. This is hard and painful but must be done. You are going through a period of healing.

"They are talking about a pipe or a drain blocking?" [I laughed and told him about the toilet blocking that morning.]

"There is a gentleman coming through. He is mentioning a car not starting properly." [I confirmed that we had indeed had a problem with my parents' car.]

"He knows you would love to be able to talk to him physically. Write him a letter, then invite him to sit and be with you and he will be there. He says, 'I will be there with her spiritually.' Then read him the letter. He will always try and bring the answers to you.

"Sometimes you feel awfully alone even when you are around other people. You must not think this. You are never alone; your guides are only a thought away."

It feels as if there is an almost daily barrage of white envelopes with innumerable questions from solicitors, trustees, accountants, etc. All of this is entirely outside of my comfort zone. But I have to learn. *And I have to learn fast.*

It is as though there is a continual wave of pressure, which accentuates my loneliness while dealing with the CIL issue. It feels as though I am riding a rising tide of insurmountable fear. Quite how I would cope without the continual reassurances from Malcolm I hesitate to guess.

It makes me ashamed because I feel so in need. In order to keep going, I have decided to renew my acquaintance with Diana Summer.

Reading ~ Diana Summer

"This is an important time; a gateway is beginning to open. Energies are bringing things to a conclusion, individually, planetary and universally. All is interconnected and every individual movement affects the whole.

"You are releasing various thought forms, feelings and conditioning that have followed you. Slowly, these are beginning to recede. Gently, you come forward step by step, knowing that each step brings realms of the unknown. The visions that you experience, the knowing that grows ever deeper inside you as pen goes to paper, brings you true wisdom. These sacred and beautiful creative forces flow through you readily, even though there may be periods of resistance. You are a conduit and a channel preparing for greater things and for change.

"Change will enable you to make hard and fast decisions. The new energies will bring you fresh inspiration and ideas. By the time that this year is out and the following year has passed by, you will find yourself in a new place of being. You will tap into the energies that lay within the landscape, the depths, the roots, all are waiting for you to connect with them. Messages that have been brought to you through the words of others, the synchronicities that you experience, all bring acknowledgement and readiness, in order that you may open up to a wider perspective as your consciousness expands. The

strength that you carry deep within you will remain strong.

"Through this transition, you may experience difficulties with those around you and those under your wing. It is not an easy pattern and resistance is strong; you are rebirthing at this moment in time. Transformations are never easy but the new pattern that is emerging will enable you to become more sensitive.

"There will be people you will meet, and some you have already met, who will guide and give you confirmation of things that you question. Information will come to you through the words of other people, through things that you hear, see or feel. Open yourselves to these things and they will become stronger and more obvious in order for you to accept. Travellers will find their way to your door and will know that they are in safe hands as they receive your words and serenity, balanced with your directness and integrity.

"The sensitivity that begins to explode within you like buds on a tree will awaken you deeper and deeper. Your path is a learning curve and you are now in the centre. You must make those decisions which initially caused you to hesitate but understand that there is an inner surge of energy pushing you forward which you are unable to resist. Trust your instinct and intuition, flow with the very energies of time and space. Your guides and guardian angels are close; they watch over you gently.

"There is a guide, cloaked in a beautiful azure blue, who will bring communication skills. He desires to work with you. He will inspire you and communicate through you. In good time, he will make his presence felt through dreamtime, meditation or awareness. He is directed through the Archangel Raphael, the archangel of teaching, communication, healing and all creative forces.

"Water—looking across water—I feel you may spend time across water. You could spend time travelling; there is a new beginning, an awakening of your real inner depths that will help you understand your ancient past.

"You will be taken on these journeys, finding yourself visiting various places because either they need your energy, or there is a need for you to connect with a certain country or culture. Every journey will have its higher purpose.

"Allow the universe to assist you. Declare your intent then allow time for things to manifest and greet you at the appropriate time. As you prepare to move forward, let go of concerns. Do not hold any doubts or fears.

"It is time for you to stretch your wings and see the larger picture on all levels. Let go of things that you would desire to keep under your control. Windows of opportunity will present themselves.

"You are one who will hold the energy and help to balance things. Many are now becoming aware that, unless changes are made, the destabilisation will continue and create such chaos that it will go into a spin of no return. This can be controlled by those who are open and awake by holding onto the consciousness, stabilising the earth, bringing peace to those who are confused and fearful.

"You will realise that many others are becoming aware and will fulfil this need also. These energies flow now in order to awaken mankind as a whole. This is a slow and laborious process of awakening and realisation but over the next three decades much of this needs to be in place.

"There is a young girl with whom you have a great bond [Karen] *and I feel she is going to find her path and it will resonate with yours. The connection there I feel, will keep repeating itself as you keep separating then come together on this path ahead.*

"There are periods of your life when it is going to be very busy, then there will be periods where it will go quiet. These quiet times are to be taken advantage of. These are times to spend on pampering yourself and doing what you want to do because your life is going to become busy in a different way. You will need to recharge your batteries and reconnect with who you are. This is vital, or your energies will deplete and will be wasted. Be really strong and say no to whomever it is who is demanding of you, when you need this time to yourself.

"I can see so much happening for you; there will be major changes during the next year or two and it is all beginning to move into place. You are going to be a prolific writer. I see you as a healer and passing this on to others."

At this point I was invited to ask questions and I said, "How much longer is this nonsense with my brother-in-law going to go on for?"

"This is going to continue but you will deal with it! You will stand your ground. He is determined and stubborn but you are standing on much firmer ground than he is. He is beginning to sink, to lose his grip. It is tough but you won't cave in, don't worry."

Chapter 16
Reassurance: Channelled and Personal

Reading: November 2000 - Shane

Having been told more than once that I should find a teacher, I arranged to meet Shane again in the hope that he could help me. Initially I kept silent, for I figured that Shane would happily work out for himself why I was there. After all, isn't that what he does?

"There is a gentleman here who is saying he wants you to stand your ground. He is saying not all of what is happening is negative. See it as an opportunity to finally put things right. This person that you fear is not to be trusted and needs to be challenged. You have been pushed around, now is the time to find your voice, don't hold back. Face your fears. The spirits want to push you to make that step, to make you cross that line.

"There is a lady present; she is saying that there are changes that need to be made. Now is the time to confront your fears. This is paying a harder toll on you than you realise and they want it to stop. It has been going on too long. They wish to give you strength.

"They are eager to speak through you. They want their harsh words to come through but know you will find that difficult to do. You are not expressing your feelings of anger. You must say, 'This is not on!' Spirit is really pushing for you to express your real feelings. You are often very strong for those around you and are able to put on a brave face. You put on a mask but inside it is very different. However, you are in a strong healing curve; this is an opportunity for you.

"You quite often just pick up where you leave off and march forward but you must remember feelings need to be felt. You do not forget them but look the other way and they are caught inside you.

By acknowledging them you can heal and let go. When you suppress them, they build-up. Meditation will help you to do this.

"When your husband died you did not really work through your grief. It has caught up with you now and it is time to heal. You feel lost and tired because spiritually you are calling out and asking for help and admitting that you are not as strong as you would like.

"You have not allowed your tears. Sometimes we need to surrender. For many years you have had responsibility. You have held yourself together because you felt you had to, you have been strong for your children but now you should have more time for you.

"Spirit wants you to meditate and think about yourself. In the future you will have much work to do. Now is the time to make yourself complete so you can pass on that help.

"The name Malcolm is coming in now. He is always there with you and he is showing me doves and saying you would understand." [He bought me white fan-tail doves and a dovecot for my birthday one year.]

"He is also showing me a pen and this is gold-coloured but not actual gold and he is also mentioning his wrist." [Just before he died, Malcolm was given such a pen by a grateful client.]

"He is speaking about Scotch and raising a whisky glass to you and wants to say 'thank you' for all that you have done. He is saying you are doing the right thing and he is behind you.

"He is speaking about his brother now and he wants him to back off. He feels angry and is saying that Ian has always been very manipulative. He is not looking after the children's interests; he is looking after no one but himself.

"Malcolm is pleased that he is able to make contact with you in this way. He is close to you now and trying to comfort you. You know that you need to step down hard and challenge Ian. Malcolm is sorry that you have to deal with this alone. He is around you every day but there is nothing he can physically do and this makes him sad. He knows what his brother is trying to do and this frustrates him.

"Malcolm knows that you did not only lose a lover, husband, and father to your children but you also lost your best friend. But he is saying that you haven't, 'I am always there, you cannot always hear or see me but I am standing beside you. We made that agreement a

long time ago. Nothing has changed.'

"He says, 'Don't worry about other people who may judge you for your belief in this evidence. It doesn't matter what others think, all that matters is what you know, that he is still with you.' Malcolm is saying, 'I always knew that there was a great deal more to life.'

"His brother is projecting unpleasant thoughts and feelings in your direction. There is so much negative energy behind his thoughts, your home needs cleansing. It has been the focal point to which he has sent bad energy. This has caused you to wake during the night. You are not to worry, we will remedy this. Be aware of it and protect yourself and your home.

"You have done many good and spiritual things for other people lately by supporting them. Now it is time for you. You are a catalyst, but remember you have your own journey and at present yours is a powerful healing one. You are being guided to many different people for the healing that you need.

"All that is happening is the effect of your affirmation. I know you are not conscious of it but you have a lot of power and spiritual strength around you. When you attuned to the universe by way of your affirmation, it brought you what you needed to progress. You are now working with pure light. This guide wants to teach you all.

"Malcolm is speaking about your writing. You will share the experiences of your journey. This alone will be healing; people will be able to relate to it and it will astonish them. Your work will be truly grounded. People will be drawn to your work and your writing. You help them to remember who they really are, and will give people hope. It will be a blessing and a gift, all will come into balance. People who are lost will be directed to you. This is the work of a shaman.

"Listen to spirit and to your instincts, you will find the strength to face your fear. You are on a true path. Malcolm hears you all the time, both in your heart and through your words. He is always trying to answer but not necessarily in the way you would wish or understand. It is often through the words of others.

"You are to stand firm, not waver and stand your ground. Face your fears even though they are strong. You are worrying but not feeling. Worry is an emotion that takes a grip over us. Malcolm is

smiling to reassure you. Keep looking at the long term. You are like a ship going through a storm and you will get through that storm. The clouds will break, all will be well.

"He is saying, 'The entire scenario is an opportunity and a gift for you. Face it. Your guides will be doing much work with you. I am here. Remember that love, true love, lives on.'"

Journal entry: Wednesday, 20 December - Surrey

I have been lying awake for hours. I went to bed at 11 p.m. and it is now 2 a.m. I have been listening to the roar of the wind and the sound of my son setting the house alarm, his climbing the stairs and then the hourly chiming of the clocks. Through it all, I have been wide awake, lucid and capable of independent thought.

Yet, for the last hours I have been bathed in the most wonderful, reassuring love. For months, I have been living through personal trauma and have cried out for reassurance so many times. Tonight, at last, it came.

My questions, doubts and fears I have finally managed to hand over to The Source. After months of failed meditation attempts, finally in my quietened pre-sleep state, all my concerns were answered.

My requests for reassurance were met by wave after wave of energy. My whole body was *electrified*. Time after time, the most incredible energy bathed my body, my whole being, calming my mind and soothing away doubt and fear. It was far stronger than I have ever experienced before.

I lost count of the times that this energy coursed through me. My entire physical body was touched by this experience. During it all, I heard the clocks strike, the wind continue to roar. I was mentally awake and yet, simultaneously, bathed in absolute delight. I envisaged a white protective light around our home as I feared for both its safety and our own.

For months I have been disillusioned with myself (not the concept) and with my repeated, failed meditation attempts. Reassurance was certainly given to me this night. I *thought* the questions I wanted to ask and was then replied to by a most fabulous *energy*. This has nothing to do with fantasy but everything to do with the most all-encompassing feeling of reassurance and the deepest love.

I felt myself being held very tightly and telepathically I thanked Malcolm for his love, presence and reassurance when needed most. I was grateful for the enormous amount of energy I knew he was using to deliver this. I kept my eyes closed. I knew that if I opened them, these moments would pass and I wanted to hold onto them forever. Eventually, I spoke my words of love out loud and then he gently slipped from my arms; it was over. There were no moments of desperation or sadness; I was simply grateful for the joyous experience we had shared.

These are not the words of a woman whose mind has been destroyed by grief. These words are the truth as I have actually experienced it. One cannot doubt what they *know* has taken place. If I were able to conjure up such an experience, I would do so daily.

It was the answer to my many prayers, questions and requests for help these past months. I really did not want to sit up in the cold to write this tonight but it is part of the deal.

It was explained to me during the question-and-answer session that this same love is available to us all, including the planet itself. It is the strength of this amazing power, which, multiplied by us all, would be able to rejuvenate earth and get us all back on track. It is this all-encompassing, unconditional love, which can heal our attitudes towards each other's race, and creed; it could end the senseless wars and clean up the harm we have done to the planet upon which we live. The earth has been abused almost to the point of destruction. The ferocious weather patterns we are experiencing are to make us take notice. It is time for us all to wake up before it is too late.

I was told that I have a part to play in this. We all do. We cannot take our place in the healing of others or the planet until we have healed ourselves. We have our own lessons to learn and overcome before we can be of use to others. Tonight was a time for reaffirming my intentions. I am here and I am ready to get on with the job. There is no turning back.

Chapter 17
Mischief Making and Talking to The Source

Journal entry: 27 February 2001 - 11.57 p.m. - Surrey

Regardless of all the proof I have received, whenever there is a period of quiet, as there has been recently, I still long for reassurance. I cannot understand why I have such a constant need for this. I don't doubt my own experiences. I know only too well all the things which have happened to me. When there is a lull, I fear that I have been abandoned, have done something wrong or failed to do the right thing, which makes me worry that I am of no further use.

What a very human feeling is lack of faith in oneself. I never doubt the concept of life after death and of the spirit world. It is always, *always* me that I doubt! This is such a hard lesson. Will I ever overcome this? I wonder.

Something strange did happen though. I went to bed early but was woken by an ongoing painful tooth problem. Yet another ear infection had begun to irritate me. I went to my bathroom to use the tube of antibiotic cream given to me a day or so earlier by my doctor. It was not in its usual place. I had used it just before going to bed and was puzzled that it was missing from the windowsill where I had placed it.

I returned to the bedroom and looked for it on all the surfaces but couldn't find it. I re-entered the bathroom, where I knew I had placed the tube hours earlier. It was becoming annoying. All I wanted to do was go to sleep, not play hide and seek with a tube of cream. I returned to the bedroom once more and tipped out my washbag in case I had inadvertently placed it there. No luck!

I entered the bathroom for the third time and searched everywhere, including the most ludicrous places. Still no luck!

Returning to the bedroom again, I searched my shelves and top drawers in case it had fallen into one somehow. I even emptied my rarely used travel medicine kit. Again, there was no sign of the tube. I was becoming very annoyed for my tooth and my ear were becoming increasingly more painful. I knew that I needed to treat them before I would be able to sleep.

Upon entering the bathroom for the fourth time, I dejectedly cast my gaze once more over the windowsill and, to my utter astonishment, I found myself looking directly at the errant tube which was in *exactly* the same place as I recalled putting it. I *knew* I had already checked it many times. I felt rather piqued and wondered if it was some sort of spirit 'joke'. If it was, I was unimpressed!

I recalled that Shane had warned me that I would experience things being moved around at home and sometimes they would vanish then reappear. He explained that it was another type of proof but I had forgotten until now. This must be an example. I wondered if I was being shown a variety of proofs and that by logging everything that happened, my journal may one day be of help to other people who have similar experiences.

Journal entry: 31 March - 11.58 p.m.

After months without any experiences at all I have just had an amazing electrical surge. It was as though it was causing my physical body to ripple, so much so that it took my breath away, literally.

Simultaneously, there was a *huge* crescendo of sound in my ears, particularly my left ear, and I noted I was lying flat on my back so there was no pillow to interfere with my right side.

I expected to hear a voice speaking to me but was so astonished by the breathless feeling, which I had never experienced before, that my thoughts focused on this. I was most definitely not asleep. In fact, this episode occurred only minutes after I had fetched a glass of water. I had also opened my bedroom door to see if my sons had gone to bed, realising that their doors were still open and guessing that they were downstairs catching up, after the long school term apart.

When this very strong experience occurred I looked upon it again as healing and gave thanks. I knew I had been in a state of total relaxation, thinking about my sons and focussing on pleasant thoughts of the Easter holidays ahead.

Journal entry: 1 April ~ 1.19 a.m.

It's happened again! This time, it was quite like being 'plugged in' to an amazing source of energy. At the onset, lying awake, I could feel it starting. Initially, I seemed to 'click into silence'. I was still aware of the noise of the heating pipes, of the boiler firing up and even the hall clock striking. Yet I felt totally detached, as if I was elsewhere, and that anything which took place in my immediate surroundings no longer concerned me. It was as though I was being lifted, propelled by this incredible energy and taken at an exhaustive speed from my bed. There were three definite power surges.

At the same time as I was mentally noting all this, there was a crescendo of *rushing* noises in my ears and a voice speaking at tremendous speed in my left ear. The sounds were indecipherable; the speed was far too fierce.

During this, I saw nothing throughout. The entire experience was all heard and felt. The speed was such that I began to feel nauseous and I *spoke* to The Source, telepathically. I am fully aware that where there is light there is also dark and I wanted absolutely no mistake where my intentions lie. I was thankful for this proof of healing power and repeated in my mind part of my own prayer two or three times:

> I call upon my guardians and my guides
> To cherish and protect my mind, body and soul
> And to fill and surround me—always
> With the white Christ Light of God's power.

I also repeated 'The Lord's Prayer' three times, not in a hurried frantic manner but slowly, deliberately and determinedly, with great meaning. I felt cherished.

I was, however, puzzled that I could be thinking this prayer so earnestly and yet continue to experience the power surges. This had not happened before. Normally, when my thinking kicks in, all else ceases and fades away. *Not this time.* When it ended, I lay calm for several moments before preparing to write. Slowly, the nausea abated and I lay revelling in the intense joy and peace.

It was a great shame that I had to move, for I could so easily then have fallen into a deep and peaceful sleep. However, I know the rules now. What point would there be if I experienced these proofs, which must use a huge amount of energy, if I am too idle to record them for the benefit of others in the future?

After this I slept well, and nothing more happened during the rest of the night. It may have been April Fools' Day (a joke instigated by man), but the events I am taking the time and trouble to record come from a far greater and more reverent sphere and I *know* this— deep within my core.

The paperwork is building up and the pressure is intense. Fear is ever prevalent and I know that the toll on my own health is a real risk. I try not to panic but it is almost impossible when there is a constant barrage of phone calls, letters and decisions to be made.

Shane is trying to help me keep calm and to rise above it all.

Reading: Shane

"I feel your husband coming in here very strongly. He knows you have been feeling disconnected and wants to reassure you that he is constantly with you and you have been very connected indeed. In your everyday life you are working with spirit and have been speaking to a lot of people on a level which they would benefit from but not understand. You do a lot of healing through conversation. He is illustrating you putting pen to paper—and writing, writing, writing.

"He is saying that your words can touch many people; you should not feel that you need to be doing 'hands-on' healing. You can work in your study and reach many people that way.

"Your strength is in your writing. Malcolm is inviting someone to stand next to him and there is a very old Native American present. He

wishes to work with you and allow people to understand the simple truths which they can apply in their own lives. Your own journey will touch many different people who have had such experiences but have not known how to knit them together. By reading your story, their own will all begin to make sense.

"The Native American is showing me a feather that he says holds wisdom. I am being shown you holding the feather then using it as a pen on paper. You must trust your abilities to be able to channel this wisdom. There is so much in your poetry—learn to trust yourself. You don't always need to see to channel wisdom; you can feel it and express it on paper.

"There is a lady coming through—it is hard to make her out, all I see is white—she is more energy than physical. Her wisdom is on a very high plane, she helps to shape our lives. She wishes to give you confidence.

"They are calling you the 'scribe'—the voice of spirit. I see people coming to you in a group and you are telling them of your experiences. You will begin to spread your story further afield. It is the normality of the story, the fact that you are an everyday person just like everyone else, that will have the greatest effect. This is your work and your direction.

"This is important, for it is the vast majority of normal, everyday people whom spirit need to touch. This is where the changes are needed the most. You will be sharing your journey and this will create healing in its own way. You must keep writing and share the wisdom. You are a messenger to help bring balance into people's lives. Through your writing people will find signposts and their own direction.

"I see books being despatched to people. Malcolm is saying that you will travel—he knows that you like to visit different places. You will meet many people and give your story to them all. You have a natural gift to communicate with people from all walks of life."

This is a very difficult time for me, which is why I am turning to various mediums for help. I need constant reassurance and guidance. I am petrified of the enormous emotional and financial risks I am taking in continuing with the *Irvine v Irvine* case, which is building daily. However, my instincts tell me I have no choice.

Shane is right about my feeling 'disconnected' and just as I was prompted to speak to him I have also contacted with Diana Summer. Although I am reassured by Shane's channelling, I have decided to keep the appointment with Diana.

Reading: 5 April - Diana Summer

"Situations which have worried and concerned you, you have dealt with admirably. Love flows to you continually, from those who watch over you, it is unstoppable, like a river. Malcolm comes to you now, graceful and full of light, as one of your guides.

"Nimue rises to present you with the sword, which represents sacred truth, wisdom, strength and power. It is essentially a sword of protection and, while you carry this, you will be protected for that which you are here to do. You will need to be aware of the precious beauty of such a gift.

"Angels are in the consciousness and people are now awakening to their presence. Born from the heart of the divine these energies are opening and will match the released energy bringing heaven to earth. This work is of utmost importance.

"The places you travel to—towns, cities and villages—you will be instrumental in allowing their energies to rise when required. You'll find yourself in areas that need your light in order for energies to flow. You will visit cities steeped in choked atmospheres and heaviness. Sometimes you will be given a ritual or ceremony to perform and at others you will just be walking where you are divinely led. This may be a visit to a church, a garden, or a place of interest. But, in truth, it is more than that; you will be allowing the energies to flow through your feet and your crown chakra, bringing balance, light and truth once more to these areas. This is the task that awaits you.

"Spirits are mentioning the channellings that have flowed through you, by your putting pen to paper. Those are realms of knowledge and wisdom that you are now guardian and keeper of. In a past life, you have indeed been a keeper of scrolls; of sacred truths and knowledge that has flowed from a divine force. These need to be put into order so that others may have access to them in due course.

"You are a channel, a conduit, and by connecting with The Source and being steeped into the earth itself, this brings a balance that many others are striving for. Perfect balance is beyond those on the earth at this time, only when all have moved into a state of ascension is perfect balance experienced.

"There is one who would seek to be difficult around you. This is not someone you have felt close to but who has presented himself as a thorn in your side; not a child but an adult connected to you but not directly part of you. This is moving through a progression and the stability that this particular individual seeks to claim will begin to fall away.

"In a past life you were an Aseem, one of a group of individuals within the community that had access to The Source. With enough will flowing from The Source into those that are ready and able, there will always be hope."

There was a very long pause and I thought she had ended. Eventually, Diana continued but in a totally different speaking voice which sounded very unusual. It was gentle and I could not really describe it as being either male or female but it was hugely powerful. Only five words were spoken by this voice, with long pauses between each:

" 'Adonai—Shalom—Shekinah—Blessed one.'

"There is a confrontation with someone around you who keeps stirring up the mud, just see him as a challenge. He is not going to get anywhere. It will be settled in whatever way it needs to be.

"Challenges ahead could come in the form of people's attitudes. They will try and distract you to stop you growing. Visualise the sword of protection and a white light around you. In the past, and also the present, there are those who will discover your work and there will be jealousies and fears. You must remain strong and protected to withstand this."

Chapter 18
Riding the Power

Journal entry: 20 May 2001 - Port Solent

Because of my inability to meditate, I am now in the habit of listening to a Harry Edwards tape each morning. It is a pleasant habit to have adopted, because of the peace and strength it gives me and I find it is well worth the effort to wake up early enough to listen to it before I begin my day.

Last night, Linda and I stayed at my flat in Port Solent. I am now writing a little after nine on Sunday morning. I first woke at seven and decided to listen to the tape. I must have listened to it several times during the past two hours but certainly didn't bother to count. Much to my delight, during the last twenty minutes, I have received a glorious confirmation and healing.

Slumbering, and vaguely aware of the voice of Harry Edwards through the earphones, I noted that his voice, though still in the background, was much fainter than before. However, I could hear the intonations of the rhythm of his speech. Lying still, with my eyes shut, I became aware of my hands *floating*. The feeling then spread and encompassed the entire top half of my torso, and I felt my head *opening* as if to *receive*.

Suddenly, energy rocketed through me. There were four quite definite waves of energy, which began at the base of my torso and rippled through the top half of my body at great speed and seemed to burst out of my crown. Simultaneously, I heard modern music in my left ear and, with my eyes still closed, a picture of a small CD player flashed into my view, at the same time in my right ear I could hear a voice which, if pushed, I would say was female but I was unable to decipher the words being spoken. It was as though I was being given further proof of my increasing connection to the spirit world, that things were being confirmed once more.

There was another flash and I clearly saw a book—no words—simply a symbolic illustration of an open book. The fourth and final surge of energy was so strong that I physically *rode* with it. Within my eyelids a tremendous glitter-coloured array of firework patterns exploded and then slowly ebbed away. I had never experienced this before. Harry Edwards' voice, which was faintly present throughout the entire experience, now returned to normal volume and, once I'd recovered, I picked up my pen.

I wonder if this is my husband's way of confirming to me that he knows that this is the first time I have stayed in the flat at Port Solent for over a year. Is he reassuring me that he is in tune with me at one of our favourite boltholes? Our 'love nest by the sea', as he once called it. Is this his way of confirming that he is also aware of the emotions I am experiencing and knows how greatly I miss him?

There are so many questions!

Reading: 31 May - Shane - Surrey

Following my recent meeting with Shane, Clare was intrigued and asked if I could arrange for her to meet him too. On Tuesday last, we went to see him together. All three of us were in the room at the same time and Shane simply spoke when he felt guided to do so.

"As I link with you, Patricia, I can see several people. I am just clarifying these before I pass on the messages. I can feel Malcolm very strongly as he joins us. Next to him is an Asian man. He is shadowing you. When you speak, some of his knowledge and wisdom comes through you. Malcolm is laughing because this is flowing naturally through you. You are not aware of it at all.

"You ask for help every day and when you are with people you automatically ask for assistance in order to help them. You are not always conscious of introducing help into situations and spirit wants it confirmed to you that you are heard. You ask for help unconditionally and quite naturally.

"This Indian gentleman is very humble. He worked with books. You will also be doing this and he will be strongly working with you.

Some of your writing will be coming directly from him. You will go right to the core of people's problems. You will introduce humour sometimes, in order to enable them to approach their problems in a more acceptable way. You will do this without effort.

"Westfield will be a very creative and healing space. Healing comes in many different ways. Water is also prevalent. You will have water features in the garden, together with a great deal of bamboo. These create healing and they trigger things inside people.

"Everything you need, you now have in your hands, Patricia. It is all there, all you want is ready when needed. You have arrived at that point in your life. Follow your instincts even when they are not as strong as you think they should be. These instincts are the voice of spirit. Trust them, you will not go far wrong.

"You teach in many different ways and have been doing so unconsciously for some time. Spirit now wants you to be more conscious of this role and for you to take more responsibility and know that you are a teacher.

"A boundary of white light has been placed around you and Westfield. It is full of healing and light. Spirit wants to keep this place alive and wants to ensure the right people go there. It will radiate so much pureness. It is your responsibility to keep the light there strong.

"Because of yours and Malcolm's love of the house you are beginning to unlock its potential and reawaken the light within it. Spirit wishes to thank you for bringing so many people together both past and present. You are continually doing this.

"You have this particular Native American guide who wants to work through you and other guides too. They are standing behind you and people will begin to notice and may even stare because they are trying to work out what is different about you. You are shadowing the energy of these guides. This is okay; it means you are connected to your role and to spirit."

This reminded me of a card I had received from a friend. She had written *"it was marvellous to see the new you—long may it continue."*

It also brought to mind the words of another friend, whom I see rarely, at our recent meeting: *"Patricia, you are positively shining!*

What on earth has happened to you?" Initially, I think she suspected a new man had entered my life. (No thanks; I'm more than happy with spirit of the original!)

"Malcolm is laughing now and saying, 'I want to become part of the party too.' Did he ever smoke cigars?"

Clare and I replied together, "Yes!"

"He is watching over you. I am asked to pass to you both great love from the spirit world."

Journal entry: 6 June - Devon

After a glorious day yesterday, in garden centres and at Totnes, Clare and I returned to a flooded kitchen caused by the hose coming off the outside tap. It took a while to sort out after which we watched a light-hearted film and finally went to bed just after midnight.

I lay awake. There was too much going on in my head. It was pitch dark when, in order to calm my thoughts, at about two thirty, I went downstairs to retrieve my meditation tape.

It is now 5 a.m. and for the entire past hours Harry Edwards has either been speaking clearly in my ears or (for most of the time) he has been in the background while I have experienced the most amazing forces of energy. Oh boy! I now know the meaning of 'May the Force be with you'!

This has been a night without sleep but no matter, I feel wonderful. I feel refreshed and fully alive. It began gradually, almost as though it were a gentle reminder of the possibilities ahead. There was no sound at all. My eyes remained tightly shut throughout—I did not open them for fear of putting an end to it all.

Energy began to course through my upper torso once more. Harry Edwards' voice began to recede into the background then, like a wave, returned. This happened many times yet each time, the energy became stronger. The sensations would present themselves and then recede, allowing Harry's words to become clear once more. This was repeated time and again. I lay on my back, incredibly hot, but I had no desire to move for, apart from the heat, I was very comfortable. Eventually, as the sensations increased, the heat no longer mattered or registered. I simply no longer cared.

The energy surges lengthened. I was amazed at how long they continued. My breathing remained unaffected and I simply 'rode out' the experiences, albeit at tremendous speed! The intensity increased. I found myself thinking and asking (still with Harry speaking in some far corner of my consciousness), *Please let Gloria and Clare experience this too! They need the reassurance.* I asked this three or four times during the increasing of the sensations and was astonished that it did not cease. This is progress! Normally, when I begin to *think,* everything stops. Not so this time. This time they reached a crescendo. It was utterly fantastic.

I had a number of telepathic conversations. Some were about Malcolm, some about Clare and Gloria. I lost count of the thoughts projected. The replies were always accompanied by an intensity of energy. My thoughts were *acknowledged* by increased energy but not replied to physically. On and on the energy flowed at incredible speeds until it reached a point when I could feel my arms lift and rise up. My eyes remained firmly closed. I could feel myself rising and, as I did, the intensity of the energy was beyond words. I felt elated and, quite literally, uplifted. (And believe me, at my weight, that's no mean feat!)

At the absolute dizzying height of this amazing joy, I saw a kaleidoscope of colours. After a few seconds, a pattern began to assemble into picture form and what emerged was a clear picture of a naked baby. The child was suspended amidst deepest royal blue and there was a golden halo not only around its head but also around the entire body. It was crystal clear. It was like a picture of a stained-glass window but not factually correct as we understand it, for there was no mother holding the child. It was simply suspended in a sea of colour. I was overjoyed and murmured, "Thank you, thank you," over and over again.

I was surprised that actually whispering these words, as I felt compelled to do, did not put an end to the experience as it has in the past. Instead, I was telepathically asked, "Boy or girl?"

Initially, I replied, "Boy." Then I hesitated before saying, "No! Both" (which surprised me rather). However, as soon as I said the word 'both', the baby, which I could see throughout, slowly changed first into a young man then immediately afterwards into a young woman. There was a tremendous surge of energy, which elated me entirely then things began to recede. I could feel my torso slowly lose height until I was solidly flat on my bed once more. Harry Edwards' voice gradually became clearer (I have no idea how many times the poor chap had repeated himself) and I lay perfectly still hoping it wasn't over yet. But it was.

I remember asking for help to accurately record the events of the past hours but I was reluctant to return to the real world and lay luxuriating in the gloriousness of it all. I pushed the words pen and paper away for as long as I could, until they finally became foremost in my mind. I reached over to turn off the tape and was surprised to discover daylight was now obvious through the curtains and, as I glanced at the clock, that it was 5 a.m. It then dawned on me that the greater part of my time in bed, on this particular night, had been one total *energy* experience.

Throughout it all, with the exception of Harry Edwards' voice (sometimes prominent, sometimes faint), I had heard nothing else at all. Communication was telepathic and what I *saw* was in my mind's eye with my lids firmly shut. However, the kaleidoscope of colour and the emerging pictures, I could never forget.

I won't pretend that I understand much from the above but I know I would gladly experience it all again. There was absolutely no fear and I genuinely feel, without any doubt at all, that I am a step further forward on my spiritual journey. I seem to be living an amazing life at present and travelling a very exciting journey. It is all beyond words and my meagre vocabulary doesn't do it justice at all. Still, I continue to feel compelled to record these happenings in the best way that I can.

It was by now 7.30 a.m. There was little point in trying to return to sleep for I felt so fully awake. Instead I decided to find the computer and get typing.

Journal entry: 9 June - 12.51 a.m.

In the past, I can remember some people describing others as being 'touched'. Those using that particular description were doing so in a derogatory manner, when they wanted to explain the unusual behaviour or belief of another. It was an expression used unkindly, indicating that the individual in question was mad because his or her behaviour or beliefs were quite beyond what constituted as being 'normal'.

I am not mad. I continue to care for my family, run our homes and go about my everyday business. I am also having to deal with what I am terrified is likely to become a major court case. In addition, I continue to record these experiences as they happen to me, regardless of the fact that this takes a great deal of time and energy.

Shortly before writing this, a rocket of energy coursed through me without any preamble whatsoever. There was no warning, no gentle building up of the energy, it simply happened. And I do feel as if I have been 'touched'—by something quite wonderful. I cannot hope to properly explain but it really is the most beautiful, comforting and yet powerful surging of energy.

This latest experience lasted only minutes but I found it impossible to sleep afterwards, so reached out for pen and paper.

Journal entry: 10 July - 2.56 a.m. - Surrey

It has been several weeks since I have been required to add to this journal. Little has happened and therefore no notes have been taken. Perhaps I have been given these weeks off in order to concentrate on the rising tide of legal issues which are mounting hugely.

I find it incredible how two brothers can be so different. I suppose that is the reason why they were so successful in business. Sadly, I am left with the one who clearly believes that he is the only one 'in step' when it comes to the controversy over our family business and I fear that we shall have to go to court to settle the matter. This is far from what I wish. However, I simply can't see my husband's hard-won efforts, on behalf of his sons and I, dissolved as if they count for nothing. Malcolm paid the highest possible price for our combined futures and I will not allow his achievements and reputation to be ridiculed and ignored.

Thinking an early night would be sensible, I went to bed at 10.30 p.m. but I was unable to sleep. Each time I closed my eyes my vision was filled with colours and shapes. I guessed that, after a long period of silence, further experiences were imminent. I was right.

Things are changing. The electrical power surges are now only faintly recorded in the base and solar plexus areas, yet reach indescribable crescendos in the third eye and crown. This time, they lasted much longer individually but there were fewer of them. The crescendos remained effective for some moments and were so powerful that I was quite breathless at the end. Again, there was no fear. It is a most glorious, powerful feeling and I am grateful for the reassurance it brings and the renewed feeling of *connection*.

During the entire process I was able to discern shapes and colours within my vision, before my closed eyes. This was not like a video screening, as I have read that others sometimes experience, but more like a continual offering and fading of outlined shapes and items with no coherent connection. It was as if I was simply being shown the possibilities.

So much for the early night!

Chapter 19
Words, Books and a Kindred Soul

Journal entry: 19 July 2001

I had not heard from Dilys for some time when she called out of the blue. She told me that she had been feeling Malcolm around her and she felt that he was trying to get a message across to me.

I was a little surprised, as Dilys does not need to tout for business, but realised that she was just trying to help. She proceeded to tell me that someone called Nigel would be helping me in the very near future. I thanked her but said I knew no one with that name. Dilys simply said, "Well, hold onto it." I said that I would and, after a brief chat, the conversation ended.

Within half an hour I received a telephone call from someone with the Christian name Nigel. He informed me that he had been placed in charge of my file at his company's office, with a view to ensuring that the recent tree work at my Surrey home would be redone and carried out correctly.

Minutes later, I dialled Dilys' number, who joined me in hearty laughter. I decided that perhaps I should organise a proper reading with her and made arrangements for the following week.

Telephone Reading - Dilys

"I have had Malcolm with me for a while. I am to ask you to go through analytically what is going on around you and did Nigel help?

"There is a water problem you need help with."

"Yes," I said, "We are battling with the council over how to drain the Mulberry Down drive properly."

"Malcolm has given me a line, which looks like something you might have read somewhere—'Material wealth is not the only kind'."

I was astonished at this. Following my trip to Goa in 2000 I had written a poem and one of the lines reads 'Material wealth is not the only kind'. I told Dilys this. She said that it was Malcolm's way of proving that he is aware of what is relevant in my life and of my poetry, and was using one of the lines to help me focus. The poem reads:

Wealth?

As I sit in relative 'splendour' on the plane home
How quickly shall I forget those I've left behind?
Dreaming of cool sheets and lying prone
I remember welcoming smiles sincere and kind.

Little was expected of us on our trip
Simply to enjoy the country where we'd chosen to stay
Our host's natural acceptance of poverty's grip
Rendered indecent the haggling they expected each day.

It seems very wrong that we have so much
When in comparison, our hosts have so little
We could afford almost all that we touched
Yet most of our purchases were totally fickle.

A major point missing here though
Is that material wealth is not the only kind
Allowing greed to control us, we'll harvest woe
Perhaps like them, spiritual wealth we too should find?

Dilys asked me to send her the poem so she could perhaps use it with her students during her workshops. She then continued, *"I have a silk bag with an elephant on it being presented to me. I feel that this is a message to you; it is time for you to make another pilgrimage. Malcolm is telling you it is time to go travelling again. Do you read Shirley MacLaine books?"*

"No," I said.

"Well, have a look at them, there may be a message there for you. There is also a link with Spain, perhaps she has written a travel book. Do check this out.

"I am seeing a postcard of beautiful poppy fields 'La Rioja'. I think this might be a wine region in Spain. He is showing me a wine bottle and saying it is a region.

"Malcolm is saying go on holiday—go and do something now—you have achieved the best you can, go and enjoy yourself, it is time.

"There is a pathway you could tread towards and feel totally comfortable with. This will help you move forward on your spiritual path. Take this, it is important. He wants you to feel freedom and travel. You must go to China."

"I am going to China in the New Year."

"Malcolm is telling me, 'You've got organisational skills; you've got efficiency skills; you've got 'manly' abilities which throws people; you've learned a lot with what you've had to deal with in the past few years. I am serious about her abilities; she could ultimately have success if she would only recognise what her gifts are!'

"He has a gentleman with him who has a Celtic rolling accent. He is helping him and sending you his love and saying that you called your son after his son." [This would be Malcolm's father, Ian, who was a Scot. We did indeed name Alastair after his uncle of the same name.]

Dilys continued, *"He is showing me a green-coloured tartan."* [The Irvine and Campbell tartans are green/blue.]

"I have the name Audrey written on my list and my attention is being drawn to the Beatles, does this mean anything?"

I confirmed that I am going to Scotland to visit Audrey and Geoff in August. They live on the Isle of Mull ... Paul McCartney wrote and sang 'Mull of Kintyre'.

Journal entry: 17 August

I have again been feeling disconnected and, consequently, rather disgruntled. It is very unsettling to feel like this when I have struggled to come to terms with the idea of being *connected* in the first place.

I have also been feeling unwell. Unwell is perhaps too strong a word; exhausted is perhaps nearer the mark. Heaven knows why, I don't have to work each day like most people, as well as coping with their everyday lives. But I certainly have felt out of sorts. That horrid word 'stress' rears its ugly head.

The annual gathering at Westfield was a wonderful success and I was happy to have so many like-minded friends under the same roof. It was a magical evening. Even Kellen and Paula were in the vicinity and able to join us. After this, though, the exhaustion set in with a vengeance and most of my final week in Devon was spent clearing up and sleeping.

Afterwards, I travelled to Kent to visit my parents as it was their anniversary. I sleep well there. It is so quiet and I feel protected and entirely safe in their home.

The first night I slept soundly without interruption. The next day was busy and at 6 p.m. I went to lie down for a while, as it was so hot. I slept until 8.30 p.m. This is highly unusual for me. After joining my parents for a while we all retired at 10.30 p.m. Again, I slept well until a neighbour's dog woke me with a loud bark at 4 a.m.!

I lay dozing for a few minutes before I felt the faint stirrings of the electrical energy rising from within. It became very strong for a few seconds and there were two main rushes of energy. While this was happening I clearly heard a male voice in both ears simultaneously. This is unusual. Usually, I hear something in one ear or the other, not both at the same time. I say it was a male voice simply because it *felt* as though it was male. I cannot say what was said and it infuriates me that I seem incapable of understanding the words spoken at these times. However, the truth is, I can't—yet! Needless to say, this reassurance after weeks of silence was most welcome.

Since returning home to Surrey I feel better than when I left. The exhaustion is not as great and the negativity, which I had allowed to seep in a little, has now been totally rebuffed. I continue to be amazed at these experiences and the new course that my life is taking. I am particularly delighted at the wonderful people I am meeting and feel very privileged.

Reading: September - Diana Summer

Weeks have passed without any further action. I dislike this feeling of being disconnected. I don't for one moment *believe* that I have been abandoned, for I totally accept that this path is not taken lightly on either side. I feel there is no turning back but I am human and my many weaknesses include a lack of patience and a constant need for reassurance. Perhaps it's just another learning curve.

So, I made an appointment with Diana:

"You are the counsellor; you are the guide, the healer and the channel. At times it will appear that floodgates have opened and there is a constant collective of souls that find their way to your door.

"They will be drawn by your energy and by that which has been said about you, through recommendation and by word of mouth. At such times, when you feel that you can give no more of yourself, then you must take a break. Shut the door. Retreat into a state of calm, enabling yourself to rebalance and refresh your physical, mental, emotional and spiritual selves."

"I have plans for a holiday in Cyprus on 10 September," I said.

"The frustration you feel is understood but it is to do with self-will. Because you have a strength of will that surpasses many, it is difficult for you to let go, to release and allow things to unfold universally. Patience is difficult to align yourself to and administer as a virtue. All is not lost for things are due to open again.

"You are an anchor and power point. Once you have accepted and believe in yourself more and have opened yourself to your own ability and potential, this then will move things further. It is a matter of self-empowerment, of not concerning yourself with the egotistical aspect of things but a quiet self-awareness. You will then be seen. Your energy begins to shift even as we speak.

"At times you may feel that all has disconnected, inspiration is lost and there is nothing to say. The pages remain blank. It is just a moment of rest for you. Appreciate these times, relax and know that, when appropriate, the inspiration will return and the words will flow

again.

"*You have acknowledged and are aware of your catalytic energy, drawing others together. Not just from the surrounding area, but from far afield. People will gather, converse and work together. This will take place on many different levels and this information is meant to be shared. The gathering is by design and is not simply a coincidence.*

"*There is a situation which will manifest and losses you have incurred will be replaced. There is abundance coming here for you from a different area. There is also a warning that you must learn to use your discernment. A situation may appear to be good but there is an illusion, which makes it not all it seems. If you are being pushed to make a decision then you must hold on until you are absolutely sure things are all as they should be. Don't be pushed into it by someone trying to persuade you. There will be a head to head with someone but you must listen to your own intuition and stand your ground. You will know what has to be done and it will not please everyone. This must be done in a certain way; you must be your own person. There is a strong influence trying to get in to affect your judgement. But all will be well and your experiences will help others in the future.*"

Journal entry: 25 October - Devon

I returned from Cyprus with nothing of a spiritual nature to note. Clare and I returned to Devon as we felt the need to be at Westfield.

Breakfasting at Somerton we continued via Broadhembury on route to Dunsford. We wanted to visit Dunsford church and sit in the ancient, carved wooden chair there, which is mentioned in *The Sun and the Serpent* by Paul Broadhurst and Hamish Miller, a book that Kellen had been reading when she visited in August.

She told us that the chair is reputed to have great energies attached to it and suggested we visit it at the earliest opportunity.

We found the church plus the chair and duly spent time sitting on it. I can't say that I noticed anything at all except that the horrendous headache, which had troubled me for the entire journey, vanished. Beyond this, there were no mind-shattering experiences.

There was nothing seen, felt or heard which was out of the normal. (Perhaps we simply expect too much!)

We decided to continue to Totnes and look in Arcturus, the spiritual bookshop. We made several purchases including *The Sun and the Serpent* and I showed Clare the picture of the Dunsford chair. While waiting to pay, I glanced at the counter and saw 'Shirley MacLaine' on a book cover. Memories stirred.

I recalled that Dilys Guildford had mentioned Shirley MacLaine's books and a connection with Spain in a telephone reading back in June. Until this moment I had forgotten all about this. I picked up the book, titled *The Camino,* and turned it over to read the blurb. In the book Shirley MacLaine writes about her own journey along a famous pilgrimage path called the Camino, which begins in France and spans northern Spain. Needless to say, I added the book to my list of purchases. I also picked up two copies of *South West Connection* magazine for Gloria and myself.

Because things spiritual have seemed silent again for a while I am beginning to understand that, although hard, this is something I need to get used to. I believe I am in a time of change. Whenever I come to Westfield, particularly with Clare, I always expect something amazing to happen. I have to confess, though, I cannot imagine quite how I would cope if it did. Particularly if I were to see an apparition of Malcolm, sitting on the veranda with his feet on the railings, a whisky glass in one hand and a cigar in the other!

Last night I felt particularly low for I was conscious that the meeting on Friday, with yet another architect, is to be a momentous decision time for me, with a view to extending Westfield and leaving behind in Surrey all that I am familiar with. Doubts about moving so far away from family and friends flooded my thinking. I know such concerns are inevitable but I went to bed with these teeming in my mind and barely slept.

In the morning, Clare sat down to study and I went out alone to complete a few chores. I was astonished when I began to realise how all the simple things were just falling into place that day and everything seemed to be going my way.

At my first stop I found a CD I had been searching for, for some weeks. I also needed to buy some picture frames; three of one size and four of another. In the same first shop, I discovered exactly the right type of frame and on the shelf there were precisely three of one size and four of the other! There were no other supplies of these particular frames on the shelves. I wanted to get the car cleaned and, unusually, there was no queue.

I then went to a beautician's shop which I had just discovered. I had not been there before and was delighted to be admitted to a spotless and tastefully decorated room where I was welcomed by a charming young woman. I relaxed and began to enjoy being pampered.

Halfway through the treatment I noticed a certificate on the wall stating that the young woman was also a Reiki healer. I was very pleased and said so. She was equally pleased to have a client who knew what it was and we had a long conversation about the whole concept of spiritual healing, with each of us describing our various experiences.

I was able to tell her some things which seemed to give her a measure of reassurance and she also told me about a place in Plymouth called 'Unity House' where like-minded people gather to give treatments, learn more and to offer reassurance. I took down the name and address and decided to follow-up this connection at the earliest opportunity.

All in all, it was an enjoyable day which seemed to be 'for me'. This simple run of things, all going so well, gave me the most wonderful reassurance and the doubts of the previous evening were left behind. I resolved to face and overcome my fears. I now feel free to walk more confidently towards my future.

Journal entry: 2 October - Surrey

Because of my recent travels I had missed two sessions of my photography course at college. I was, therefore, pleased to return and catch up with old friends and get back into the darkroom.

One friend, Derek, was there no more. He had been greatly admired by the rest of the class as he bravely fought his way to class each week on crutches, aided by his wife, Sheila, and a strong determination.

Since Derek's death I had seen Sheila only once when she visited briefly and had left looking emotional. After months of absence, she had called in on this particular day and I was pleased to actually be there and enjoy chatting to her.

Initially, we were speaking alone and I am still uncertain of how things occurred, but I do remember her saying that she often feels Derek's presence around her. She said, "You know, Patricia, sometimes I could swear he is just in his study and, at other times, beside me in the same room."

To this, I replied, "He probably is—he's unlikely to move on until he is satisfied you are going to be okay." Immediately, she smiled. Then followed a most animated conversation, and swapping of experiences and beliefs, which clarified that she and her daughter have both had many proofs since her husband's death that spirit does indeed live on after the physical life is over.

What astonished me most of all, though, was that another classmate and friend of mine for seven years, with whom I had never discussed spiritual matters, joined us. She stood nodding her head in agreement regarding much of what we were saying.

Puzzled, I mentioned this to her and, to my absolute delight, she proclaimed that not only does she, but also her younger brother and her mother, see spirits regularly. When they are going about their normal everyday lives it is nothing for each of them to see spirits walking about with the rest of us. She told me that her old uncle regularly walks up her parents' garden path towards the family home and gives her a wave and a smile, yet he has been 'dead' for over fifteen years. I was stunned and thrilled by this revelation.

We have been friends for all that time and only now do we discover that we share similar spiritual experiences. My friend was also delighted. She never discusses such things with anyone but her mother and brother and she is pleased to discover that she now has an accepting ear much closer to home.

Sheila was pleased that her bravery had begun such an earnest conversation. She told us that her daughter would love to meet us and discuss the concept for, since her father's death, her experiences had opened her mind to such phenomena and she wasn't sure where to look for support. We have arranged to visit the Harry Edwards

Healing Sanctuary together later in the month.

There was no emotional exit from the classroom this time as Sheila left. In fact, she was wearing a broad smile as if she were sharing a secret. In the meantime, I have sent the extra copy of the *South West Connection* magazine that I picked up in Totnes to Sheila's daughter. It might help her.

Journal entry: Sunday, 7 October - Dymchurch, Kent

It would appear that all the time I have been expecting to *hear* or *see* something I have been blind to the numerous synchronicities going on around me. I seem to be in the midst of a period of 'coincidences' which I prefer to think of as synchronicities. I no longer believe in coincidence. These I read as ticks on my life's chart which confirm that all is proceeding as planned.

Recently, I discovered a shiny, new 100 Peseta coin in my purse, which is similar in size and colour to a £1 coin. I had picked it up in error, as my son had just returned from Spain.

On this particular morning, I had taken my parents to a village boot fair. It was a fantastic autumn morning with golden sunshine, a buffeting wind and a kaleidoscope of puffy, coloured clouds. The rain showers were hard, yet over quickly, whereupon the sun would reveal itself once more, bathing the wet grass and drenched trees in glistening gold. The stallholders had taken refuge in their cars but they now began to step outside again to brave the elements.

I had had another lucky morning. I had been searching for a pair of Turkish coffee cups for a friend for some time and found the perfect ones. I bought more shrubs for the Westfield garden including one which will forever remind me of my parents. I even managed to find an electrical extension with six separate plug sockets for my father. (I took this and tested it in the village hall kitchen before parting with the princely sum of 50p!) It just seemed to be another day when things were going my way. I was so grateful and enjoyed the simplicity of the glorious morning, my parents' company and my many bargains.

I bent down to look at a box of books and was pleased to see two Shirley MacLaine titles among them. Then I heard a voice say, almost apologetically, "I collected those when I became interested in the religions of the world." I glanced up at the speaker, smiled and resumed looking at the books, wondering why she had stopped being interested in them.

The voice spoke again, "Some people say that Shirley MacLaine 'went a bit funny'."

I looked directly at her and replied, "Well, I think they were wrong." I had by now, of course, read *The Camino*, the book I bought in Totnes, in which Shirley MacLaine documents her brave, personal quest for spiritual understanding while walking the Camino trail in northern Spain, on an arduous voyage of self-discovery.

A fleeting hint of recognition flickered in her eyes and then she said, "That's right. She didn't 'go funny' at all. I know that and you know it, too, don't you?" I nodded.

Then I asked, "It's unusual for people to part with spiritual books like these. Do you mind if I ask why you are selling them?"

The reply was instant, "I'm moving to Spain, to live there permanently, and I can't take everything with me."

I selected six of the books and handed them to her. I gave her the relevant coins and glanced at the 100 Peseta piece still in my hand which seemed to shine even brighter in the golden light of autumn. I picked it out of the change and thrust the remainder back into my pocket. The lady handed me the books in a plastic bag.

"Did you say you are going to live in Spain?" I asked.

"Yes."

I handed her the sparkling coin and said, "Well, take this as a talisman to bring you good luck. Never spend it. Never give it away. Keep it forever and, when you get to Spain, make sure you buy more books like these and keep reading them."

Her initial shocked expression changed into a broad smile as she studied the coin and she leaned forward, gave me a firm hug and a kiss on the cheek. "I will," she said, "thank you so much. I shall keep it always." Then, staring directly into my eyes, she added, "I am so very pleased to have met you."

And that was it—in a flash—it was over. I still cannot think, for the life of me, what made me say such a thing to a complete stranger but all I do know is that we were equally glad to have met on that beautiful autumn morning. And I am quite certain that she will continue to read spiritual books in Spain.

Chapter 20
In God's Name

Several weeks ago I contacted an astrologer in Devon, recommended by Gloria. Unfortunately, through her being unwell we were unable to meet personally but she sent me her comments based on the reading of my charts.

'I hope that you believe in reincarnation because I shall speak a lot about it. We believe that we have had lots of different experiences [lives] and the aim of all these lives is to go on learning more about the nature of God, and the position we hold in the evolutionary pattern. We believe that you chose this particular life, with particular circumstances, to learn lessons. These charts symbolise a path from past to present to future.

One of the outstanding features of your chart is the conjunction between Venus and Jupiter; those two are closely linked together in all three charts. They are the symbolic depiction of good fortune and mean you are wealthy, good looking, have a pleasing personality, or all three. This is strongly indicated.

In the 'Nodal' chart of your past you were indeed an important personage and you used your gifts to be in the public eye and to do unusual things and became a bit of a rebel. You were meant to do this and had a great influence on the people around you. You used your gifts to great advantage and achieved a lot of acclaim and wealth through it all.

At the same time, you were quite sensitive and did not particularly like yourself all that much. You had an enormous influence on other people but you realised that people were not necessarily happier through it. You were not sure why this was. You acted impulsively, you did what you felt was right at the time, you influenced people enormously.

But you were not quite sure what your life was all about and whether you used your gifts rightly or not, and wondered what else you could, or should, have done. In a way you were carried away by your own success and this took over the direction of your life. You did the things at which you were successful whether you yourself approved of them or not.

So, in this life, you made very sure indeed that you should learn to use those gifts of yours in a responsible and constructive manner. This, of course, takes time. You did not want to follow the dictates of other people's value systems. You could have. You would have been the ideal head girl, for instance, if you believed in the system that your school adopted. [I was the head girl at my school.] *You could also, in this life, with your gifts and strength be an asset in any business.*

You have enormous capabilities but you are trying to use them in the way you want to use them, not in the way others want you to. You can sway people to think the way you want them to think, you have that ability. You could manipulate them, quite deliberately, but you don't want to. Nor do you want to abide by anyone else's rules, nor by any church, or other people's family values. You have to work out your own values. This takes time, courage and knowledge. You don't want to base your life on any faith because you know, through previous lives, that church people can fake a lot and you became quite cynical about the established values of any particular group. You do not want to have much to do with faith and belief but are trying to establish your value system based on facts.

You are a go-getter and full of energy. You could organise anything. You have the ability to look into other people's minds and hearts and this worries you at times. When you try to help people, which is something you like to do, you have to decide whether you want to help people to stay as they are and make people feel as comfortable as possible or, alternatively, you could help them to progress in learning something. This would be less straightforward, less convenient and could be quite painful for them, though it may at times be necessary and quite advisable. Because you are so efficient and so effective, you know the value of time and your own energies. You are extremely keen to use this ability to the best advantage once you know what this is.

The balance of colour in your chart says quite a lot about you. You have a very healthy balance of red, green and blue. You have enormous gifts and energy plus the willingness and keenness to learn. Once you know what it is that you are here to learn, you will use all this energy to set about and learn it. You will read, think and talk to others about it. It will be something of the modern way of looking at life. It will not be orthodox, therefore you will need the courage of your convictions, which you have. But it takes a long time to be clear in your mind what it is you want to concentrate on. It will be something which takes other people's long-term welfare into consideration and you will learn by experience.

I think you might have had some fairly startling experiences which make you realise that the orthodox way of looking at life leaves out a great chunk of reality. This is very real to you and to a lot of other people but society, as a whole, covers it up and doesn't want to know about it. You are very keen to acquaint yourself further with this and study it more. There are lots of groups now which explore the unorthodox ideas from many points of view. There are many views; some are constructive but others phoney. You need stimulation from ideas.

Your chart shows you are just about to reach the stage of going within when it comes to philosophy and ideas. This can be a difficult time and quite depressing because you are isolated as you have to do this on your own. Others can help but cannot do it for you. You are a searcher after the truth and are interested in the ideas that groups have to offer but you prefer to work by yourself.

The path is the goal. It is the actual search which is of value rather than the finding. The purpose and path of life is so vast and so complicated, nobody can know it all or even attempt to know it. But we may know the right direction and this is your forte. Your need to learn, your urge to learn is outstanding and rules your life. You have got it all together and you have enormous power and are a trendsetter. Once you know which way you want to go, you are able to take people with you and inspire them. You are a born leader and can assert yourself if you want to. You have been assertive but now want to help others to assert themselves, which is a step forward. You want to help others to work out their own values and their own paths. You no longer want them to follow you like sheep.

You are very keen in this particular life to speak your truth when you have something constructive to say. You are very conscientious about trying to be as responsible as you may be. If you do have a truth that others cannot share with you there is no need to hide it these days but we can mention it without trying to bulldoze people into following us.

You are fed up with leading sheep into believing what you want them to believe. You do not want this, this time round. You did that the last time and now you want to inspire others to think and to ask questions in a constructive way, so that they can enjoy discovering their own paths and truths.

There is an issue of power here. You had a considerable amount of power in a previous life through the wealth you had, through the personality, and also the social position you held. In this life you want to be quite sure that you don't act just to increase your power. You have it and want to use it. In fact, it is your duty to use it but what you can work for, is to achieve a powerful transformation in others, after you have achieved a transformation in yourself.

You feel you must find something or someone to whom you feel responsible. The word God is rather hackneyed; people mean different things by it. Whatever your concept is of the Godhead, there is no need to be able to put it into words. It is beyond words, yet it is an energy that is definitely there. (If you can talk about it in a way others can understand you are a genius!) You feel very responsible to whatever it may be and if you can pass that on to other people, it would be of tremendous value.

In the previous life you were dependent on other people's adoration of you and you played to the gallery rather to get their admiration and adulation. In this life, you deliberately do not want that. You try not to upset people but you do not say what they want to hear for their own sakes, if you do not feel it to be the truth. You try to share your struggles and uncertainties with other people. In this age we know that the whole universe is so vast, the knowledge *that we could have, and should have, is so enormous.*

Sharing our reverence and awe is an important message that we can give to others. For quite a few people it is essential that they express their doubts and negativity and this is part of their learning process. People will eventually have to widen their horizons beyond what they consider now to be rational and reasonable. People will slowly accept it and begin by denying and decrying but that is part of the process too. You have the ability to influence them but deliberately hold back and slow yourself down, to allow people time to learn in their own way and at their own speed.

Lots of people are longing to be healers. There is a difference between curing and healing. A person who cures takes away a physical symptom. A person who heals, smooths out the underlying trouble which causes the disease.

You have a special gift to be a teacher, not of facts but of the value and aim of life. Also of reincarnation and the consequences this has for you; and the wisdom needed to deal with the potential of our lives. You will be able to use your gifts in such a way that you can influence people most constructively. Your ability to influence others will show itself as an ability to give others the tools to manipulate themselves. It is your heart's desire to help others to be spiritually healthy. Inner cleanliness comes first. Once people know the meaning of life it will be easier for them to cope with the difficulties that come to us all and recognise them as lessons that we have to learn.

Once you know the direction that you believe life takes and what is underpinning the whole of life, you will be able to help others to come to the same conclusion. I think you will do a great deal of good and be a facilitator for others to learn what you are learning now.'

Journal entry: 30 October - 1.44 a.m. - Surrey

Something strange happened to me tonight. After months of silence and little or no spiritual occurrences at all, I have now been prompted to pick up my pen.

From the centre, the very core, of my being outwards to the extremities of my physical self I have literally come alive with power. This didn't come in waves, nor was it solely concentrated in the spinal area, as it has been before. My entire being was simply infused, including my head.

Had I been brave enough to look, I would have expected my entire body to be glowing. I was fully conscious and had no desire to risk opening my eyes, as I did not want to jeopardise the experience. I was not in a hurry for it to end. It lasted a long time but I have no idea exactly how long.

The power didn't *consume* me; I was the power. It emanated from within me. I saw nothing but patterns and masses of purple yet *felt* as though I was receiving great knowledge. It seemed as though there was a question-and-answer session happening inside me. I believe much was being explained but, sadly, cannot remember what. I felt as if this power emanating from me could conquer and overcome anything at all. Absolutely anything! I kept repeating in my head over and over again, "Lord God, in heaven above. I *know* I'm a channel for thy healing, thy light and thy love."

It was as though I had reached an important stage in spirituality. It was as though I was being *charged* ready to encounter the next step forward. In fact, it felt as though all my guides and protectors were with me not only pouring energy into my being, but receiving what I was emanating also. It was a two-way experience. It was as though I have turned an important corner, safe in the knowledge that I'm supported and far from alone—but I don't pretend that I fully understand what went on. I do know, however, that I was being taught to *listen* and quieten my own overactive thoughts— this was in order that I might *receive*.

I am also aware that 30 October was my husband's birthday. I would love to be writing that this experience stemmed from him but I don't feel that. I think this was from something *beyond* Malcolm ... something greater than him. I felt wrapped in peace. I hope I am not misjudging his efforts or his own advancement in the overall scheme of things.

Journal entry: 7 November

I am at a Health Hydro in Berkshire and, unusually, for my character and upbringing, feel no guilt whatsoever about the amount of money I am spending on my own well-being. I am enjoying time out and the autumn splendour which surrounds us here.

On the first night here I was sitting alone at the dining table armed with my book (a sure indication that someone is not expecting company) when a lady approached me and asked if she could share my table. Before we had even completed the main course, she was speaking about spirituality.

Yesterday, I asked the therapist who was treating me about the Reiki healer employed at the Hydro. It appears that she only comes in at special request as Reiki is a recent innovation here. I decided to book a treatment to meet the lady in question. My initial enquiry led to the therapist confiding in me about her own spiritual experiences. (I have ceased to be surprised now!)

I checked the notice board to see what lectures or meetings might be of interest to me and I noticed that a clairvoyant, Yvette Tamara, is coming on Friday.

Journal entry: Thursday, 8 November - 6.10 p.m.

I attended a hypnotherapy session, naively thinking that I would emerge from it totally put off eating all fattening food forever. Instead, I found myself in floods of tears, furious with myself for not being able to relax and allow the hypnotherapy to take place.

It became more like how I would imagine a grief counselling session to be and I found myself blurting out my fears and sense of loss to a complete stranger. I felt like a fool but the therapist seems to think that it will have done me some good. Judging by the way that I feel at present, I can't say I'm very convinced.

I then went and sat in the pool area with my notebook, too embarrassed to go to dinner but too hungry not to. Frankly, I could have done with a jolly good laugh. Eventually, the girl I had welcomed to my dining table on the first day returned from a walk and suggested that we eat together. Luckily, the lights were low in the dining room.

Journal entry: Friday, 9 November - 16.45 p.m.

I wasn't totally honest yesterday. Part of the reason for feeling so wretched was that I had also been a coward.

At the Hydro there is a chapel. This is my fifth visit over twenty years, and each time I have been there I have been appalled to see that the beautiful chapel is used as a table tennis room. On the first day of my present stay, I again visited this chapel. I noticed that the table was still there. I had this dreadful feeling and *knew* that I was expected to do something, speak to someone about this but what could I say?

During the course of those first few days, I always seemed drawn to visit the chapel. This feeling of expectation for me to do something about its inappropriate use became more and more exaggerated. In the end, I made a pact with myself that, if I should see the manager three times in one day, then I would summon the courage and speak to him about it. Yesterday—my dreadful day—I saw him three times but my courage failed me.

My heart was already so low that, although I knew what was expected of me, I was too cowardly to proceed. After an emotionally wretched day and tear-stained supper I went to my room early, watched complete trash on the TV, retired hurt at 10.30 p.m., deeply upset and feeling sorry for myself. I was so low, that it reminded me of the bleakest days following the loss of Malcolm.

I was truly in despair and called upon every guardian, angel, guide and helper I could muster to pull me out of this awful black hole. Finally, unable to rest, I listened to the consoling voice of Harry Edwards and eventually slept.

I woke shortly before 7.30 a.m., feeling a little better but not exactly great. Rocketing back into my mind came the question of speaking to the manager about the chapel. I knew I couldn't leave without fulfilling the promise. What he chose to do about it would be up to him but I knew what I had to do and it troubled me.

My treatments ended at eleven in the morning, after which I showered and changed and prepared myself physically and psychologically for the encounter. At the reception I asked if I could speak to the manager, stressing that I had no complaint. I read instant relief in their faces. Within minutes he appeared. I asked if we could speak privately and he led me to the first floor and showed me into his office. Finally, we sat opposite each other in vast leather chairs. The moment had come.

I began by thanking him for being so understanding and continued, "Mr ... I am here for a week and I am trying to have a peaceful holiday away from everything but, the fact is, I am a medium. [I had actually said it!] Every time I have seen you in the past few days, it has been pressed upon me to speak to you regarding a certain aspect of the Hydro. I am here to ask you, if you wish me to proceed with this message or not?" I could barely believe what I was saying.

He was concentrating completely and looking gravely at me. Then, to my great relief, he asked me to continue. I told him that I would not look directly at him while speaking but proceeded to say everything that came into my head. I cannot remember all that was said but the following is the gist of it:

"This Hydro has a great opportunity to become a major metaphysical centre. The jewel in its crown is the chapel, which is currently inappropriately used. This chapel could be put to far greater use. For this to work well it would require the addition of symbols from each known religion of the world, to be incorporated in the décor of the chapel, so that each is justly acknowledged. The energy in the vicinity of the land around the Hydro, particularly among the trees, is very powerful and of the highest source. This is currently untapped.

"Among your staff, there are many that are interested in metaphysics. Some of these you are aware of, others are, as yet, unknown to you. It is advised that you speak with all your staff and reassure them that you welcome their knowledge. At present, because of the sacred nature of their work, some are fearful of being exploited because of a lack of understanding and greed.

"It is suggested that log cabins be positioned within the trees, in particular, one large cabin for metaphysical meditation and group work. The chapel should also be a quiet room and a centre for such work.

"It is important that you understand that this is a *request* not an order. However, should you concede to the request, it will be looked upon as a gift to the universe and such gifts are rewarded with abundance."

When I had finished speaking, it was as though the clouds of the previous day vanished completely and I felt absolutely great. I didn't even fear his response; this wasn't initially important to me. All that mattered was that I had had the *courage* to carry out that which I felt compelled to do.

The manager had been taking notes ardently throughout the entire episode. At the end he looked up, put down his pen and sat back in his chair looking intently at me. It was my turn to be surprised. He began by thanking me and said, "That couldn't have been an easy thing to say."

I assured him that it wasn't at all easy and that part of me was still wondering what on earth I thought I was doing! He laughed, thanked me again and then said, "It's very odd but I have noticed you several times this week. I keep seeing you in corridors, by the pool and other areas and we are almost always alone. I have been prompted to speak to you but couldn't think why. There was no reason to, yet the feeling was strong."

Yet again, I was shocked. Why on earth would he notice this overweight, robe-clad, fifty-one-year-old among so many others? I replied, "Perhaps, that was your own intuition working?"

Later that evening, I noticed that the manager was present at the clairvoyant lecture and demonstration. I overheard him telling someone that he had never attended such a thing before but that he had recently become interested in the subject. As I listened to him speak, I recalled our encounter earlier in the day.

Part of me could still not help wondering, *What in God's name did I think I was doing? Then* it dawned on me. The whole episode *was* in His name, in fact, in His many names. That *was* the point!

Chapter 21
The Courage of My Convictions

Journal entry: 1 December 2001

Things are coming to a head in respect of CIL. I have a great deal on my mind and I know that, soon, I shall have to follow through on my major decisions. But do I have the courage?

This is not an easy situation and I feel great need for reassurance and guidance. It has been some time since I have experienced close personal contact with The Source; there has been a distinct lack of energy coursing through my body.

I asked Diana Summer for help.

Reading - 30 November - Diana Summer

"There is deviousness going on here. Your adversary will present himself in one way but underneath that there is the underlying aspect of him. He is clever and a bit of a chameleon. He can present himself as charming and kind but when the other aspect of him is in control, he can be shady and dark. It is this dark side which seems to be working against you. It is coming to disrupt. He wants to cause you worry and anxiety. He can't leave it alone. He is like a terrier, once he gets hold of it, he wants to keep shaking it and cannot let it go. This is the energy of this situation. It is not pleasant.

"With all your knowledge and ability, there is an opportunity here for you to take action and by so doing you will achieve what you need. But it is indeed a leap of faith and trust. You just know you have to do this, whatever the outcome. This is ahead of you. The situation around the court case is not easy.

"Be on your guard. There is someone out to try and destroy you. There is a burning jealousy here, a feeling of wanting to cause damage. There is intense irritation, which dwells deep within this person because of how strong you are. This plays havoc with him. He cannot believe that he can't just walk in, take, and then walk away. The fact that he is up against this huge amount of strength, that this strength is feminine and that it is in control, is unbelievably painful for him. It is causing him damage and is eating him away inside. It is almost like hatred. Take heed and be aware. Have your eyes and ears open and protect yourself.

"I cannot tell you how incensed he is. He is looking for every trick in the book to manifest his wishes and desires. He is a misogynist, so you are up against it in all ways. I cannot believe how angry he is, with you having this control over him. He is steaming. He is learning a very difficult lesson. All you seek is confirmation of what you already know but this will not be easy. You must think this through. He will be as devious as he can possibly be.

"You are maintaining a huge influence just by sitting tight. You really are holding energy there. He cannot believe how powerless it makes him feel. I do see you achieving what you want, success is there but it is borne out of battle. Know that you will be looked after and that it is right.

"This is karmic. This man has been in your previous lives. When you marry, you take on karmic issues. There was a really intense karmic issue between your husband and this man. Your husband completed his part and returned to spirit but this triangle has been around before and you are now taking on the karma that is left. This man wants control and it is almost a cry for help in a very strange way. He wants to be heard and wants to be seen but he wants to be in control. He cannot accept help from you but might, much later, from another source. At present he is in such a dark space he is not open to anything.

"But, Patricia, you are immensely powerful. Just your very presence can have an impact on people; you don't even have to speak to them. You have a real energy. You are never unnoticed. You never sit unnoticed unless you choose to. Others can feel your strength and that is what he doesn't like. He feels threatened by you

and that is half the problem.

"You are a constant reminder of his insecurity and his own sense of inadequacy. This is your role. These are his unresolved issues. Do only what you feel is right in your heart and only when you feel it is time.

"You are here as a catalyst and as one who will overcome the challenges presented to you. These will, at times, appear insurmountable or overwhelming in their very nature, and the intensity of all that they represent. But you are here to challenge ... to fight for what, in your heart, you know is right. This will bring balance and will redress each situation. Each time you overcome your doubt and fear of your ability then another step forward will be achieved. It is no easy path.

"Your path continues to unfold. Already you are, at last, acknowledging the help you are giving others. You are drawn and inspired to share with them what you have experienced; to guide them.

"You will be using the written word, brought through from the higher planes of consciousness, inspiring you to write and record that which needs to be shared. You have a gift and are beginning, gently, to become consciously aware of it. A greater sense of self will be acknowledged as time passes. Your light will touch many. It will be an individual choice of how they use it and make good of it. You can only guide, but know that you are never on your own.

"This present situation is your challenge and once you overcome this, you will progress spiritually. Nothing lasts forever and each week or month that passes, is a step nearer to resolution."

Journal entry: 4 December - Surrey

Today has been a trying one. Early this morning, I attended a meeting with counsel regarding our impending battle with Ian over the company affairs. I came away from the meeting feeling alarmed. Everyone agreed that, morally, we have a case but are uncertain of the outcome and fearful that I may not stand the pace either financially or personally.

I dislike the idea of giving in to Ian's bullying, but I'll be honest, part of me was relieved to hear my eldest son declare, "Write it off, Mother—it's not worth it." Peter Darby, who was also present, was of the same mind.

However, it is not as easy as that for me. I feel very confused and dreadfully unhappy. Returning home, tired and irritable yet again, I ate too much (of course!), which made me feel even more miserable. Finally, hauling myself upright, I decided to do something positive.

I telephoned a friend and she invited me over for a cup of tea. We talked about spiritual matters, which have bound us now for several weeks, and moved on to discuss my current dilemma. It was helpful to talk about it. As I left, she said, "Don't you worry, Patricia. Give yourself time. You will receive help with this, I feel that very strongly." With these words echoing reassuringly in my ears, I returned home.

*****

I went to bed at 8.15 p.m., vowing to achieve much more the next day. I dozed a little and felt grateful for the refuge of my bed. I could hear Duncan's distant voice using the telephone and remember being mildly annoyed at the length of time he was talking. I could hear the clocks striking periodically and fetched some water to drink, which is how I know that I wasn't dreaming.

I began to sense the faint stirrings of the electrical sensations I have experienced on many occasions before, although not for a long time. I welcomed this; I was in the mood for reassurance.

The rippling began once again and continued on and off for some time, all the while I continued to hear the familiar sounds of the house. I glanced at the clock, it was nearly midnight. I remember thinking that it was late for Duncan to still be up and knew that I'd not heard the alarm being set or his footsteps on the stair.

The sensations suddenly increased in intensity. I welcomed them but was surprised at the speed at which they occurred. It was as though my entire body was infused with power. There was such a terrific surge coursing through me that I felt as though I was fainting and sinking into oblivion, which, quite frankly at that point in time, I would have welcomed.

My entire body was alive with this input of power. Then, slowly, it faded. I kept my eyes firmly shut. I did not want the sensation to end because I was grateful for reassurance after months of inactivity. The feeling ebbed. I lay there quietly, for in the furthest reaches of my being, I knew there was more to come. And come it did!

There was a *massive* crescendo of the sensations. It was so enormous that I thought I might be physically sick. This was accompanied by a loud *rushing* in my ears, both ears simultaneously, which eventually receded, leaving me feeling nauseous.

After a few moments—it could only have been seconds—the electrical sensations increased to such a degree that it alarmed me, but in the recesses of my mind, I *knew* there was nothing to fear. I simply *rode* with it. In fact, it was like riding a huge surging tide of electrical power. I cannot think of another way to describe it. I felt as though I was being lifted higher and higher. I was spiralling upwards and was perfectly happy to allow it to happen. Then, there was a massive crescendo in both ears simultaneously and I clearly heard the words, "We want you to fight, fight, fight ..."

The voice was soft but the diction was very clear. It was neither male nor female. The actual words, though, could not be denied. I could actually decipher them! I lay there for a short while, possibly only minutes. Eventually, I knew that the experience was over. The heat my body had generated during this was intense and I was soaked in perspiration. I threw on my towelling robe. I knew that Duncan was still up and went downstairs to tell him exactly what had occurred.

I realised that to take this as a serious instruction upon which to base our entire future would be foolish without invoking the 'spiritual law of three'. I need this to happen three times in order for me to discern between frivolous, mischievous or, possibly malicious intention and the *absolute truth*. Mentally and verbally I asked that this instruction be clearly presented to me three times. If this is done, then without any shadow of doubt, I will step forward and fight.

This power, that I feel so privileged to experience, is very strong but I must be sure that it is for our good and is not engineering our destruction. I am fearful of the unknown. I don't want to fail my sons, my husband or myself. Nor do I wish to fail The Source of all that is ...

Journal entry: Wednesday, 5 December - 4.08 a.m.

It has happened again but for a shorter length of time. Two terrific surges of energy coursed through my body and the words—not *heard*—but intuitively *received* were, "This is our moment." *Our* moment, not *your* moment, it was very precise.

This is not enough. I need to relive the major experience twice more before I can proceed, safe in the knowledge that what I am doing is right for all concerned.

In desperation, I decided to call Yvette Tamara, a clairvoyant who recently gave a demonstration at the Health Hydro. I am not trying to 'pass the buck'. I am not trying to ask someone else to make my decisions for me. I simply want to call upon all the help I can to make this very difficult decision. I am fearful of upsetting my sons and need them with me on this. But I am also very afraid of failing to do what I believe in my core to be right.

One thing only is certain. I have to live with my decision and I have to have the courage of my convictions. I cannot allow fear of the unknown to control my life, either now or in the future. This is not a decision I take lightly. But I don't want my whole life to prove fruitless if I fail to make the right decision at the eleventh hour. I asked help mentally, verbally and now in written form; *please, may I clearly hear and understand the way forward.*

Reading: Sunday, 9 December - Yvette Tamara

Yvette asked for a photograph of Malcolm, which I took. The following is from the tape of our session.

"A May anniversary, does this mean anything?" I confirmed that 1 May was our wedding anniversary.

"What is it you want to ask me, Patricia?"

"I want to know whether or not I can trust my brother-in-law, Ian."

"No, I don't feel you can trust him. What I am being shown is a worm in a box trying to dig himself out. He will do everything not to face up to a situation and everything to get out of a hole. Be very careful with this man. I feel he is quite devious.

"The spirit world is coming through very strongly. Ian is up to no good. I'm also being shown a Rob connected with Ian, Rob short for Robin."

I said nothing but instantly thought of the company accountant.

"There will be lots of reshuffling and reorganising to do with the company and around Ian. He has ideas of bigger and better things. He values money over family. I am being shown pound signs as if this is his God, as though he would cut his arm off if it meant he could keep his money. I am now getting a 'thank you' from the spirit world for speaking to you.

"You are thinking of going away in April, you should go. Decisions will have been made before then."

I replied, "I have to decide whether or not to take Ian to court."

"Yes, definitely! There are a few sly things going on. The situation must be resolved. Ian doesn't think you will pursue him. He thinks you are going to keel over. You have got to take him to court, otherwise you will never resolve it. I feel it is a necessity."

I responded, "I feel it is but, sometimes, it is difficult to put the fear aside and do what you know is right."

"Once you have, you will feel as though a weight has been lifted. At the moment your stomach feels as though it is ill." I nodded.

"But once you have done it you will know you have done the right thing. You must take Ian to court because he is going to try and wriggle out of something. I am being told the company will be divided into three sections in some way."

I confirmed that Ian, the children's trust and I all own shares.

"'You must protect it,' I'm being told. You must do this now because I feel if you are not careful he will do things to ruin the company and try and manipulate things.

"Instructing a solicitor is a must. Ian won't like it—he will say 'damn that woman!' But don't be frightened. You must do it to

safeguard things, otherwise you will lose out.

"It will turn out all right. You must take this man to court, though.

"Your husband went very quickly?" I confirmed that this was so.

"I'm hearing, 'I'm very sorry to have left you.'"

Chapter 22
New Resolve, Old Arrogance

Reading: Saturday, 22 December 2001 - Janet

I have discovered a clairvoyant, Janet, living in Rye. All she knew about me was my Christian name. Again there was no prior discussion although Janet required Malcolm's photograph.

"There has been an imbalance for quite some time, not just this last week or two but for most of the last year. I am being told I can go back a little further than that. Indirectly, it does affect finances. You have been trying to plan things, separate things out.

"I am getting this information from the gentleman in the photograph. He was a very clever man who would have worked with his brain and in a position of authority.

"He says, 'One moment I was there and the next I was gone.' It took him a while to understand what had happened. In lots of ways he was full of vim and vigour. Do you understand that? These are his words not mine. There was a birthday around the time that he went." [My nephew was born six days later.]

"He walked his own pathway and was in charge of his life. He was a man of precision. That was part of his job, getting things right. He is bringing calculations in here but these are for both of you, not just for him.

"He says that your home is in turmoil, do you understand? It is as if you want to go but you have to stay. He is saying you must do what you want because it is your life and it passes by very quickly. You must remember that. When he looks back at his life, he realises how fast it went by and how little he really did of what he wanted to do. He had plans for many things he wanted to achieve and these didn't materialise because he didn't live long enough to put them

into play.

"You have got to think of your future. You can be giving up things now, only to lose out in the future. Is he making sense? Get a piece of paper; this is good advice, put down the good things attached to your life, the possibilities and the bad things. He is saying things are going round in your mind, the same things all the time and you are coming back with the same answers. You are not going to clear the thoughts unless they are on paper. Only then will you create the space for other thoughts. You have got to be more open-minded. You are looking at here and now and six months ahead, would you understand that? You have got to look at the bigger picture.

"There is more than one problem. There are three in all. He says you must make it clear in your own mind and heart that it is really what you want before you act. He is saying, 'Think seriously. Feel what is right but don't just look at now, look further ahead.'

"He is concerned about you and the family. He is talking about the hurdles you have had to jump already to get where you are, which were very difficult and have hurt you emotionally. This pain has made you feel rejected."

"He says there have been many tears. You did not know which way to turn at the time but you found daylight and you climbed even though it is an uphill struggle. The impression that he is giving me is that you will progress. You will not stay where you are. You will not stay stationary. He is showing me how he wants to put his hand on your back and push you forward. In his mind you haven't got a lot of choice. Those are his words, not mine.

"He is taking you abroad for some reason and I see you working overseas. You will travel a lot more. It is almost as though you are abroad in the same respect as TV crews who have special permission to photograph the unusual. This is to come. There is excitement here and expectation, looking ahead. It is like a newsreel reporter taking photographs of different things. He has opened the sky as if to say, 'everything'. This is the future for you.

"He would have been very good at figures, without doubt. He knows what he is doing, his brain was like a calculator. A lot of the work that he did he was self-taught. He is saying, 'I started off on my own, I worked my way up and the money I received was mine

because I worked for it.'

"He seems to be handing out money but it is not just to one person. There is a legal document of some sort, which needs to be addressed. He is saying the sooner the better. There is a clause in it that has been misinterpreted." [Malcolm left the one share that is causing us such trouble in his will to his older brother, expecting it to ease our path, not obliterate it!]

"He is doing this ... " Janet clasped her hands and began rubbing them together—one of Malcolm's habits when he was indicating someone who was greedy.

"He is telling me to do the same, saying, 'Just prove to her that it is me.'

"Malcolm liked nice shirts. He is saying, 'It was important to me, I still like nice shirts and shoes ...' He says, 'I am giving you a picture of me, it's important.'

"This gentleman would have had a keen sense of humour. He complained about the chair that he sat in. Was it in the wrong light or wrong position?" [I confirmed that he complained about his chair at home being in a draught.]

"I get a good feeling from this man. I feel happy and safe with him. Regardless of anyone's position, whatever class, he could blend in and work along with different types of people.

"There has been some problem to do with the boundary line?"

"This is true," I confirmed, "I have paperwork to sort out regarding the boundary fence between the Gospel Hall and our home."

"He is saying, 'All these things I know.' This is proof that he knows what is going on in your everyday life. He has wanted to talk to you for a long time but you toyed with the idea and then gave up."

"Not intentionally, but meditating is not my strong point."

"He says, 'Life is what you make of it. What you put into it, you get out of it with luck.' He put a lot into something at one time and it didn't materialise in the way he expected it to. This is to do with business, not home life.

"This gentleman is so on the spot. It is almost as if he is observing things and was very quick of the eye. You would think he hadn't noticed something but he had.

"He liked to read," Janet said. *"You like to read but you don't get the time. The material you read is different to what he read. You have quite a few books, so many he is saying you could start a library."* [A family joke.]

"He is pointing to a watch and saying he wants you to buy it for Christmas. It is as though it is a gift from him to you." [Malcolm wanted to buy me a gold watch to stop the metal ones making black marks on my arm.]

"Malcolm is pleased with himself because he has conveyed to you the things that mean something to you both and these help to prove who he is. He has not needed to bring anyone else in.

"You have got one window in your house in Kent that is different from the others." [My bedroom has an unusual window—it is an overhanging bay—all the others are integral with the walls.]

"He says, 'I know all that there is to know. You cannot tell me anything that I do not know. I have grasped it in my hand.'"

At this point, I asked if I could ask a question: "Am I right to pursue Malcolm's brother regarding the company?"

"Yes! Because you are a woman you are looked on in a different light and they feel you haven't got the ability to forge forward. He wants you to move forward. You need to push harder than you are and get more help legally. He says, 'Right is right and wrong is wrong and what has been done is wrong. But you do need more force. It will pay dividends.'

"There is more involved than you anticipate. He wants you to open your eyes wider. There are things in existence at this moment that you have no idea about, underneath not on the surface. You know within yourself what is right and what is wrong. You must stick by what is right. It is a hurdle to overcome and it will take time. It will take longer and is more involved than you anticipate.

"You must not feel guilty about the decision that you have to make. You are feeling guilty. There is no guilt there ...

"Someone is trying to brush you off and, because you are a woman, he thinks you will give up. He thinks you won't persist. Your husband would like you to see it through until the end.

"I am sorry, I am losing him. He has gone."

Journal entry: 26 December

I have written to Ian. He needs to know exactly what I feel regarding his treatment of us and to have a final opportunity to put matters right before I pursue him through the courts:

Dear Ian,

The last time we met amicably was on 8 December 1999 at the meeting in the Westminster solicitor's office regarding the proposed purchase deal. At the close of that meeting you told me clearly to get myself some 'independent advice', which I did immediately. Because of my lack of involvement and understanding of such business affairs I have needed to use such advice ever since.

However, I have decided that it is now time for me to write to you directly and state to you exactly how I view this entire scenario. I thought it only right to make a few facts about my personality to you perfectly clear.

I do not tell lies

I will not be bullied

I wish to cause no pain or hardship to anyone

I wish to receive no more than our fair share of the company's productivity and assets

Let us get back to basics.

Yes, you began the company a few months ahead of Malcolm's involvement but we both know the truth; that without Malcolm and his cool, impassive ability to organise the smooth running of the administration and travel schemes (and I do mean all travel schemes) then Campbell Irvine would never have grown to its current size. No one parts with 50% of shares in a company unless they acknowledge that there is a need to do so. It was not because you were being kind to your brother—it was because you needed his very real abilities. You know this and I know this.

I totally agree with the four-sevenths/three-sevenths split in company profits and would always honour this. I know that this was the way you and Malcolm marked the fact that you did begin the business a little ahead of him. This fact is undisputed.

Regarding your work in the Army, we are all very proud of your achievements and so was Malcolm. The weekend following Malcolm's death you came to me at our home in Surrey. You were worried, that the amount of time you had taken out of the office to spend with the Army had put too much pressure on your brother. You asked me whether or not Malcolm had ever complained. I could see the concern in your face and knew that we all had more than enough to deal with and that nothing could alter the fact that Malcolm had died. I simply chose to tell you, how proud Malcolm was of you. He was. However, please do have the grace to honour the fact that if you had not received the utmost support from your brother during your long absences from the business, then your achievements would have been far more difficult to realise.

You need to understand how incredibly proud we are of him. We are proud of the quiet, resolute manner in which he constantly and consistently worked for us all. Malcolm poured his heart, soul and mind into building up assets he could enjoy together with his family. Just prior to his death he wrote a letter to all travel clients introducing them to his PA, in this he stated that the company had reached such a stage that he could now afford to step back and take more 'quality time' with his wife and family.

In this letter, he explained that he would be relinquishing some of the work and his PA would be taking on a greater part in the future. He had begun to spend time introducing her to a large number of the travel clients during the course of the previous year so that this could be achieved. This was during 1995 and the last months of his life in 1996. You, of course, now prove this point. Prior to the year of Malcolm's death there was not the time to visit the company in Australia, as you now do annually, for a month at a time. Just as everything was about to come to fruition and we were all to, jointly, reap the rewards, Malcolm died.

You have recently met my three sons in person. It was their wish to meet you face to face and try to put some of their points across to you and to listen to your viewpoint first hand. Both at this meeting, and the previous one with Alastair, you told them that their father's interest and work towards the 'provincial' offices was his own volition and that it had been a costly and terrible mistake which you have struggled to resolve since his death. You seemed to take a pride in the fact that you showed no interest at all in these provincial offices and visited them rarely, if at all.

There were six provincial offices at one time I believe. And you know it is a fact, that none of these offices would have been opened without you and Malcolm discussing it fully. Has it never crossed your mind, Ian, that if you had offered Malcolm a fraction of the support that he gave you with your Army pursuits, these could have been a success? You have never visited one of the offices at all, and others, only to store your excess furniture in at weekends! Yet, Malcolm, resolutely rose at 5.30 a.m. daily, and made it his business to visit each one while travelling either to or from London. His attitude was that staff needed to feel the presence of one in authority. It was important that they all felt supported. Even if he had visited the office long before they actually arrived at work, it was important that they knew he had his eye on the ball. They welcomed and respected this.

It was Malcolm's greatest regret that you took absolutely no interest in the staff of the provincial offices whatsoever, nor offered any support to him in this direction.

Malcolm left you one of his fifty company shares in his Will. This was something he discussed with me and, because of my total trust in him and his in you, this was agreed.

He chose to do this in order to ensure that you could continue to run the company unhindered and strong in the confidence, that he could trust you to protect his family.

My sons and I derive no pleasure from this current situation. We are not greedy. Our only desire is for my husband's lifetime's effort to be justly acknowledged and that the wife and sons he so steadfastly supported, should be protected now he is gone and should be allowed to enjoy all that he worked so hard to provide.

It saddens me that when this whole matter began you could not have been more open to discussion. If communication had been easier we may have resolved this more quickly. Previously I made too few demands and asked for no explanations when I should have.

We have acted in a united manner and with faith in the sound professional advice we have received. Your attitude has been one of absolute non-negotiation. Perhaps if you had made room for our questions, and we had not been expected to silently accept whatever decision you made, this situation would never have come about.

I am driven only by an intense loyalty to see Malcolm's efforts acknowledged and justly rewarded for his entire family.

My husband would expect no more—and absolutely—no less.

Yours sincerely,

Patricia Irvine

Chapter 23
The Decision

Journal entry: 12 January 2002

Much has happened since I last wrote up my journal. The fact is, although I have clearly asked for a third confirmation of the instruction to 'fight', I have not received it. I keep asking to be shown the way to resolve this awful mess satisfactorily.

I believe in The Source and The Light and in continued spiritual life after physical death, through my own experiences. However, I am not convinced that I should take second-hand instructions from mediums as the absolute way forward. I am horrified at the thought of letting my husband and sons down. I also despair when I think that my spiritual growth may be thwarted by a 'wrong' decision now.

I am fearful of losing myself and rendering this journal null and void because I fail to have the courage of my convictions. I am trying to find my way out of this black hole and honesty has to be the key. I have to be totally honest with myself. It is my rock.

During the past week my mother has been terrifyingly ill, which shocked us all. Although thankfully, she is now improving, it caused me to ponder a great deal. This circumstance made 'life' as we know it rocket into perspective. The fact is, life *is* too short to waste. I have been tied in knots of fear, not wanting to let Malcolm down by not fighting his corner and insisting that his life's work be honoured. But then, am I not letting him down more by allowing this disharmony, fear and misery to disrupt and destroy the peace of the home and young family he so adored?

My sons have lost their father. Am I not letting them down by continuing to put my own health, and theirs, at risk with this continual battle? Which matters more, to see Malcolm's efforts honoured properly and financially? Or inner peace, happiness and harmony in the home? Can we have it if I don't fight for it?

I am confused by the messages received and am fast becoming of the opinion that it is only the direct contact with me that I can truly rely upon. I cannot deny what I *know*.

I went to see Paula yesterday, for healing, in an effort to try and calm down. At the end, she told me that she clearly saw my husband and his father smiling broadly and throwing boxes of paper in the air. These papers flew everywhere and disappeared from view. This could indicate that we are near the end; on the other hand, they could have been making confetti!

I know we are told 'all answers are within, we just have to search'. Well, believe me, I'm trying. I search. And I don't sleep. I spend hours alone thinking of little else. I endeavour to be still and in the silence to allow things to happen, trying to find the way forward. I just feel hopeless. When I think of this journal, it saddens me to think that something I do—or fail to do—could render it useless. If I don't take Ian to court, is it all wasted?

On the other hand, I am continually told that our gut instincts are our spirit, which knows the true way forward for us all. Well, my gut instinct is fearful of risking our family security. Would this not be letting Malcolm down? Or is this the 'leap of faith' required to test my resolve and see whether or not I am capable of fulfilling what is expected of me?

I am tired. I am fearful. I am lost and confused.

I have received a letter in response to the one I wrote to Ian on Boxing Day. The only time I have been absolutely certain that I was doing the right thing was the day I spent writing that letter. It *felt* right. I have now received a calm, lengthy response, which may be a chink of light. Communication is the only real way.

I sat alone mulling over the whole mess. The thought that entered my head was that I should give my shares to my sons. Ian has no time for me at all but he seems anxious to keep in touch with his nephews. Is this the way forward? Or will I just be passing the buck?

All I want is for this to end and for us all, including Ian, to be free to get on with living. I need clear, precise, definite instructions made to me. I have repeatedly heard that we have to let something out of our lives in order to allow fresh things in. How many times have I read 'let go and let God!'? Well, is this the time to let go?

I woke this morning at 6.30 a.m. The initial calm, as I awakened, was replaced once more by fear. My arms felt as though they had permanent goosebumps and my stomach was churning. The fear was the same whether I thought about going to court or whether I chose not to. No spiritual help came in the 'quiet' of last night when I needed it most. *Why?*

Years ago, when I was head girl in my final year at school, one of my deepest regrets is that I let my school down by failing to remain until after the final speech day. I took a job instead because I knew I should try and support myself to help my parents. This meant that the task of making the end of year speech went to the deputy head girl. Prior to Christmas, I met this girl in a garden centre in Kent for the first time since we had both left school.

Why? Is someone trying to tell me something? And if so, why can't they tell me more directly? I do not want to do the same thing again and let everyone down at the last moment.

I must have been introduced to all of these spiritual friends during the course of the last two years for a reason. So, I am going to ask for their help. I shall turn to them in this, my deepest hour of need.

*****

After the emotional outpouring onto paper this morning, I visited Betty Blackburn. During our conversation she told me I was wrong to expect the same message to be repeated to me three times *in exactly the same way.* It doesn't work that way. The messages can be repeated in a variety of different ways. *This has already happened.*

I read her large chunks of my journal, some of which she was able to explain, and I was relieved to discover that some of the awfulness predicted has already been lived through.

While we were sitting, occasionally Betty would interrupt with words and the odd sentence, which were given to her from Malcolm. The first was *'auditors'*. The second phrase was *'there must be no further direct contact at all with Ian. Deal with this matter only via solicitors'*. The third, *'you are a thorn in Ian's side'*.

At one stage, I was saying how difficult, in my current state, I find it to meditate or attempt to tune in to hear anything directly myself. Three times during the course of the afternoon I was told, *"I am always there—you will hear me."*

Sometime later, Betty burst into tears! Worried that she might be unwell, I quickly asked her what the matter was. She replied, while removing and wiping her glasses, "He has just said, *'Thank you for being such a good friend to her.'"*

Journal entry: 2 February

It has been an agonising week following a non-negotiable letter from Ian. I read through pages of our sorry tale and have asked the solicitor to proceed, so that each side may be heard and a decision made, and Ian and I can go our separate ways.

I have spoken with my sons and, although I cannot expect them to agree, they have said they will support my decision. Not long ago, I received a letter from my eldest son that ended, *"You have had enough and I have had enough. We must slap a writ on him, cut a deal or keel over."* Well, their uncle will not 'cut a deal', and their mother is not for 'keeling over', which, sadly, leaves only one route.

His appalling behaviour cannot be ignored and I have no wish for any of us to be associated with Ian in the future.

Once the decision was made I felt calmer. This doesn't mean I am unafraid but I feel less inner turmoil. I now have to get on as positively as I can. Friends have been supportive. In particular, my spiritual friends all feel positive about the outcome but no one says it will be easy. It may not get as far as the courtroom. I hope not. But I have to be prepared. I do fear this man but I intend to face up to him in a calm, balanced and centred manner.

I went to bed early last night. I have to care for myself and sleep is much needed. I found this very difficult indeed and lay bathed in fear which seemed to penetrate my very core. My skin seemed to be permanently raised in goose pimples and was actually sore from the weight of the sheets.

Praying more earnestly than I have ever prayed before, I spoke out loud about my dilemma. These were not mechanical, repetitive prayers but an earnest conversation with The Source from the heart asking for protection and strength.

I repeated the deep breathing exercises Friday had taught me. These helped for a short while but then the fear would come flooding back. Again the feelings of panic rose. In my mind there seemed to be a battle between the scenes I feared and the reassurances of my friends. I have *never* felt such fear. It kept rising—but I just kept praying!

I thought I was dreaming at first. I heard many voices, almost like children in a playground. I couldn't decipher whether they were for or against me. All I knew was that twice I most definitely joined them in calling out. I joined in. I have no idea *what* the words were. I simply know I took part.

What ceased the calling out was a rocket of energy which somehow cleansed my entire body of the fear. It happened several times and I murmured, "Thank you, thank you," aloud. I was awake and grateful to be able to bask in the peace that saturated my entire body.

It spiralled up once more, this energy that I had not felt for so long. Afterwards, I lay bathed in reflective peace. I didn't want to move at all. I didn't want to lose the feeling. I felt cleansed and full of joy. Eventually, I realised that it was over. I sat up, gathered my pen and notebook and began writing.

I now know that whatever I have to face in the future, and whatever the outcome is, I have made the right decision. I also know that there is a powerful source of help, which is not in my control at all but most definitely working with me.

After weeks of silence, painful deliberation and real agonising, I had finally made a decision and it had been confirmed. The power that rocketed through me was a strong physical sensation, which left me overflowing with peace. I am deeply grateful for the much-needed reassurance.

It is now 8 a.m. I have heard every hour strike so have got up. I don't even feel tired. I feel totally relaxed. It is so very powerful, this help. Opening the curtains, I looked out in the dawn light and wrote the following:

The Heartbeat of Spring

Thank God ...
The snowdrops are out
At first light
They peer through the hovering mist
Like tiny beacons ...
Nodding rhythmically in time
With the heartbeat of spring
Each tremulous wonder
A spark of light, of hope ...
Thank God ...
The snowdrops are out.

Journal entry: 28 February

Things have been quiet again but I have begun to feel stronger. Pleasant things have begun to happen; what a marvellous change!

I have, for a while, been designing photographic cards. They have been well received and one particular card company has invited me to view their operation and have lunch. Perhaps I have turned the corner?

Earlier I read in the local parish newsletter that an Imam from the Islamic faith was being invited to take part in this year's Lent course. I was immediately interested. A night or so before the actual course was about to take place, I was woken once more with words in my head, which were demanding to be written down. I guess it's only at this sort of time spirit can be sure of getting my total attention! I wrote:

Perspectives

'If one were to lay a rose in the centre of a room then invite ten people, placed at equal distances in a circle around the flower to describe it, similar descriptions would occur but they would not be the same.

Each person would have *his* personal perspective of that flower. Similar words might be used to describe it but the wording could not be exact.

Each person's perception would be slightly different but the flower would not change.

It is only when human ego is introduced that things begin to go violently awry.

When one human perception is forced upon another, trouble ensues.

With ego involved, each individual around the flower could become convinced that only *his* particular viewpoint is the right and only one.

In order to prove a point, he might rush to take up arms and endeavour to force the other nine individuals' opinions into his own mould, hoping to make theirs mirror his own.

As each individual becomes determined to prove that *his* way is the *only* way, little would be achieved. Mayhem would follow and a writhing, unstable, pitiful mess would be created.

There would be no winners.

However, had each of the ten decided to quietly live with his own perception and allow the other nine to do the same, much would be achieved.

If each individual, by living with his own perception of the rose, The Source, became a fine example of how to live life, then others would give credence to each viewpoint because they couldn't help but to be impressed by the various achievements.

The names of each perception would not matter. What would make the greatest impression would be each individual's ability to *live* his viewpoint in a peaceful manner and in doing so, allow the others to do the same.

This would bring happiness to himself and to the whole. Gandhi advised us, *"It doesn't matter which book is being read as long as God is being worshipped!"* This simple understanding, should we ever be able to accomplish it, would ensure that we could all, collectively, move on in our perception of the whole of life.

Individuals would learn to view the rose, 'The Source', from *all* perspectives and we would therefore learn to understand each other more fully.

The rose, 'The Source', remains unaltered. It is like a tree with innumerable branches, which jostle and shake in the wind and appear to be separate but the fact is ... each leaf, each twig, each branch, can be traced back to ...

The same trunk,
The same root,
The same Source of all.'

The following evening was the first of five meetings of the Lent course. Clare and I were going together and she gave me a lift. I told her about 'Perspectives' and she asked me to bring it to class.

During the interval, I congratulated the vicar on his initiative for providing us with an opportunity to learn more about the Muslim faith. I told him about the piece I had written. He asked if he could have a copy.

The following week, the vicar said how much he had enjoyed reading it and asked permission to use it in *the parish magazine.* I agreed.

I guess the light is slowly beginning to dawn. I really can see now how the concept of spirituality has begun to work through me in the form of written and spoken words.

Reading: 19 April - Diana Summer

"There is someone who is really trying to unearth something, and it is like they wish to present it as a fait accompli. There is deviousness and skulduggery around you; someone is trying to dig deep to try and find evidence or proof of something against you. This is underhand and going on behind closed doors.

"There is a sense of betrayal here. Someone is not being as open with you as they might be. This person is in his darkest hour and is drawing a huge amount of his dark side to him. He is a controller and cannot stand the thought that he is not in control of you. He is incensed. A connection is going to be severed.

"You are going to rise above it and steer your way through. Even though all this is going on, what you have got to do is stay firm and be strong. There are issues here, which must be brought to an end before you can move on. Life will begin again.

"This is your challenge for you to move through. It is the final step before you can get on with the work that you are going to do. You know that we have choices in life. In order to do the great work, we have to overcome a major challenge. Your challenge is this. It has been an ongoing thing and this is the final stage. This is the breaking point, the severing of the ties, and it will free you."

"The path that the other person has chosen is not a good one; they are manipulative and unpleasant. You will have lots of help from spirit and you will gather the right support around you also. It is an important time. Prepare yourself for that which lies ahead, call on the powers of communication, integrity, inspiration, knowledge and wisdom.

"This task, when completed, will enable you to bring closure. Opportunity will arise for you to walk away, to embrace the light

of the work that you are here to do. Already you have experienced things and begun to recognise that what you have been told has a semblance of truth. The synchronicities you have experienced have demonstrated the truth of this.

"Your future work will involve helping people to unravel their own difficulties. The healing gift that you have will be received more readily. The mediumistic gifts will blossom and you will be drawn towards those who will help you to embrace all that you are.

"There is work for you to do with the angelic realm. They will teach how righteous anger has its place. You are a powerhouse of energy. Your presence brings strength, stability and growth to wherever and whomever you connect with. The wisdom that flows from you, messages, sounds and the very intonation of your voice, all these things have a wealth of communication within them.

"The power of communication as counsellor, friend and businesswoman hold you in good stead. The power of words is unheeded by many. Words are the key to unlocking problems.

"The documented reams that you have carefully manifested will have a use at the appropriate time and will assist and help those that are given the opportunity to read them. At this moment they are to be kept safe and secure.

"This then, is the path that begins to unfold. The final duty you are here to experience. Be at peace with yourself."

Chapter 24
Artistic and Spiritual Experiences in China

Journal entry: 12 May 2002

Carol O and I travelled to China and met up with Gordon, Malcolm's cousin. While we were there, a definite spiritual follow-up to the cultural, religious tolerance and education theme occurred.

In Xian, I met two Imams. One was from the Great Mosque Xian and the second, the Great Northern Mosque. Xian was one of the main Silk Road cities, so travellers from other countries and cultures have settled there.

At the first mosque, we were invited in as the Imam was known to Gordon and his friends. Carol and I were just outside the Imam's main room, waiting at a garden table when, from inside, I heard the Imam say 'Canterbury'. Tired of being left out of the conversation and ignored because we are women, I asked Gordon to tell the Imam that my three sons had been to The King's School, Canterbury. When he heard this, Carol and I were immediately invited into the inner sanctum of the mosque, given tea and almonds and invited to look at the Imam's photograph collection! One of these clearly showed the much younger Imam welcoming a previous Archbishop of Canterbury to his mosque. We were then allowed to take photographs of him, and the gardens of the mosque, and I promised to send him copies to add to his collection.

We then walked through narrow, dusty streets to the second mosque, the Great Northern Mosque of Xian. A brother of one of Gordon's Chinese friends had been responsible for overseeing its renovation following the damage suffered during the Cultural Revolution. The renovation had taken ten years and the mosque had only recently been reopened to the public. Much to our delight he also invited us in to take photographs and we were impressed by the beauty of the calligraphy that decorated the entire central section. We were told that, eventually, the calligraphy would decorate the whole interior of the building. Gordon asked if we might be able to meet the calligrapher.

Again, we were shown into the inner sanctum of the mosque to await his arrival. As female visitors and not of the Muslim faith we felt very privileged for the second time that day. Waiting in a cool ante-room we were asked to sit on splendid, carved wooden chairs at a marble table. The men were one side and Carol and I the other.

When the calligrapher arrived we were surprised to see that he was also the Imam. He was a young man, perhaps in his late thirties, and it transpired that he and Gordon had met previously in Singapore. The calligrapher had, in fact, stayed with him while taking part in a calligraphy competition there. However, since then, he had been made Imam of the Great Northern Mosque. Gordon congratulated him and after a lengthy chat, much laughter, numerous reminiscences and a great deal of photograph taking, we prepared to leave.

Then we were asked if we would like to join the Imam at his favourite restaurant that evening. It was incredible. Meeting two Imams that day, and being made so welcome even though we are non-Muslim, white women, was a surprise in itself. To be invited to eat with men, let alone the Imam, was very unusual indeed.

Later that evening we arrived at the restaurant. As a 'thank you' I had written a line or two of poetry in three of my photographic cards. I handed one each to the two brothers and one to the Imam. After much discussion, which Carol and I couldn't understand, of course, Gordon explained that he had been asked if we would return to the mosque the next afternoon to take some official photographs. They had tried to take some good shots themselves but their equipment was not as sophisticated as ours. We agreed that we'd love to and would do our best for them. The Imam promised that, after the photography shoot had been completed, he would give us a demonstration of his calligraphy. It so happened that the next day was also my birthday.

The following day, I began by concentrating on the exterior gardens. There were many stone carvings. There were also natural stones placed within the garden, which deserved merit. It was hot work and I had to move quickly because the light in China is not good at the best of times and in late afternoon it fades quickly. I was a little nervous of this photographic brief and terrified of letting them down.

Eventually, I was shown into the prayer hall itself and (with a young boy in tow to help me by moving things and turning lights on and off, etc.) I concentrated on the interior decoration. At one point, the young man ripped open the cellophane packaging of a new face towel and thrust it at me, for me to 'mop my fevered brow'! This greatly amused Gordon and Carol and there was a lot of jesting and comments about my 'international photographer' status later. I just hoped that the results would please the Imam.

When the light had failed and we could do no more, we walked with the Imam to his home. We stepped through a hole in a courtyard wall and climbed stairs to the first floor. We were greeted by his wife and shown into a large room, then invited to sit at the dining table and joined by the Imam's two brothers. The male children were called in to meet us and we took some family photographs for him but only the men and young boys could sit with us. The poor women and girls were in a cramped scullery and were only allowed to eat the leftovers of our finished meal later. Carol and I were appalled at the discovery of this—it really didn't sit well with us at all!

After we had drunk a delicious tea of fruits and herbs and eaten our fill, the room was prepared for the calligraphy demonstration. The Imam wrote a piece for Carol and another for me. He wrote in Arabic and Chinese. The words on mine translate as follows:

This is a gift to Patricia of England
In springtime the most beautiful are the flowers,
For mankind, the most beautiful is friendship.
(An old Chinese and Arabic proverb) 2 April 2002

What an amazing birthday gift.

The evening was fascinating and we felt privileged to be invited into such a home. Although it was very humble by our standards, we could not have felt more welcome. As we stood to say goodbye, the Imam shook hands with us all, including we women. Then, in his very gentle manner he spoke quietly yet profoundly. It was translated to us, of course, but we easily felt his mood.

He said, *"Here we are Christian, Buddhist and Muslim; male and female; we are from the East and from the West. We are eating together, drinking tea and delighting in new-found friendships. I am doing my job and you, in your way, are doing yours, and we are each paving the way for fresh possibilities. Now my friends consider, in the Middle East at this moment, they are doing what precisely?"*

It was a very poignant moment and he had made a very thought-provoking statement, for we knew full well the depth of rage that was running through the Middle East at that time. We all fell silent.

I recalled Diana Summers' reading, which had told me I would be *"travelling and meeting people in different lands and of different cultures. Also, occasionally, I would be asked to take part in certain rituals and, at others, I would simply be a guest in their presence..."* This had certainly been the case in Xian.

Chapter 25
Catalyst and Facilitator

May 2002 - Devon

I woke at 6.30 a.m. It was unnecessary to get up that early so I lay there stretching and consciously trying to *breathe in the Light* and *draw in energy*. Immediately, my hands began to feel as though they were floating. Then a rippling of energy began to course through my torso. I lost the connection once or twice but it returned. I lay there, conscious of the rippling gathering momentum and, all the time, listening to the gulls squawking outside my window.

The rippling became stronger and more frequent and a pattern developed. My eyes remained tightly shut. It felt as though my arms were outstretched on either side of my body. I faintly heard a voice but again was unable to decipher what was being said. I was wide awake and remember thinking that I was glad I had decided to simply lay relaxed and not get up when I had first woken.

As the sensations became stronger it was as though my entire body from the base of my spine was leaning forward, with arms outstretched either side. The colour purple deepened behind my eyelids and the energy soared. The voice became clearer. The rippling became stronger. It felt as though I was riding a tide.

Each time, the energy heightened and the voice became clearer. I did not recognise the voice, nor could I say whether it was male or female. The sounds were becoming clearer but were still incoherent because they dipped and soared as my body seemed to rock to and fro. It was a glorious feeling and the energy rose higher and higher. As the pitch of the energy remained level, I mentally asked the same question about going to court. The energy remained constant and I clearly *understood* the reply, *"You must all learn in your own way."*

Dissatisfied with this, I intuitively asked, "Even when we feel that we fight a just cause?"

The reply was instant. *"Will you never learn? I am not able to answer your question directly. I will guide you as best I can but you must learn in your own time and your own way."*

With that, the voice disappeared. I felt chastised, no doubt deservedly, and the energy, which had remained constant throughout, began to fade.

The alarm, set the previous evening, rang once and I put my hand out to cancel it. The experience had lasted for roughly an hour and was different to previous occasions but gave me welcome reassurance.

✶✶✶✶✶

Back in Surrey, I opened the mail and discovered, to my delight, that the Prince of Wales had replied to a letter that I had recently written to him. While I was in China, Clare had kept a newspaper article from *The Times* for me to read. It was calling Prince Charles 'The Prince of Faiths' in connection with the launch of his Respect initiative, a way of 'supporting and helping the community through the mobilisation of faith'.

As this was in line with my own thinking, I thought I'd send him a copy of 'Perspectives', adding a note saying, "A great idea! Congratulations—you are easily capable of making this work. You have the ability." I signed it but wasn't expecting a reply. It was merely sent as encouragement. (We all need it from time to time, including royalty.)

The reply had been forwarded by the Prince's private secretary:

The Prince of Wales has asked me to write to thank you so much for your very kind letter of 18 April about Respect. His Royal Highness is delighted that you felt encouraged by the initiative and suggests that you may like to get in touch with Mike Waldron, the Diversity Manager, to find out more.

Respect is meant, above all, to be a practical way of supporting and helping the community we all serve, through the mobilisation of faith and encouraging others to do the same. Reflection, tolerance, respect and a readiness to listen to and help our fellow man are—as they have always been—basic and universal requisites of a civilised society. For all those reasons, the more who can be involved in Respect in a practical way, from all faiths and none, the better.

This comes with The Prince of Wales' prayers and best wishes.'

I was thrilled with the letter.

*****

Following my return from China, Dilys came into my mind several times as did Kellen. I then received an email saying that Kellen was considering returning to the West Country.

So I telephoned Dilys and said, "You've been on my mind for several days and so has Kellen, a friend of mine from Goa. I think you and Kellen are meant to be introduced. I can't say why but I think it is important."

"If you are telling me, Patricia, then I think it is important too," she replied.

I continued, "Kellen lives six months of the year in Goa and six months in Devon. When she returns to the UK, she wants to work as a nurse in the Plymouth area. I have the feeling that I am to tell you this and pass on her details." This I did and then we said goodbye.

Moments later the telephone rang. It was Dilys. "This is incredible, Patricia, you don't know this, but I have a daughter who also lives in Goa for six months of the year. Because of this, she is hardly ever at my home. Today is my birthday and she is here. I have told her about your call and it appears that she attended one of Kellen's workshops in Goa. Kellen had to rush off at the end and she was unable to ask her any questions. Now, you have called me and given me her contact details. So thank you from us both."

Somewhat stunned, I wished Dilys luck and rang off.

Later I received an email from Kellen which read:

I thought it was about time I wrote and thanked you for making a connection between me and Dilys. Has she told you the link between her daughter and me in Goa? Spirit never ceases to surprise me! The connection with Dilys came at a time when I was feeling that nursing was not for me but I couldn't see what was going to happen.

I now know why I am going to Devon. I also know why I am going to Plymouth. Thank you!

Journal entry: Friday, 5 July

I am beginning to feel that my work is connected with tolerating, understanding and bringing people of different cultures and religions together. More and more this is beginning to make sense to me and I think it is a great purpose in life and I'm delighted to be part of it.

Perhaps we should respect people of other faiths more and not see our own view as the only legitimate way to The Source. People can worship together in silent prayer and, simultaneously, be 'at one', regardless of the names they use. Surely, we could benefit from learning about the traditions of other faiths and respect just being together? It might be enough to break down the barriers.

I have been urged to write the following two poems on this subject:

Silence

Step into silence ...
And allow yourself to hear

Step into silence ...
To a place where there's no fear

Step into silence ...
Where you will be reborn

Again, into silence ...
Welcome your new dawn

In silence ...
Your soul is made anew

And there once more
You will find the real ~ you

Be silent ...
Still ... quiet ... calm

Precious Silence ...
Where God keeps your soul from harm.

Guidance

I ask that you teach me to be still
And to learn how to listen
Help me to hear and once I have heard
Give me the courage of my convictions.

Help me to acknowledge
And accept my past
So I may be able to step forward
Into my future.

Guide me so I may achieve all that we planned
And all that was agreed
Keep me calm, balanced and centred
So I can remain steadfastly on my path.

Journal entry: 12 August ~ Kent

A friend and I were listening to some old tapes. One was *Time* the
musical.

Sir Laurence Olivier's narration welded the show together. He
had some amazing speeches which now strike a chord with my own
experiences and discoveries. I give credit to the writers Dave Clark

and David Soames and I believe that the work was way ahead of its time:

My favourite line is *"There is a power greater than logic and stronger than fear that nourishes hope and lights the way home. It is the power ... of love."*

(*TIME*—the pop musical, 1986, Dave Clark and David Soames)

Last Sunday night I was totally fed up. I felt unwell physically and more out of touch than I have felt for some time. I had one of my conversations with God. It wasn't prayer in the normal way but a frank, one-to-one.

It was desperately hot and I tried to sleep but the heat made it impossible. I lay as quiet and as still as I could and then spoke aloud about how I was feeling. I have no idea what the time was when the energy began, wave upon wave, very gently and then a terrific feeling of speed. It was as though I was flying! It was such an incredible, exhilarating feeling, simultaneously cleansing and calming. But the *speed* ...

I was afraid to open my eyes in case everything stopped. I kept them closed and saw a myriad of colours and shapes, ever-changing. There were intuitive words. To my great shame I lay for such a long time drinking in the experience, I did not immediately write them down. I remember hearing the hall clock strike twice, then the next thing I knew it was morning. By which time, of course, *I had forgotten the words.*

Unbelievable! This is the first time that I have not kept my part of the bargain and it will be the last. In future, I will record everything as soon as it happens. I was feeling unwell but that is a poor excuse and I do feel ashamed of letting down the other participants.

Chapter 26
A Matter of Faith

Reading: October 2002 - Diana Summer

"There is a garden here, which is being looked at [Westfield]. *You are being told not to worry about it but to concentrate on the issues closer to home in order to give yourself the energy to dedicate yourself to what needs to be done.*

"You have all the information that you need now. You are gathering it together from different sources. The final bits and pieces need to be sorted out because they are affected by the underlying issues.

"You are pulling out all the stops and you are doing the heavy mental activity by using your wisdom, knowledge, expertise and business acumen to make sure everything is as it should be.

"I feel it is all being put on you to sort out. There is another person who is sitting back waiting and almost enjoying the fact that you are scrambling around to find evidence and positive affirmation in order to prove your point.

"It is not a cut-and-dried situation. There are finer details, which are ongoing. It is like a karmic situation and you will be released. You will know that you did what you had to do. You have dealt with the deception and subterfuge and you will be seen as the one who was right, the one that knew.

"You have a huge determination to see things done properly. You will do your utmost to achieve, but must give yourself space and time in order to fuel your fight. Accept that some other things may have to be sacrificed just for a while so you can put your energy in what you need to do.

"You have found a really close friend who will give you the right information, knowledge and advice. He will help you allay any fears you may have. There is a lot of wisdom here. A lot of things are coming to light. Someone has tried to manipulate the situation but they have not been successful. They will try this manipulation, but it will not sit happily. Questions will arise. It is about balance.

"When you have achieved this, it will be a huge relief. It will set you free. When that happens, your real ministry will begin. I can see you working with many different religions and cultures, looking into what they believe and seeing that their objective is the same goal."

"Sometimes it can feel very lonely," I said.

"This is not known to be the most popular path or one where you make the most friends. With the work that you are here to do, sometimes you can be seen as the challenger, someone who sacrifices things like being popular. In many other ways, it is the most rewarding path. You will meet a new peer group and others very similar to yourself. You will know they have the same beliefs. You will sense that you have a resonance with them.

"You and your higher self have decided to end this and you will feel so free and light once this is over you will wonder how you got through it. You are going to travel and will be reaching out to do this work. In fact, this work has already begun. It will be a wonderful journey for you. You will change completely and the joy will come back into your life. This situation has been taking so much of your energy. Even when we feel disconnected and nothing is happening, working through a karmic connection is basically what we are here to do. Things are going to change. It will sort itself out.

"It is not the most enviable or the most popular task but you are here to do it. You were born to do this job and you agreed to do it before you reincarnated."

Journal entry: 2 November, Surrey

I woke feeling very despondent and the weather matched my mood. The rain was lashing relentlessly against the windows.

I was travelling to Kent later that day and telephoned Janet in Rye, whom I had met once before but had not communicated with since then. Her initial reading was one of great comfort to me. We arranged that I would visit her on route.

I drove through Sussex across country, via Rye. To cheer myself up I decided it would be a fine opportunity to look for nautical curios in the antique shops there, with which to decorate the old boathouse currently being converted into a fourth bedroom at Westfield.

I drove through the lashing rain, hoping that it would stop during the journey. But the afternoon sky became increasingly dark and foreboding. This slowed the traffic even more than usual. The weather and my mood remained firmly in step.

Reading: November 2002 - Janet

I arrived at Janet's in good time and her welcome lifted my spirits. We commented on the dreadful weather, for its mood had increased in intensity, keeping pace with my own.

I handed her a photograph of Malcolm and, after a number of poofs were given, she began, *"Malcolm is talking about your dedication. You have been very unfortunate, you have had one hit, tried to recover from that, then something else hit you and you are now trying to recover from the second one. You have an inner strength that you don't even know is there but it is so strong."* [Malcolm's death, followed by the pending court case?]

"He has given me a paper, it is almost like a Will, it is a legal document. Your signature has to be on it. Malcolm is saying, 'Do it and have done with it.' This person you are up against has overstepped the boundaries but they would not have done that had he been here because he would have put his foot down. He is saying you must do as he would have done. You have got to realise that, although you feel alone, you are not alone. He is with you and trying to help you. Common sense must come into play now. This person has a hold over you. This worries Malcolm and he wants it finished.

"He doesn't want to have to constantly help you with this same problem. Malcolm wants to help you in a different way. He says, 'Love is a bond that never dies.' You must always remember that. He will be there to support you, this gentleman, and to help you in any

way he can but when it comes down to it, only you can make the final push and he wants you to do that. Now is the time, it should have happened before. He is right behind you like a rod of iron.

"Malcolm keeps giving me the feeling of money, there is some concern over money, which should have been sorted out a long time ago. It is as if one person is grabbing and the other is standing there watching it happen and is unable to do much about it. It will be sorted eventually, but not immediately.

"He is saying this problem you have to deal with has got worse lately. He is dividing something up and saying, 'Fair is fair, how could they have misunderstood what I wanted?' Somebody is deliberately misconstruing his wishes. Malcolm is also saying, 'God doesn't pay his debts with money.' Someone is in for a bit of shock; it will make them stop in their tracks. He is talking about loyalty.

"You have made a decision recently, it is the right decision; you must go forward and not step back hoping it will alter the situation. You go forward and stay in the front firing line, this is what he wants you to do.

"This gentleman believed in the divine spirit. He has brought in a Bible to show to you and is saying, 'Have faith in what you have done and stick by it.'

"I have you going across water ... he is taking you by the hand and leading you across the water. When you do this have a thought for this gentleman because it is him who has made it possible." [He made everything possible.]

"This man is almost too good to be true. He wouldn't have done anybody a bad turn, he would have helped anybody and everybody given the opportunity. He is saying, 'You are praising me too much, I wasn't that good.' But, as I get into the spirit of the man I feel the kindness, the depth of love, which he is radiating out to me from his heart.

"Malcolm had a brother? Who is he calling 'Tin head'?" [Ian was a colonel in the TA.]

"He is saying, 'He could boast himself into anything but there always comes a downfall.'

"If I put this man in a dinghy, would you understand?" [Yes! The only time Ian ever showed interest, or indeed actually took

the trouble to visit Malcolm's beloved yacht, was when he took a number of his regiment on board. It was an army exercise and they used our inflatable Rib dinghy to land Ian's men on the Isle of Wight.]

"I'm sorry, my dear, but I am losing him ... but he wants you to realise that he knows all these things and it proves that he knows what is going on in your life. I have got to tell you to hold fast.

"He is saying, 'Don't let me down, I am relying on you. Don't let him get away with it. You will gain much by standing firm, not just in the monetary sense but also the principle.'"

Journal entry: 29 November

Last weekend I attended a drinks party in Surrey, where I found myself cornered by a man that I recognised and knew his name but that was all. We had never conversed before, although we'd met on similar occasions. I was beginning to wonder if I had done the right thing by attending when suddenly this man said to me, *"I am a Reiki healer, Patricia."*

I was surprised that he simply blurted this out. He then went on, *"I am a Reiki healer and I knew I could discuss it with you because I could feel your vibrations from across the room. They are very strong."*

After the party, I drove to Kent to stay with my parents. Valerie Kirkham is taking a spiritualist service in Ashford and has asked if I will read one of my channelled poems. I have chosen the following:

The Colours of Life

Light ... is all
Nothing flourishes without light
And without light ... nothing '*is*'.

One small candle flame
Gives hope in a cavern of darkness
And it gives positivity, one of life's greatest gifts.

Positive thinking, is a foundation for you
Build on this ...
And strive to live your life to the full.

Do not allow yourself negative thoughts
These will snuff out your flame of hope
And that is too high a price to pay.

You are worth so much more
So ... from today
Look for the colours of life
For they are yours.

During the past few days I have been reading a book called
Entering the Circle by Olga Kharitidi. It is about a young Russian
woman doctor's discovery of her own natural healing powers. She
was being taught about a natural ability to heal, held latently within
us all, that could be awakened and used to heal, not only ourselves,
but others.

I kept my appointment with Valerie and read the poem as
requested. I felt completely calm when reading and enjoyed doing
so. The platform demonstration delivered by Valerie was very
professional, distinct and to the point. She helped at least five of the
congregation and it was clear that she is highly thought of.

We drove to a hotel for a late supper. After discussing the
service and catching up on news, I told Valerie about the book I was
reading. I explained that I still had the final chapter to complete
but suggested that she might like to borrow it. She enquired what
the book was about and I told her. She immediately asked, "Is it
called *Entering the Circle*?" I confirmed that it was, upon which she
announced, "I, too, am reading it at the moment. It is an amazing
book. I have virtually finished but I have the last chapter still to
read."

How's that for a synchronicity? Not only are we reading the
same book but we have both reached the same place in it at the
same time. I am constantly amazed by this fascinating subject
that has brought so many of us together. I believe that it is the

continual evolvement and discovery of the numerous and varied synchronicities like this that confirm we are where we should be on our life's path, and are doing exactly what is expected of us, at that precise moment in time.

Journal entry: 5 March 2003

I think it is important to record synchronicities when they happen. I recently visited a friend in Lancashire. While we were there we drove into Kirkby Lonsdale to browse in a crystal shop where, I noted, they still sell locally made cards, some of which I had bought on a previous visit.

I returned to Surrey and attended the Jack Temple lecture at a hotel in Sussex. Immediately I walked in the door of the hotel, I noticed a framed selection of exactly the same cards I had seen in Kirkby Lonsdale. This indicated to me that I was in the right place at the right time and there was undoubtedly a point to my being there.

The lecture was interesting. Jack Temple was then eighty-five years old and had more energy than most of his audience combined. He was on his feet the whole day with brief breaks mid-morning and afternoon and the customary hour for lunch. At the end of the day he was still buzzing with energy.

Another synchronicity has occurred. While I was travelling from Durham to Lancashire I stopped the car to take a call from the solicitor. I was told that the QC wished to be furnished with information from an expert witness, in order for us to be able to prove what amount of salary my brother-in-law should reasonably expect to reward himself. In other words, we should pay someone to do a survey of directors and their salaries in order that comparisons could be made.

On the Monday, I received a further call from the solicitor, advising me that it was time for me to sign the Statement of Truth, which was necessary before the Petition could be issued. The magnitude of the action caused the old fear to stir once more. The solicitor then went on to say, "By the way, Patricia, an amazing 'coincidence' has occurred. I went into a colleague's office earlier today and lying on his desk was a copy of a law magazine that this company subscribes to. The outside cover drew my attention to the fact that printed in this issue is an up-to-date survey of directors' salaries!"

The solicitor went on to say, that unless Ian was the managing director of one of the top fifteen public companies in the country, he should not reasonably pay himself such large figures. He continued, giving me examples of the salary figures for a man in a similar position to Ian's and what he could reasonably expect to allow himself. This news cheered me enormously.

"That," I said, "is not a coincidence but a synchronicity! It has come at just the right time to reassure me that I am expected not only to sign the Statement of Truth, but also to see this sorry business through to the end."

Chapter 27
The Right Place at the Right Time

Reading: March 2003 - Janet

With the first hearing of the court case due on 1 April, I have been thinking more and more about Malcolm. Knowing that I was travelling to Kent on Mothering Sunday, I arranged to visit Janet. I handed over a different photograph of Malcolm to her this time.

Janet began: *"I have this gentleman smiling at you. He says that you have done something today that you haven't done before."* [That day I had been allowed free rein to travel the line and photograph the Romney, Hythe and Dymchurch Railway trains.]

"There is to be a hiccup with the case, I don't feel that this is anything for you to worry about because Malcolm is just brushing it on one side. He is telling me, 'The answer will take time. It won't be decided there and then. You have got to remember, the ordeal will be then but the decision will follow.'" [Judgement doesn't come immediately—the judge has to have time to consider all cases.]

"He is saying, 'Keep your chin up because you have more spiritual help on your side than the others have.' There would have been some kind of agreement before this situation arose. This is where you have to do your homework. It wasn't written legally on paper. But if you allow it to stand, it will be a point in your favour. It will help." [This refers to a gentleman's agreement between the brothers, which I would always honour.]

"He is saying, 'When the time comes, you are not going to be alone.' It is almost like you will have somebody as a backup, would you understand that? You have to sign a document, definitely." [The Statement of Truth.]

"Malcolm says that in this world you can't trust anybody. He trusted this other person with his life and he has let him down, so his words to you are do not trust anybody as he did. He is doing a lot of writing. It is as though he will give you direction or words in your head, which will help. It is almost as if this is in two or three days' time from now." [The first administrative hearing is in two days' time.]

"I feel that whatever happens he is going to be there in court with you to give you the strength, courage and willpower to say something you would not normally say. He is looking at me and smiling, saying that you do not stand alone, you have never been alone ... since he passed over; he has always been there for you.

"I feel that this court situation is not all your brother-in-law's own work. He would have had two women pushing him. He is not a bit like your man! Even though they were brothers, they are not alike. They are so different. The way they think, the way they do things and their personalities are opposite. They have totally different interests. One is so much more caring. The other is very full of himself.

"There has always been a dividing line between them, which goes back to their childhood. One would be continually arguing and the other would just stand by and just watch in puzzlement. Their personalities and intelligence were different, not less than the other but different. Your man is a thinker; the other brother does things on impulse then thinks later. Their values and way of living was entirely different.

"He wants you to know that he is aware of what is going on in your everyday life. He is saying, 'Have faith.'

"I'm losing him now, I'm sorry, my dear, I am losing him."

Journal entry: 15 May

I have decided to embark upon a course of detoxifying treatment in order to get myself feeling as well as possible before having to face the onslaught of the court.

I arrived at the clinic on the first day and met the therapist. She said she was also a Reiki healer. Needless to say, minutes later we were in deep discussion about all things spiritual, including healing.

She said that the following day she would be visiting a medium in Sutton. I was very interested and asked her to let me know how she got on when we next met.

This she did. She said that she had been very impressed with the medium and also said, *"She asked me if I knew anyone called Patricia, to which I replied that I have no friends or family of that name. She pressed me further and I said, 'I do have a new client called Patricia, but I have only just met her!'"*

After this, the medium leaned forward, looked her directly in the eyes and said, *"She is going to be enormously useful to you."*

I took this to be another one of those situations, which requires me to follow it up, so I asked her for details of the medium. During my ongoing treatment, our friendship grew and I have introduced her to the work of Jack Temple, Harry Edwards and many others, through my ever-growing collection of books.

Intent on remaining as strong as possible to face the court, I decided to visit Diana.

Reading: Diana Summer

"The threads, connecting you to a certain male individual, with whom you are having a difference of opinion, are beginning to unravel. It goes back beyond this lifetime as the connections are old. There has been unfinished business, which has not been resolved in past incarnations. There is a control issue here which is working its way out. His intent is to manipulate. But this time you are remaining strong, maintaining your integrity and using it.

"The natural strength from the core of your being, your awareness, is continually growing. You have now accessed the teachings of your soul essence. You are fully empowered and wish to declare it.

"The individual is moving through a lot of fire, anger and frustration. Change is imminent and nothing can stop it. This experience is part of your path. It is that which you agreed to do. Once completed things will settle and the past will be set right. This is the final work to set both of you free. As you move forward, you will finally feel able to extract yourself from this ancient pattern.

You have the intuition, vision and knowing to facilitate this and are equipped with the strength and courage to achieve it. This unravelling will enable a clearing, which will help you obtain a sense of calm and peace. This karmic release will help to reconnect you to your divine abilities. The threads connecting you to the high consciousness will be activated again.

"Know you win, whatever the outcome, because you will have set yourself free. That is the really important knowledge to take on board. It will create the abundance which is rightly yours and this will come in so many different ways.

"New forces of power will connect with you. You will be empowered and know who you really are. Whatever you desire you can bring into being. You will be balanced and move into your divinity. Your work will truly begin. This is waiting to unfold for you. Knowledge will begin to download. It is for you to share by giving talks and workshops to empower others and to open them up. You have the keys to unlock their spirituality. There are many you have yet to meet."

Diana then asked if I had any questions.

"My journal is now quite large," I said, "and people keep saying I should get it published. But I believe that I will know when the time is right."

"This manuscript is not complete," replied Diana. *"It is not quite ready. When it is, you will know and you will be inspired to do what is necessary. There is a lot of energy around it and when the time is right it will be done. This situation has to be settled first. When it is completed it will flow at the right time."*

Reading: May 2003 - Pamela Wellsman

I kept my appointment with the medium suggested to me by the therapist at the clinic. Pamela welcomed me, invited me to sit opposite her at a table and asked me to place my arms on a cushion, palms up. I had no idea what to expect and this was very different to any other such meeting I had attended. There was no conversation and we had never discussed anything before.

Pamela began: *"I look at the lines on your hands and read what is written with regard to you as a personality. On the lifeline, I see milestones and can highlight them and show the history that makes you as you are. Each step you have had in your life is responsible for how you are today, physically and mentally. I look for all the creative areas, career opportunities, relationships, children and so on. When I link to you, I link to your vibration and information source which is coming from your ancestors, your loved ones and, predominately, your guides.*

"We all have guides who are designated to us, by God, from the minute we are born until the minute we die and they use a medium to relay information. They talk to you all the time but it is very difficult for you to differentiate between your dreams, your feelings and what is actually being said to you. So when you come to a stranger like me and are told things, it is easier for you to listen. Your guides will prioritise what they need you to hear.

"Dreams are made up of three areas of clairvoyance that tell you things about the future, which is why it needs to be recorded on tape. The mediumistic level is when you have a link with your guides and loved ones and get proof and validation about life after death and invisible support. Psychic is what most people have inklings of somewhere along the line; synchronicities which prove that there is an almighty force around, that can see and link everything.

"You have healing coming through your hands. I also see you have the ability to put people on the right track mentally, physically or both, by your interaction with them on a personal level. You have had tears and heartache. I can tell this from your heart line, but all will be sorted. There has been a great feeling of loss, something to do with your mother or a partner?

"Mary is being mentioned [my mother]. *They are calling for her from the spirit world but your mother has the resilience of an ox and her guides are not letting her go, so you will keep enjoying her company at present.*

"When we do go, we only go to a different vibration. We get rid of our bodies, that is all. We don't actually go anywhere. We are still around our loved ones. We shed our hair and our skin daily but we don't worry about it, nor should we with our bodies. Sometimes

loved ones may be strong enough to communicate with you but you may rationalise it away and not believe that it really is them making contact.

"At age ten or eleven there was a blip in your life; there was loneliness and isolation at this time. At school you began to accumulate your abilities and you were quite scholarly." [Yes, I went in one direction to school and the entire village in another! I loved it even though I was always fat and treated badly. I had to prove myself.]

"At sixteen you made a major change in your life and probably went to college. You had great independence and it shows that you have a serious skill in this way. From eighteen until about thirty-six, you did what you had to do but it didn't fulfil your potential." [True, I loved being a wife and mother but always felt as if I could have achieved more than I had.]

"Is your mother spiritual? Only I get the feeling she would enjoy this tape and would be interested by it." [Yes!] Pamela put down my hands. *"Now hold that,"* she said, giving me a crystal.

"The crystal I have given you acts as a transmitter from you to me and will tell me about your physical health. Spirit will tell me whether a doctor's intervention will be required. You have extreme tiredness, which runs right through you from time to time.

"You need some Reiki healing. You also need the dentist." [I had discovered during lunch that one tooth has become sensitive.]

Pamela began looking around her. *"There is somebody milling about here. I get a man and he is saying you are to cheer up and he wants you to know that there is life beyond him. 'Till death us do part was the statement, although we can meet again, you can also have your freedom and you are to make the most of it.'*

"I can see a lot of grief and anger here about your parting. Is this in the last seven years, this parting? Sometimes, the missing is greater than it was in the beginning, it is as though it is finally sinking in and for some reason we miss them and need them more.

"Peter is mentioned. Who is Raquel?" [I didn't, at that time, know anyone called Raquel.]

"Now we will have a look at the cards, please shuffle those." Pamela handed me a pack of well-worn cards. *"You need to pull out*

twenty cards and place them face down, keeping them in order as you take them …

"You have money coming to you, so there may be a resolution to something very soon. The first line of cards shows me what your fears and dreams have been, and what your actions have necessitated in changing in your life. It shows those whom you have been interactive with."

Pamela continued, *"The middle line is the present time, which is upon you and this last one* [she indicated] *is the near future."* She paused again and looked about, *"There is someone walking around me here. Do you often feel his presence? Only, I feel that at the moment with all that is going on he would want to make his presence felt very strongly."*

I replied, *"My husband, if he could, he would be here for me."* Pamela turned back to the cards and continued explaining as she dealt each one.

"You are being supported; maintained romantically and emotionally. It could be the memory of him and you and fighting for something? Spirit is engaged in helping you in two respects. We don't just have one guide, we have numerous guides depending on how much strength we need at the time. Different guides at different times specialising in different areas. There is a man in your life who is unfathomable, hard work, and difficult to communicate with.

"You are weighing up different options. Something is definitely interfering in your life, causing you to be upset. You are trying to estrange yourself from somebody who is, basically, a male chauvinistic pig! It is favourable because there is a lump sum of money coming your way. The money comes through inheritance, settlement, redundancy or a win. This is settlement.

"There is celebration of your life, your heart will feel content and fulfilled. There is a professional man who has some involvement in your life and helps you with a monetary issue. Whatever your goals or ambitions or aims are at present you will succeed personally or professionally.

"There is a woman in the background who is a two-faced female, fond of her own way. She creates a problem behind a man and pushes him when probably he doesn't want to be pushed.

"This [she indicated] *is the best card in the pack, security, harmony, happiness and contentment. It would be impossible for this to be shown here if you had ongoing sagas or burning issues that aren't resolved.*

"I am now going to look ahead. If you fight the case, what it shows here is that you are winning. It is favourable and I think you needed to come here to hear that because you have had a terrible and uncertain time."

Pamela began looking around her again and said, *"I am being distracted all the time I am trying to speak to you, it is like I am on remote and I can hear people trying to talk in the background. It is like a dull radio station. I can't quite make out what they are saying but there seems to be a lot of people in the spirit world trying to come forward for you. I suppose, they could be your partner's family, maybe. They are certainly there in force and he seems to be the one called upon to organise everybody.*

"Does this saga involve you getting a lump sum of money? Only, it shows here that you will be receiving money. It is showing that things are working out and this card shows financial security over and above your needs.

"I don't know whether your husband had cancer but there is a chap standing here, but no, I think there are two people because I am being shown problems with the chest and the stomach. I am not sure whether it is one person or two people with two different complaints. There are two people blending together, trying to work together." [The chest is my husband. The stomach cancer was his mother.]

"Elizabeth, who is that? [Elizabeth, 'Betty' Trussler, a dear old friend, who helped look after the boys.] *There is a feeling of real love and warmth coming from her, bless her. She has a heart of gold and thought very highly of you and you did of her. She put you on a pedestal and you had a very good relationship.*

"You have felt a degree of loss; there have been issues going on regarding money or status. Loss has been constant in your life for the last many years but the tide is turning. You are a widow and you have felt that lately very much, with all that has been surfacing regarding your husband's memory.

"The constancy eye here means that you have constantly pursued fairness and justice and a dream to feel happy, settled and secure in a great future for yourself and your children. It is not in vain; spirit have aided and assisted you whether you have realised it or not. Your home is your fortress and you will fight to keep it.

"There is closure to do with a man being portrayed, certainly in your eyes, as an enemy. But with this card you have renewed hope; it renews everything because hope does do that.

"There is growth, expansion and improvement in your status. Everything you have gained you will not lose. The owl here shows wisdom and that is you; you are truly wise, clued-up and patient in the face of adversity.

"There is a book you are writing, which is to do with learning. This has been a learning exercise for you. You have creative ability. And you go where you are drawn, don't you? You follow the synchronicities. You are the same as me, and it's magical, isn't it? It is such a lovely warm feeling and you think: My God, that was wonderful, I was really meant to do that.

"You get pointers all the time and, if you follow them, you discover that you were really meant to do certain things and you won't go far wrong. If spirit wants to get your attention and they can't get to you directly, they will use someone else, for we are all using each other to achieve universal understanding."

Journal entry: June 2003

Earlier this year, I spent a week in Devon with my sister, Carol.

One night I joined Kellen at Gloria's where we immersed ourselves fully in this subject which binds us. During the conversation, Kellen asked me if I had read *A Course in Miracles*. I hadn't and Gloria lent it to me. By the following morning I had decided to buy my own copy.

Carol and I went to Totnes where there is an exceptionally good spiritual bookshop. I asked the lady behind the counter if she had the book in stock and as she walked away to check, I heard a whisper in my ear, *"I have it and I want to sell it. If you are interested let's meet outside!"*

I completed my purchases, excluding *A Course in Miracles*, and then went outside to meet the stranger. I was greeted by an apologetic and smiling woman who explained that she was moving and selling some of her books as she couldn't house them all in her new home. She further explained that she is psychic, but also dyslexic, and found it difficult to get on with this particular book, therefore, she was happy to sell it.

We agreed to meet later that afternoon at her home when I bought the book from her. I felt a strong, unexplained, affinity with her and was sorry to learn that she was moving quite a distance away and that we wouldn't have the chance to talk further. We completed our holiday, and I returned to Surrey and assumed the matter was closed.

Two months later I received a message on my telephone in error. It was meant for someone called 'Penny' and was about a lunch date. Realising that some poor soul would be in trouble if I didn't respond, I replied to the text saying, "Sorry, wrong number."

I then received a further text thanking me for bothering to point out the error. Then a third message arrived saying, "I have just realised who you are, I sold you the book!"

A few text messages flew back and forth and we decided that, as I was about to return to Devon again and she was still there, we might try to meet for lunch or dinner. I couldn't remember her name but recalled that in a recent reading from Pam in Sutton I had been asked, "Who is Raquel?"

Remembering this, I sent another text saying, "I have forgotten your Christian name, is it Raquel?" and the reply came back, "Yes. That's right, it is!"

So ... *this* was Raquel!

Sadly, things didn't work out for us to meet as the timings were not quite right. After a few more text messages Raquel gave me her landline number in Liverpool and I went to Devon as planned.

The following morning we had a great conversation. I am really pleased that the 'error' helped us to get in touch a second time as we appear to have much in common. I said that I was currently reading a book by Shirley MacLaine *It's All in the Playing*, which details how MacLaine set about filming her book, *Out on a Limb*, the story of how she discovered her own spiritual path.

I told Raquel that Diana Summers had suggested I read *Out on a Limb* as the book was the result of Shirley MacLaine keeping a diary of her own spiritual journey. I also told her about my own expanding journal. I explained that *Out on a Limb* was currently out of print and I was having trouble finding it. To this, Raquel replied, "I think I have that book. I'll look, and if it's here I will send it to you." Yet another synchronicity!

Chapter 28
A Need for Reassurance

My father has been seriously ill and the last six months have been a period of major adjustment for us all. I have spent a large part of that time endeavouring to be supportive to my mother. The following are notes logged during this period.

Reading: 8 September 2003 - Janet

"There have been many cross words, some necessary, some unnecessary. I want to go back to approximately four weeks ago and the man in this photograph [Malcolm] *is picking up a glass of wine and holding it in front of you and wishing you luck. This is where something has been added giving a different slant on the whole picture and he is pleased that you did this because it took courage. You were not alone, you had backup.*

"I am being given some legal papers, which have to be exactly right in every minute detail. You are one-third of the way through. You are digging your heels in deeper than you anticipated. It is almost as if you are finding the minutest detail to bring forward. I am being told that you are making a very good job of it and you should have been a lawyer because you are working on the pieces that will make the balance of the scales go in the right direction.

"This gentleman is patting you on the back and saying, 'Well done.' It is as though you have brought a point to the forefront, which would have been overlooked and not come into play. There has to be some proving of money. [I have found some papers that should help our legal case, which delighted the solicitors.] *You have recently signed a document. You have two more to sign that are coming up very soon, which are all in connection with the same thing.*

"I have three people wearing wigs and they are all conferring, three, not two. Something is not quite as straightforward as it appears. It is almost as if they have to ask an opinion of another. They are carefully looking at papers and referring to them." [The judge and barristers no doubt!]

"I want to give you the number seven." [This has been going on for seven years.]

"You have clever sons and this gentleman is saying you would be very wise to listen to what they say. It may not have anything to do with what you are dealing with but indirectly it can come into play. This will help you." [I do listen to them.]

"You have had a birthday in the family recently—this man is raising a glass." [Duncan's in August.]

"If I gave you Rome, would it mean something to you? [I have been there with the friend who accompanied me on this day.] *I have somebody moulding clay."* [My friend is a sculptor.]

"I am being given the name Frederick." [My father; he and Malcolm were very close.]

"Would you understand the name Caspar?" [Not at the time, then five years later Alastair and his wife called their firstborn son Caspar, a Danish name.]

"You are trying to get under the bed for something?" [Recently, I retrieved Malcolm's homemade burglar deterrent—a wooden baseball bat—from beneath the bed.]

"You are reading a book, which is taking a long time." [I'm trying to study *A Course in Miracles* which is tough going.]

"You are also going to venture out into a new direction, possibly turning a hobby into a business." [Yes, combining photography and poetry in books.]

"I feel that you are setting the table for an extra guest. They might be invited I don't know but the table has to be set for someone extra who is going to turn up."

A few days later my dear father, suffering with the first stages of Alzheimer's, became very confused after my sons took him out for a drink; he was convinced that he was expected at my home for lunch. Realising his distress, we hastily rearranged the table and made room for Granddad.

"This gentleman is grinning all over his face. You are to pat yourself on your back and be very proud of yourself and the courage you have shown. Your husband is raising a glass to you because he never thought you would have such courage and the strength to do what you have done. He is saying you are on the right pathway. With his love, he will continue to guide you."

Journal entry: Sunday, 23 November - 4.15 a.m.

After months of zero happenings, during which time I became impatient and frustrated, things stirred again last night. I have no idea what the time was; I'm out of the habit of glancing at the clock now but it was certainly pitch dark. As I lay listening to the driving rain, the sensations stirred. At first I thought I was dreaming then realised that the clock was striking. I noted that the rain was beating relentlessly against the windowpane. As I was capable of listening and taking note, clearly, I was definitely awake.

I knew it was coming; I could feel it, the old sensation was there. My hands felt as if they were floating and energy speeded through my torso. It happened six times or more and was not very strong, nor did it last long, but it was there and I welcomed it!

Before, during, and after the experience, scenes flooded my closed eyes and they were of different rooms, but none that I knew. If asked, I could have described the colours and furniture layouts. There were no people in any of the scenes and as one faded it was replaced by another. I didn't count them, there were far too many. I wasn't sleeping or dreaming. I was thinking about the scenes and registering them while continuing to note the sounds of the house and the rain lashing down.

Initially, I had the same glorious feeling of calm. It then switched to a much less comfortable feeling and I began whispering the words of 'The Lord's Prayer'. It became so intense that I felt as though I was under some kind of psychic attack. I repeated, "I work only for the Light," over and over again, to an unseen audience. Slowly, the scenes abated and I felt calmer. I had no wish for them to be resumed and made this clear! In fact, I wondered if this was a lesson in *seeing*, yet because of my recent unfamiliarity with experiences in general had I, once again, wrongly allowed fear to step in?

Throughout, the sounds of the house pipes remained and the clock continued clicking, along with the noise of a train on the Betchworth crossing nearby.

*****

Towards the end of the year I received an encouraging text message from Duncan:

"I understand why you've done what you've done with this court case. You know you have to give it everything you've got; whatever it takes to follow what you love. I do the same with the thing I love. We're not so different you and I. You've had my support for a long while. Now you've got it more than ever. See it through to the finish, Mum. You know there will be knocks. Don't let anything stop you. X Goodnight."

I have not erased this message. It delighted me then and continues to give me strength.

Gloria Channelling Malcolm

"My dear Gloria, how I value this quest to create a bridge for us to communicate. It may be difficult at first but what an opportunity for us all.

"I am, as always, very close to Patricia. I guide her and steer her to find evidence of great importance to make her path more comfortable to bear. She has my deepest love as always. I give her my strength, knowledge and my patience to sustain her. Much joy will return to her with a job so well done.

"The love we share for our dear sons is of eminence and returned to us with warmth and pride. They are our greatest gifts to each other. Patricia, my treasured wife, gave me all so graciously. We shared such precious times. How I wished and wanted much more than God could give us. I am so very close to her and will be, whenever her need is there. Tell her, our love is forever and will sustain and give great strength in all situations.

"Ask her to go forward now with love and confidence in her heart and all will work out in our favour."

Reading: 22 December - Janet

As the court case was progressing, and with Christmas approaching, I again contacted Janet. We were to spend Christmas in Kent and with my father now in a retirement home, I knew it would be a difficult time.

"Malcolm says this has taken a long time because it is very involved and they have had to go deeper than anticipated. This gentleman [indicating Malcolm's photograph] *is very exact.*

"There is a paper, you have got to look for it. I feel you have already looked at it and you feel it has no bearing but it does." [I could not, at the time, think what this might be. Later a vital note was found to do with profit sharing of the company. Malcolm was right!]

"There have been two people working on this, not one? But I feel they have brought somebody else in as well?"

"Yes," I confirmed, "we are about to embark upon mediation, which introduces a third party."

"You have been scanning some papers." [Yes, the solicitors and I have visited the accountant's office to look at the files.]

"Malcolm is giving me the impression that you and he once stood and looked at a beautiful waterfall. He is saying he can still see that now. You were abroad because he is taking me to another country." [We visited Niagara Falls when Alastair was a baby.]

"Malcolm takes pride in the fact that he has helped his family to where they are now. He knows he has given them a good grounding and advice. He feels proud of them and you. He is saying, 'We made a striking pair.'

"He is clearly showing me a roll-top desk." [This meant nothing at the time ...]

"He is giving me the name 'Ian'; does that mean anything?

"Malcolm is saying he wouldn't change any of you but you have to fight for what is yours. They will try and persuade you not to carry on and to let it go but he says don't allow other people to have

what is yours unless you want them to have it.

"He says you count your blessings and talk to him. You will always talk to him and he will hear. Never feel guilty about what you do. This man is very happy for you and all those around you. His arms encircle you all, with his love. 'Enjoy life to the full ...'"

Chapter 29
Gloriously United

A friend had been to see a clairvoyant, Zoe, in Maidstone. She was quite impressed and gave me Zoe's business card, which I found while packing prior to my return to Surrey. I took this as an indication that I should follow this up.

I telephoned Zoe and arranged to call in on my return journey. I was greeted by a charming young woman who showed me into her sanctuary which had the largest roll-top desk (as previously mentioned in Janet's reading) that I had ever seen. Discovering this amused me and I promised to explain after the reading. Zoe and I had not met before. She knew nothing about me or my situation.

Turning cards, Zoe began. *"This is a card of healing in respect of recent trauma in your life. You are coming through a situation and out the other side. It is a period of grieving, of adjusting and recuperating. There is a lot of spirit activity around you; you are a very spiritual person. I feel a really strong faith with you and that's what has got you through. I also have this very driven, ambitious feeling and I can tell that you are quite focused. You can set your sights on the finish line and will persevere until you get there.*

"There has been a time of sorrow, grief and difficulties in your life.

"This is a card of karma. You have been in this situation before. However, you have an opportunity to change the outcome. You have repeated the situation because the first time round the outcome was not as it should have been. There is a situation here when there is a lot of change and fresh starts. This represents opportunity, new growth and new beginnings. If you are thinking of starting a new

business, for example, then this is an excellent card to draw because it represents you striding forward.

"This shows that, although you have a lot of people around you who you can talk to and trust, you feel very much alone. You feel that everything is on your shoulders. You don't have any reason to worry because what is coming is very much better than what has gone before, so I feel there is a lot of happiness to come. There is a situation coming when you are really going to feel as if you are being hit while already 'down'. However, it is quite fast moving so as quickly as it comes you will deal with it and all the other cards here are very positive, so it is nothing you cannot deal with. It is just a setback.

"The card that follows depicts strength, which is very positive, and you will deal with this situation and be able to cope. This depicts growth and moving forward. It could mean the birth of an idea and clearly shows abundance and fruition.

"This card is linked to work and money and is showing the handing out of money, a lump sum of unearned cash, not something that you don't deserve but a big lump, a windfall, which makes a difference."

Zoe then left the cards and tuned in to the spirits present.

"I have this man who is itching to come in here. I feel he is not particularly tall and he is really making me chuckle. He is making me smile and is quite laid back in his approach to things." [Easily Malcolm.]

"He is also showing me a party, which was just before a significant family birthday in November." [Alastair suggested a large family party for bonfire night, something we have not done for years. He instigated it a few weeks before his own birthday, which is 21 November.]

"I feel that you will soon be moving on with your spiritual journey. Spirit will say, 'Right you have had a break, now we are going to push you onto the next stage.' I feel that you should be healing; you have the ability; you have so many abilities ... you lucky thing!

"He is saying you should devote yourself to what you believe in and what you want to do. He wants you to follow your heart, follow

your passion. You are very artistic, I am being shown pictures here." [Photographs!]

"'Go to Scotland.' [Malcolm's ancestral home.] *There is a feeling of great love and respect coming from this man and you are not to question at all whether he would approve or whether you are doing the right thing. He is saying, 'I just want you to go away and enjoy it.' He would support you whatever.*

"You win the day, you can deal with this and you get what you want. There is healing and balance restored."

*****

Having arrived home in Surrey, I feel that I need to make changes. I have signed up to a computer course, which I have wanted to do since last June. I need to improve my computer skills if I am to have any success with presenting my poems and photographs. I must be able to produce some new ideas to show to potential publishers.

With the mediation regarding the court case looming in late February, I need to be as calm, balanced and centred as possible, so I have decided to see Diana Summer.

Reading: Diana Summer

"The voice with which you speak brings forth music. Those that listen will respond. With each word it becomes more powerful. You are guided by those who are ready to use you as their conduit, their channel.

"You are a catalyst and teacher. You hold the potential to blossom, with all that is your divine inheritance. The world is full of sleepers moving through their daily toil, industrially asleep, not aware of their real purpose here. But for those that are truly awakened, the divine truth begins to surface and a deep knowing becomes reality.

"This is part of who you are at this moment. You are at the very beginning of the work you are here to do. You bring the light and colour to people who otherwise would continue in their lonely lives. You will be connecting people that need each other.

"It is important for you to accept and bring these teachings through poetry to those who will listen. People will look to you for guidance, knowing that you can unlock the consciousness within them. You are on a pathway towards enlightenment. But it is the journey where experience is gained.

"It will open up opportunities for you to recover and to overcome resistance. Nerves are a form of resistance gathered by fear. Always communicate with your angelic guides and helpers. Ask them to stabilise and strengthen your intent. Declare your intent from your heart that you will accomplish that which you have set out to do. Trust in yourself.

"You are a catalyst. You connect people together and are a gatherer of souls. You are the beacon; souls will be drawn to you and you will set up gatherings. Those drawn towards you will come to learn and understand. All will share their knowledge, their awareness and each will learn from the other. Gatherings may be small at first but will grow and expand. The chosen ones will come. You will meet others on the path who are also catalysts. Be at peace with yourself and with each step on the path, know that progress is made.

"You have earned success. You have a lot on your side. You have a lot going for you. Know you are right. There is some sort of limitation, which could stop it from really being resolved. I feel it might go on for a little bit. You have to remain strong still. You have the strength to do this and are in a good position. Delaying tactics, manipulation and trickery will be employed but things will change. Everything has got to turn around. You know that this man has a real sting in his tail. You are the woman who can transform it.

"There is a connection here across an ocean. You will be inspired, invited on holiday but your guides will guide you to go across water ..."

Gloria Channelling Malcolm - 20 January

"Dear Malcolm, Patricia would be so glad to hear your opinion about the forthcoming second attempt at mediation ..."

Malcolm: *"My dear friend, how glad I am that you spoke. Of course, I am always so close to her and especially at this time, when the whole event is coming to a head. It is, indeed, a huge and important time in my dear family's life but their love and combined strength and support will enable them to come out like shining stars. The truth is, this will be their greatest ally.*

"There will be support and help from unexpected sources and, as always, love will prevail. Please ask Patricia not to fear my brother but to make him very much aware of her strength and the information she has gained over past months of investigation. Let him learn of the support she has from staff and old friends who know the situation well. Of course, he will fight, in fear of losing most of his treasures, but the time has come for Ian to face the world he has created and to accept the harsh truth he asked to learn before he reincarnated.

"Ask Patricia to stay calm and strong and know in her heart all will be well and then find joy in her life again, so very much deserved. Tell them I love them all. I am the proudest husband and father and very much alive in spirit ... Malcolm."

Journal entry: 18 April

After a meeting with counsel, I travelled to Devon as I was drastically in need of soul food! It was the week of my birthday and I hoped for some communication from spirit while there, as Westfield has been the venue of many experiences in the past.

Nothing has happened at all. I'm becoming more and more despondent. I hate this feeling of disconnection. It makes me very frustrated. Dilys keeps coming into my mind. Initially, I ignored it but it has recurred time and time again, so I have called her. We spoke for several minutes and have arranged to meet.

Reading: Dilys Guildford

"Malcolm is ready to answer any questions that you have and is giving me the names Ian and Andrew. He says that he is not sure about Andrew." [A new employee.]

"He is also speaking about a Peter.

"He says, 'I love you and miss you.' Do you have any questions he can help with?"

"What is his opinion of the first mediation?" I asked.

"He is delighted that Ian had to make a public apology to you during the first mediation because of his unacceptable behaviour." [This was a fact and because the first mediation had failed we were now facing a second one.]

Dilys continued, "Malcolm is saying, 'I should think it nearly choked him. Do you and the boys feel better?'"

"Yes," I replied, "but it meant nothing. He apologised because he was forced to not because he meant it."

"Malcolm is linking Andrew in with this. There are things which need to be straightened out."

"He is an employee. I don't know him and have no jurisdiction over his employment," I said.

"It is as if he is being 'given a seat', that is what Malcolm is saying."

"Andrew has been given a seat on the board."

"Malcolm wants to ask when will you make Westfield your home? He is saying he spends a lot of his time at Westfield because, 'I feel comfortable here in Devon.'"

"When the time is right," I answered. "I can't move until I know, financially, that I am able to and I won't know that until the court case is settled."

"'You will be able to,' he is saying."

I said, "I realise that Malcolm knows what is going on in my life. The second stage of mediation is coming up on 19 April. I don't know what the result is going to be; we could still go to court and if I lose ..."

"You won't. He is telling me, immediately, that you won't."

"But am I expected to go that far, to court?"

"Yes," Dilys continued, "because Ian won't give in. You will have to go all the way. You will have to be prepared to go that far. This is something that you cannot get out of. Malcolm is talking about his brother here, saying he is being unfair and unkind. There is no consideration for you and the boys. This is what he is showing

me ..."

"It is difficult when you are the one making the decisions."

"'But you have made the right decisions,' Malcolm keeps saying to me. 'She has made the right decisions ... tell her. Ian is the one who has made the wrong decisions.'"

"So we go all the way to court?" I asked.

"Yes, because he [Ian] just hopes that you will back down. That is what he has hoped all the way through. You are a woman ... she'll back down ... she won't do this. 'Well, she will,' Malcolm is saying. 'She will.'"

"What does Malcolm think about the boys going to the mediation with me?"

"He thinks it is a superb idea. If they want to do it let them support you. Let them see what you have had to do and achieve since Malcolm has passed. They have enough graciousness and respect. Malcolm thinks it is very important for them to go, 'Take the boys if they want to go, and I think they will want to. You have got to feel confident about court ...'"

"I am risking so much ... but I feel that I must proceed."

"It is essential that you do it. 'The truth will out,' Malcolm says. 'Ian knows you are right. The family knows you are right.'

"'It's stopped all those sad gatherings,' Malcolm is saying. 'They were always talking behind our backs. They never liked how well we did, so stop worrying about it.'

"He is showing me Gloria's essences, 'Let her help you when in court,' he says."

"I'll need help because it is exhausting. It's nearly eight years since Malcolm died and I have been fighting Ian for six of those. I know the lesson that I had to learn. I have stood up for what I believe in and I have faced my fear. Ian may still have some learning to do but I am getting tired now."

"You know Malcolm's biggest worry? It is you," said Dilys.

"Yes, my health, I should think! I am overweight through comfort eating and years of feeling desperately alone. It is making me ill. I'd like to get on with my life but it seems as though it has been on hold for the last seven years and I don't understand why it has to be this way."

"Malcolm gives me the initials WAV," Dilys continued.

"We used to deal with a company with those initials."

"There is something hidden which could be revealed."

"There is a piece of paper which someone at that company has been promising me for months but I still haven't seen it. The guy has had a heart attack. I won't press him."

"This would sway everything. Malcolm is angry."

"Is there anything else I should be doing?"

"No. You have done all you can. There are many things connected with WAV which could help you ... Malcolm is saying he is feeling down."

"So am I!"

"He says, 'I never wanted it to be like this. This has been the biggest nightmare. The only concern I have is your happiness and what is happening to you!'

"I am being shown poetry and paintings, do you paint?"

"Photography, I take pictures."

"He is showing me these side by side."

"That is what I want to do."

"More of this work is coming very clearly to the fore. He is showing me that this will begin here, at Westfield.

"'I am with you, my darling. I am doing everything I can and keep pushing people towards you, trying to help you.'"

"I could do with a lot more reassurance."

"'I love you, you know I love you, and I try to put people in place to help you.' He is speaking about someone called Amy." [Amy was his PA in the company.]

"He has come to let you know that he is definitely nearby and he needed to talk to you because it has been a long time ... He is asking you where your rings are?"

"They are on different fingers because my fingers are too large, like the rest of me!" I said. "One of the things I find depressing is that I have been at Westfield for a week and usually when I am here there is some sort of spiritual connection. But there has been nothing. It is bad enough being in a prolonged court battle without feeling that I have lost spiritual support as well."

"You haven't lost Malcolm's support."

"I'm not, personally, seeing much evidence of that either."

"Well, he is very specific. He is low at the moment as you are. But I think to make recognition of what is important in your life is the most important thing. Is it your health, is it your homes, is it your business, or is it your happiness?"

"I think it is my happiness ..." I said. "I want to feel like there is a reason for *being*. I may have people constantly telling me that I have three beautiful children. I am eternally grateful for that but they have all left home now and it is not enough!"

"I am being shown rose petals—Malcolm wants you to be comforted. It is really hard when you feel especially low and he can't do something more physical. He is missing all of that, everything about that he is missing. And also your cooking!"

"That's proof enough—he is trying to make a joke."

"'I love you,' he says, 'don't ever feel that I am not here; it's just that I can't make myself felt. There is such a barrier; you are holding on to so much, there is no space. And the violet flame work that you were doing has stopped. What happened? That brought you closer to me than any other time.' Malcolm is saying this, do you understand that message?"

"Yes, I do ... I used to repeat the violet flame prayer each night."

"'You were keeping the door open. Now I'm here ... I'm back ... and the next few days will feel different. So try to feel it because, at present, it is like trying to get through a glass wall to you.'"

Dilys asked, *"When do you go back to Surrey?"*

"Tomorrow or later today ..."

"Sleep and travel tomorrow morning. You will feel Malcolm's presence. I know that because his spirit feels warmer and lighter to me now and the frustration of not being able to come through has gone. They lose the technique of communication and I think that is what happened. That is what it was like when you were on the phone yesterday. He came through straight away and he has been coming through with blocks of information ever since. Malcolm is a believer, he knows he can do it, and the more he gets back into it, the easier it becomes, but it is very difficult working with you when you are so tense. He is still here. Your anger is so powerful that it is creating a negative block around you.

"He is saying, 'This is not the Patricia I know, this is a Patricia who is in pain.'"

"It is a Patricia who would just like to have her life back. All I really want to do is write poetry and take photographs ..."

"They will go into books and exhibitions, eventually. That is what I see you doing."

"At the moment, I feel that I have stepped into a tunnel and I cannot see the light at the end because it is around a corner."

"The light is there ... the darker and more depressed you get, the less likely you are to see it. Somehow or other, every day there has to be a candle go on, let's give it some light, 'I'll work on it too,' he is saying. 'We'll join back to the violet flame together.' Do you understand?"

"Yes, I had a book about the violet flame and in there was a prayer about being part of it. I have forgotten the words ..."

"Look through your books and find it. Please, come back to it. What you'll do is facilitate Malcolm to get through. This is why you feel so bereft and ..."

"I feel abandoned," I said.

"You have abandoned yourself, your spirit and your hope. You have no need to. There is great light at the end of this.

"There is a wedding coming up? Malcolm says, 'I'm not going to miss it. I am coming with you. We will enjoy it together.'" [Alastair's wedding is at the end of July.]

"It is going to be a very beautiful day. Malcolm will get a message through providing you come towards it. He is showing me a red telephone box and laughing—does this make sense to you?"

"Absolutely!" [Malcolm gave it to me for Christmas one year and it is at our home in Surrey, which Dilys has not seen.]

"Malcolm's definitely there!"

*****

Later, at Westfield, I wrote up my notes, whispered the words of the violet flame and then lay down to sleep. After a short while, a single, rocket of energy surged through my entire body—just one.

Clearly, it was confirmation. The following morning, I returned to Surrey with renewed hope.

On the answerphone was a message from a friend, asking if someone she knew could join the gathering that I had begun organising at Mulberry Down for spiritually like-minded friends. Invitations had been forwarded to all the people I've met in connection with spirituality during the past four or five years. The idea has been well received.

I returned the call and explained that all those invited were people I had personally met. I felt that this was important. She suggested that I meet her friend properly, at a mutually convenient time, before the arranged gathering. The next call I received was from Pauline, who introduced herself, and we arranged to meet at a pub for supper. We greatly enjoyed each other's company. I explained that I was about to return to Devon and Pauline said that she would be staying with friends in Totnes at the same time. I immediately invited her to Westfield.

When she visited, Pauline also met Gloria. We spent a happy afternoon exchanging experiences and knowledge about spirituality. I received a call from Pauline, inviting me for some Reiki healing, which I have gratefully accepted.

While in Devon, I wrote the following poem:

Alive

Roaring through the trees
Like unending surf beating upon a shore
The wind dances crazily.

It quickens
And far off
An owl calls eerily.

Breathing in the cold air
I stand and watch
The ceaseless rippling of the tide.

Rain falls
Leaves glisten on boughs
Which sway in the lamp light.

Icy fingers, dead cold,
Reach out to touch my face
And inside ... I feel so alive.

Telephone reading: Janet

"Wear blue. Someone will speak on your behalf to do with money and property and what he says will make a big difference. He wants to give you advice. Wear the special watch." [I wore Malcolm's watch last time, for strength.]

"You are not going alone." [My sons are accompanying me.]

"Talk to spirit in the quiet and ask for help, you will receive it. Things are coming to a head. If you don't do it you will regret it."

I didn't discuss any of this with the boys at all. Yet, on the day of the mediation, I made a point of wearing a blue blouse. Charles, I noticed, had also donned a blue shirt. Duncan, a little late, of course, came down in a suit and blue shirt. We met Alastair at the office in London and he was wearing, yes, you have it ... a blue shirt! The solicitor also wore a blue shirt and so did the forensic accountant we had employed as our expert witness. Everyone wore blue shirts!

Gloria Channelling Malcolm

Malcolm: *"I really thank you for this chance. I need to tell my precious wife that I'm there so very close beside her every moment of the day. The thought of tomorrow brings no joy but our sons, our wonderful creations, will give much strength to her. They will enter together and together they will stand. They will truly show everyone what love and togetherness can bring!*

"Yes, beauty, strength, much love and power will be presented there for all to see. My family, each one so very beloved by me. My wife, Patricia, who gave me all I ever needed and more beyond my dreams. Now I am there to give to her, to keep her strong, and to let

her know what true love is all about. She will do well. There is no fear of that. Please tell her once again that I love her. Ask her to show that these Campbell Irvines are really together, out in force. Show those who need to see it, what families like ours are really made of.

"She must assert herself in no uncertain manner. It is her right in every way to assert herself and say, it was my [Malcolm's] *business; my life and with my love, I'd planned and made a future. There needs to be true respect and equal share of earnings up to a certain point of time. Let honesty prevail. It is difficult to say, if only I could speak to those who need to hear my view!*

"Please tell my dearest wife to stand up and be strong. Let her know that I will be there to support her."

Journal entry: The Mediation

The second mediation day was a long, complicated and arduous one. I was present in one room with our solicitors and my sons. Ian was with his team in another. There was a third room where the negotiations actually took place, with the mediator present.

Ian totally refused to deal with me or my solicitors and insisted that he would only speak to my sons. I was concerned and said that I would not allow them to be alone in a room with their uncle for one moment and we would only conform if the mediator were present with them at all times. This was agreed.

All three sons were called in to attend with the mediator to listen to Ian. When they returned sometime later, they looked somewhat dazed, and my solicitor, conscious that it was a difficult position for them to be in, allowed them a few moments before questioning them.

Finally, Alastair, as the eldest, was asked what had transpired. He continued to look shocked and puzzled. He then turned to our solicitors and said, "It's quite simple really. Our uncle *hates* our mother ..."

And so it continued for most of the day. Fresh ideas were raised; Alastair, Duncan and Charlie continually returned to the mediation room armed with suggestions to put forward and would then have to listen to all sorts of retaliations from their uncle. They would then return to our room to be questioned about what had taken place. It was excruciatingly painful to witness and all the time, I was required to remain with my solicitors in our separate room. The mediator was the only one allowed to accompany them during this process for Ian refused to meet with anyone else. No progress was being made.

Eventually, around 4 p.m., I decided we had conformed sufficiently to the requirements of the mediation. I could see that a satisfactory way forward was not going to be achieved and could no longer bear to see my sons treated this way. Unwilling to allow the situation to continue, I decided to wrest back control and refused permission for them to leave the room again without me. The mediation came to a close.

Even though it was emotionally and fiscally costly, after a gruelling day, I felt euphoric. Alastair made my day. For when the mediation was over he walked over to me, and in front of both lawyers and the mediator, put his arms around me and gave me an enormous hug. Then he said, "I'm with you, Mother. We have got to do this and be reassured I am with you every step of the way!"

Duncan and Charlie had come to the same conclusion months before but, until that moment, Alastair had not been fully convinced for he continued to fear for my health. I believe it was the bullying stance of his uncle that day which enabled him to finally see what we were up against. Alastair's words were all that I needed to keep me going. We were fully united. Ian's own behaviour had enabled this and I was thankful.

Chapter 30
A Birthday, a Wedding and a Funeral

Journal entry: Saturday, 3 July 2004

Twenty-one people attended the Mulberry Down gathering. It went well and felt an important and useful exercise. Everyone was relaxed and enjoyed discussing their own spiritual journeys in complete confidence that they were among friends and those of 'like minds'.

I rang Gloria to let her know how well the gathering had been received. She had contacted Malcolm again and read his reply: *"My dear friend, it truly is so good to speak to you again. Times are very stressful for my beloved wife because my brother is trying every way he knows to break her spirit. Tell her, beware of Ian, give him not one ounce of hope and always show him strength.*

"Ian had hoped that all this costly business would stop and see him sitting pretty and in a state of comfort. He now sees the strength that my dear Patricia holds within. He is digging in and will find it difficult to surface.

"When the time is near to face that man in court, she'll give him more than he ever dreamed of. His name is at stake, remember, how can he hold his head up high? Be still, my dearest wife and family. Stay calm and bide your time. Do not be frightened by his tactics. I love you all so very dearly and am always close. Stay calm, take each day as it comes. Your strength, your love and your togetherness; only good will come of them. Remember, one day at a time. There will be real joy in your lives again."

Journal entry: July ~ Kent

It is 8 p.m., the week before Alastair's wedding. The patio doors are open and I can hear starlings and seagulls in choral competition outside. It has been a lovely day and I was grateful for a complete rest. I was up early and had finished cooking by the time the heat of the day set in. So, I allowed myself a rare day of lying in the garden and enjoying the warmth of the sun. I am now recharged!

The last two weeks have been intense. All witness statements had to be completed by 23 July. It was an arduous task. I went in early that day to sign the final draft and noticed that my solicitors were both still in their clothes from the previous day. They had worked all night! The costs are terrifying, both emotionally and financially.

A couple of weeks ago, Mother asked me to take her to see Janet. Mother went in first. Then it was my turn.

Reading: 17 July ~ Janet

I handed her a photograph of Malcolm.

Janet began: *"Your husband is saying it is a pity he couldn't complete his plans as they included your mother."* [Malcolm had planned a granny annex at Westfield.]

"Your husband had two Christian names?" [Malcolm Campbell Irvine.]

"He is taking off the first one." [Campbell Irvine; the company name.]

I asked, "How does Malcom feel about the court case? Am I on the right track regarding the children's trust fund?"

"You have no choice. 'Fair's fair.' You have a while to go yet because it is so involved." [Yes, they keep moving the goalposts!]

"Do I need to worry financially?"

"'God will supply all your needs.' Malcolm wants you to proceed with the court case. He is holding up a glass of wine.

"He is saying, 'You have an inner strength, which will protect you.'

*"Your sons love you. Love from their father comes through them
to you.*

"You must be having a visitor to stay? [Yes, Gordon.] *It will give
you great pleasure, you can relax with this person. It will also help
him; it is a two-way thing. This I envisage to be fairly soon, not even
a month away?"* [The following week.]

"Do you have a house with steps that go round it?" [Westfield
has steps surrounding it.]

*"You have bought yourself something new recently? Something
you would not normally wear?"* [Yes, this is correct.]

*"Malcolm is saying that you needn't have bought the second
one!"* [Amazing! I have had two outfits made; one for the wedding
and one for Duncan's twenty-first. I wanted to feel confident.]

"Well, he approves. He is approving of it all, my dear ...

*"Malcolm is talking about the tie he had on when he was in the
coffin."*

I remembered immediately. Before the problems with the
company profits began, Ian had accompanied the children and me
to the chapel of rest. Afterwards, the boys left the chapel a little
ahead of me, and Ian followed. On the way back to the car I asked
Ian to accompany the boys and returned, alone, to the chapel. I felt
strongly that I needed to be the last one to see Malcolm, not his
brother. I returned and stood looking at Malcolm. I did not want
to touch his hand as I knew it would be cold and lifeless. I chose
instead to touch his tie. It was our last personal touch. I have never
discussed this with a soul.

Journal entry: 15 August - 8.45 p.m. - Kent

Tomorrow will be my parents' fifty-seventh wedding anniversary.
Instead of celebrating we will be attending my father's funeral. I
cannot quite believe that such a huge pillar in my life is no more,
particularly as I am sitting in his home, surrounded by so many
memories. Mother's floral tribute is fifty-seven red roses. Mine is
a dozen sunflowers tied in blue ribbon. I have been asked by my
family to read a poem, one which I wrote for him on Father's Day. I
pray I can make a decent job of it.

Memories of My Father

There are many memories of my father that I shall always prize
Most definitely his smile
With love pouring from his eyes.

I shall miss all the jokes I'd heard a thousand times before
And his welcome for me at home
With him waiting at the door.

I shall miss the smell of his tobacco and the many cups of tea
And I shall miss the way
He was so interested ... in me!

I shall miss late night moments shared,
When he would speak of times when young
And the special pride that beamed from him ...
When a solo I had sung.

I shall miss the counselling he gave me
When life would go in fits and starts
And the simple wisdom, spoken clearly
Directly from his heart ...

My father was a rock
And a very, *very* dear friend
I just hope my family feels the same
When I'm at *my* journey's end!

On Wednesday, 28 July, Mother arrived at Mulberry Cottage and, at noon, we collected Father from the care home next door. Father had chosen his favourite pub for lunch and, as the weather was so glorious, we sat beneath a shady willow in the garden. My father was on top form. Although frail, it was obvious that he thoroughly enjoyed listening to stories and even told us a few of his own. It was a perfect time together.

Two days later, I walked to the care home to collect Father as he was to join us in time for his birthday tea. Our entire family gathered to celebrate Father's birthday one day early, because Alastair's wedding was on the actual day, 31 July. Father was in fine form again and fully enjoying himself with his family.

*****

The wedding day dawned and it was exquisite. My son and his bride had organised everything brilliantly. It took place in the chapel at Alastair's old schoolhouse at St. Augustine's, Canterbury, in the quadrangle.

Following the 3 p.m. service, there was croquet on the lawn, champagne and conversation. The heat was so intense that chairs were placed in the shade for my parents to sit in comfort. Father, clearly enjoying the company, looked years younger.

My abiding memory of my father will be him raising his glass, after Alastair announced at the reception that he and his new wife were sharing their special day with "Granddad, who is eighty-three years old today." The whole room toasted Father.

The last time I saw my father alive was as he left the celebration.

Mother and Father were in contact the following Sunday and Monday, and I knew that they were both terribly tired so I left them alone. I had planned to drive to France for a day or two with Carol O and decided to visit them after I returned.

I was just north of Le Mans when I received the phone call that everyone dreads. My sister-in-law told me that Father was in hospital. I did a U-turn and thundered back to Calais.

We were silent in the car. At about 5.10 p.m., UK time, I turned to Carol and said, "I feel that my father died within the last twenty minutes." I explained that for that amount of time I had been filled with the most amazing 'nothing can touch me now!' kind of feeling. It was all-encompassing. I'd been bathed in the most incredible feeling of peace, it was almost tangible and I had been basking in it, choosing not to speak until it had passed.

Carol then declared that twenty minutes earlier she had been intensely cold and that, even in the intense heat of the afternoon, she had needed to lean forward and turn off the air-conditioning on her side of the dashboard. Puzzled, at the time I'd watched her do this but kept silent.

Finally, hours later we arrived at the hospital and learned that my beloved father had indeed died of an aortic stomach aneurysm at 5 p.m. Clearly, what we had both felt was Father visiting us in the car for those minutes, in order to say a final 'goodbye' to his daughter.

If I am being sensible and philosophical about it all, I do realise that the timing could have been much worse. As an early stage Alzheimer's sufferer, Dad's quality of life was only going to spiral downwards from then on. However, to lose such an immense influence from my life really hurts and I miss him dreadfully.

Last Friday, I could hear my mother's need for company when I spoke to her on the telephone. I quickly packed and returned to her home to keep her company until after the funeral. Yesterday, I took her to see Janet in the hope that it would help her. Janet had not been told about Father's death.

Reading: Janet with my mother

Mother handed Janet a photograph—there was no conversation.

Janet: *"He* [Father's picture was used] *is showing you and him pulling a Christmas cracker."*

Mother replied, "Yes, last year at Tricia's home."

"He felt very close to her."

"Yes, she took him out a lot."

"She meant a great deal to him and did much for him. He is saying, 'We were so lucky to have her. She was always there when needed. She'll always be there for you when others go away.' How thankful he was that you and he had her.

"He says, 'Patricia's life will work out. It will take time but it will work out for her.'

"This man is saying what joy he had in those few days before he passed; 'It felt as if I was young again. I could talk normally once

more and it was so lovely.' There were people talking around a table and he could join in. He is saying, 'It is a memory I will always have.'

"He didn't expect to die when he did and was much more his old self just prior to the wedding. He felt truly alive. He wasn't frightened of dying and he loved his last weekend because he was included in everything. He enjoyed it all!"

Journal entry: 19 August - Devon

Well—it's happened! At long, *long* last Malcolm has contacted me again here at Westfield.

I woke early this morning, got up to close the windows, then lay down once more to sleep.

I was listening to the tide slapping against the hulls of the boats on the creek, the halyards clanking and the first ducks waking, when I felt the rippling sensations.

It was very gentle and bathed me completely in waves of glorious energy. There was no coursing through me this time but a sensation of rippling energy. I had almost forgotten how wonderful it could feel.

Then, I felt movement to my left and heard breathing. Malcolm was back! His leg moved and he put his arm beneath my shoulders and drew me gently to him. My eyes remained closed and my head rested on his shoulder. I knew he was speaking but could not decipher the words. I didn't want to break the spell by speaking aloud but told him with my mind that I did not understand. He pulled me closer for a moment, then, the rippling ceased and he was gone.

Tears filled my eyes at the loss once more; it was so acute after such a gentle, loving moment. But he had come to me here, at Westfield, at last ...

I wish I could explain more adequately. Sceptics would say it was a dream or wishful thinking on my part. But, for months, I have been longing for such a moment and, although there has been plenty of opportunity, nothing has happened for ages, until now.

This morning, it most certainly did! I cannot create this energy which courses through me before and during such an experience. The heat of my body at the end of the experience is so intense. If I could, I'd choose to live permanently in that state. No, it is not of my creation, either physically or mentally, and one cannot deny what happens to oneself. There is a huge difference between belief and knowing. I *know* this happened because I fully experienced it.

I feel honoured and grateful that he returned to me again.

Reading: 2 September - Pamela Wellsman - Surrey

I arrived back to letters from my solicitor, which had me plummeting to the depths once more. I spoke with all the experts I knew and decided to call upon my spiritual friends for support, including Pam, whom I visited:

"You are pretty low at the moment, the lines on your hands are feint. When they're feint it means one has lost hope, enthusiasm or a foothold in something. You ask, 'What's the point of going on?' But we have to respect that spirit has a plan for each and every one of us. Spirit likes us to keep going even if we are elderly, for we may be an integral part of someone else's learning, whether we appreciate that idea or not. Every stage is part of our body and soul's development. This life is only one chapter of our soul's evolution.

"Rupert is being mentioned." [My solicitor.]

"There is a Malcolm coming through. He is saying that he is sorry. It is only when we reflect, that we realise that maybe we could have done something different." [Leave the 'golden share' to his younger brother perhaps?]

"I get smoke wafting across." [My father smoked a pipe.]

"You are creative, you have lots of ideas but you're not sure how to settle yourself with them. There is a move with you, a house move. There is a need for you to re-establish yourself somewhere.

"A lot of healing energy is coming through. You have real abilities to heal others by just being there for people and giving them answers to their questions or advice and encouragement. Deep down you are not as confident as you portray. You give the impression of being on track and in control but you are not confident

underneath the surface. There is teaching in you, very much so."

Pam began to use the cards.

"You will get back on track and feel that your efforts are not in vain. Malcolm gives his approval; 'the fight is worthy'. He is looking after you and believes that you are entitled to what you are fighting for. Your opponent is pompous, selfish and opinionated. Malcolm's saying, 'He's got enough anyway, why he wants more I don't know.' It is the principle with your opponent and with you also.

"Choose twenty cards ...

"The queen of spades has flipped out ... At the present time you have to deal with an unfathomable man and you are in a quandary about the outcome and that is what is frustrating you. Behind the man who is troubling you is a horrible interfering woman who is causing trouble between you and this man."

Pam began turning the cards over ... *"This is you, bored with waiting, but resolving things after a period. This shows money is going to greatly improve for you. You are going to have money over and above your needs.*

"The ten of diamonds depicts a big building that you are going to visit, like a court, and it will help to sort things out. I think this may be the resolution of this business with the two-faced man and the fact that you have got the money, would indicate that you are going to succeed.

"Let's look ahead ...

"Seven of diamonds indicates that, whatever you are aiming for, personally or professionally, you're going to succeed.

"Three of hearts is you feeling content, happy, secure, fulfilled and harmonious. There is frustration around a travel issue but that is only a short-term thing." [My work in China.]

"I have something to do with languages coming through me and Jakarta and Indonesia, does this mean anything?" [Gordon is a linguist and has business connections there.]

"There is education and travel here." [I later travelled to China and helped to record a book of phonetics and phonology at Sichuan University.]

"The travel card is here. You and a man will be travelling together." [In 2005, Gordon and I attended a family wedding in

Malaysia and then travelled on to China.]

"This first card shows money coming to you. There are new beginnings.

"You have had terrible misfortunes recently in the way you feel. Your mother also feels like that, so you have been dealing with grieving females.

"Ahead of you there is anger over something that is coming to a head soon. This will entail a journey to sort out whatever it is about—perhaps to court. I think there are numerous journeys soon for one reason or another."

"This business problem will continue until you see a judge, he obviously has a hand in things. So you have got a few weeks of battling still but you are not going to lose. I think you are just about getting there, it's taken a while. You will get financial security.

"The hope card is the best card, for when you see her it means personal desires will be fulfilled. There are things coming to an end and luck is on your side and this enables you to see that it is all part of a plan. You have got hope—that light on the horizon."

Reading (by post): Saturday, 4 September - Janet

Earlier in the week I had sent a letter to Janet with both Malcolm and Dad's photographs asking if she could help. Today, I received her reply:

My dear, please don't feel guilty about asking spirit for help, that is what they are there for. I know you've said you have had a battering over the last eight years and you wonder when it is going to come to an end. I can understand that. We all think we can't take any more but, somehow, we do.

I now have Malcolm's photograph in my hand and I am tuning into him. He is saying that he is damned if he would let him get away with it! "It belongs to me and now I am not there physically, it belongs to you and the boys. You fight for what is right. I would not settle, if I did, it would be an awful lot higher than what is being suggested. I would have taken him to court because it is teaching him a lesson. He knows it is a lesson that you are learning too, and that you shouldn't be."

Both parties [Malcolm and Ian] *were very keen to join up in business. One cannot blame either side for their becoming partners because it did pay dividends. When your husband was alive he was happy with the partnership and the returns. He is saying he would fight on but, if you do, there is a little more work to do. Your husband is banging his fist down on his other hand to demonstrate how determined he would be.*

He says you have inner strength but you do not know it. He is also saying you can only do what you think is right. He is watching with eager eyes. He is saying, "I was a good business man, I was the administering brains behind the company to get it off the ground. What the company employees know about administration, basically, they have learned from me. It isn't fair. Believe me, Ian is being more than unfair."

You will go across the sea but ... I don't feel immediately. I would say you will go abroad and this gives Malcolm much happiness to see that you are going to be happy travelling. He is sending his love, his thoughts and his prayers and hopes it all works out well. Don't feel guilty over anything at all, just fight on, that is the important thing. He says that things worth having are worth fighting—and waiting—for.

I now have the picture of your father in my hand, Patricia. He is talking about your mother and the sadness his death brought to everyone. Someone was at the funeral that he did not expect to be there. [Malcolm's brother-in-law.]

The flowers were beautiful and he thanks you for those. He is saying, "You know, I really didn't die then. It felt like I died when I went into that home because I knew I was past anybody bringing me back to the state of mind and body that I wanted to be in. But I am happy here."

He says, "You don't do things by halves you go the whole way!"

And your husband is joining in and saying, "Yes, I agree!"

"You go all the way or you don't go at all!" [The court case.]

Your father says that your mother can get by quite all right and he doesn't worry about her financially. She is quite capable now because she had to learn this when he went in the home. He was meant to go into that home so that when he passed, his passing wasn't so hard on his wife.

"Give her my love," he says, "and tell her that I think she has been very brave and she is to live her life to the full because she is going to live quite a while yet. She is not going to be with me for quite a long time ..."

He knows your mother is feeling a different loneliness. "You must remember we are never alone, we are always together, like you and Malcolm are always together. There is happiness for you. There is life ahead for you both, to be enjoyed."

He says, "To feel young again before I died. Those few days, that short time, we were together was heaven on earth. I never thought that I could be so happy and enjoy my family so much and that we would all be together again. I love the memory of us all enjoying ourselves and talking. I felt almost as if I was the 'top' guest and that feeling is what I have with me all the time now that loving, beautiful feeling. Think of that when you are down, it will bring tears of joy to your eyes like it brings them to mine."

Chapter 31
Foreign Travel and the Power of Words

Journal entry: 20 September 2004 -Spain and China

I have returned from a trip to Santiago de Compostela in northern Spain. This was the pilgrimage that Shirley MacLaine completed and recorded *The Camino*. I shall reread that book now with renewed interest.

I flew to Bilbao with Carol O, where we collected a small rental car. We did not join the rustic part of the Camino until we were well west of Astorga. This section was particularly delightful. We were among walkers and cyclists who were doing things 'properly' (the hard way), and those who had obviously more time than our five days!

The road wound picturesquely through the countryside with mountain views. We stopped to explore the tiny chapels and villages on route and to experience the atmosphere with the pilgrims whenever we could. The feeling inside some of the small village churches was silent and reverent.

Arriving in Santiago during late afternoon, we found a hotel on the outskirts and rested before venturing into the city. At 8 p.m., having found a parking space, we continued into the old part of the city on foot. There were few people around and we went into a small restaurant where the kind family owners prepared, especially for us, vegetarian paella. We then continued towards the cathedral.

The city was beautifully lit and we first came upon the south entrance and the clock tower. I was drawn to the ancient tower and stood with my back leaning against it looking across a small square. Instantly, my feet seemed to be alive with energy. It was like being plugged into a socket! Carol was nearby and I called her to come and feel it too. She stood beside me but felt nothing. The vibrations continued through my feet and intensified. I stood there for twenty minutes or so, happily rooted to the spot. It was fascinating, not at all frightening, just rather curious. Carol returned a second time but still felt nothing. Eventually, we left the square and went back to the hotel.

The next morning, we arrived in good time and entered the cathedral by the south door. A service was in progress. The fact that it was a Roman Catholic service did not matter (I find religious boundaries tedious) and I accepted the communion offered. I was overwhelmed by intense emotion, which surprised me. I fought back the tears and returned to my seat. At that time I knew there was nowhere else in the world that I was meant to be. It just *felt* so right.

Once the service had ended, mayhem reigned. The initial, tranquil atmosphere was killed by the 'body porridge' and constant popping of flashbulbs. The clergy turned off the lights and, frankly, we couldn't get out of there quick enough. We walked to the other side of the old town and stumbled across a bustling local market, which suited us and our cameras far more. We were so glad that our first experience of the cathedral had been the previous evening, which had somehow been far more evocative, but my abiding memory will always be the energy charges as I rested against its wall. As inexplicable as it was, the whole experience was breathtaking.

*****

A great deal has happened since I last typed this journal. It has been a very difficult period. I needed to get away for a while, from the mounting fear of what might happen in the interminable battle of the court case.

I travelled to China to visit Gordon for three weeks. As he is involved with the language department of the Sichuan University, he asked if I would help to record a book on phonetics and phonology for a professor there. I was thankful to have my mind so positively distracted.

It was fun to be in a recording studio and doing something so very different. The professor seemed delighted with my voice, as it suited his purpose well. It was interesting meeting new people and being picked up from home in a car, then being driven through the streets of Chengdu to the studio, which gave me an opportunity to see much of the city.

I learned what a real 'Chinese takeaway' is. They sent out to a local restaurant for lunches which arrived in plastic bags with chopsticks! We ate the delicious food together, in a small studio lounge. The studio itself was located in a high rise, ugly block but it had fabulous views across the city. 'Health and safety' would have had a field day if they could have seen us enjoying the view with the large windows opened wide.

When not in the studio we were at leisure in Chengdu. We visited a food festival and a flower show where I saw chrysanthemums unlike any I'd seen before. Gordon bought some for his roof garden, which looked lovely when planted beside the small stream and adjacent tea house.

We spent a lot of time in the roof garden away from the bustle of the noisy city. It overlooked a park and, as the garden was on the fourth floor, it felt as though we were on an island floating in an oasis of green. There was the haunting and evocative sound of a flute playing early in the morning and late afternoon, when a local man chose this time to practise in the park. During this time, I wrote another poem:

Rooftop Garden

I know a secret garden
Hidden from prying eyes

This splendid green oasis
Is planted in the sky

High up on a rooftop
Amidst dense urban sprawl

The orchestra will thrill you
When birds begin to call

And from the rooftop garden
No ugly buildings will you see

This cherished garden island
Lies 'midst the tops, of parkland trees

Gentle running water,
Sounds wild as it runs free

And gives delight to those that hear it
You and me

A haven in life's madness
This garden's a gem of pure delight

If sleep calls you in the afternoon
You'll give in without a fight!

As you sit there silently
Drinking in, with all your soul,

You'll be glad that its creator
Achieved his special goal

However,
As you may not see this garden

In its pool of swaying trees
Remember,

Mother Earth's both yours and mine
And she's there for all to see.

One night, I found it really difficult to sleep. Worries caught up with me. Even though I'd taken myself across the world to get away for a while and had interesting company, I knew there was no 'getting away' from reality long term. The positive side to my escaping the trials back home momentarily was that at least I was enjoying some new experiences.

I was 'prodded' to write again that night. I jotted words down in my notebook.

The next evening we had a quiet meal at home and Gordon brought up the topic of 'time'. There followed a lengthy and in-depth discussion on the variations of the past, present and future.

After a while, something occurred to me and I remembered my jottings of the night before. I went and fetched them and read the words of 'Now' aloud to Gordon. We were equally amazed by the synchronicity.

Now

There is no 'time'
No today, no tomorrow, no yesterday
There is only 'now'
There is only this moment.
Listen for the faint and distant beating of a trillion hearts ...
There is only 'now'
The ever-present 'now'
Don't save your dreams
Don't fear ...
Humankind is weighed down by fear!
Fear of the unknown
Fear of being hurt
Fear of rejection
You must 'fly your dreams'
So fly high, dearest one
Fly 'NOW'!

When we had completed the recording of the book at the studio, I wrote a poem in one of my photographic cards and gave it to Jing, the producer, by way of thanks, because I had so enjoyed being part of the project. Jing was so moved by the card that she showed it to her father, the professor, who read it and then asked me if I would allow him to include it at the end of the recording of his book. I happily agreed and he then asked me to read it into the microphone and record it for this purpose.

Words of Friendship

A lone raindrop
Into a silent pool
Falls ...

The effect is instant
A rolling momentum
Rippling, gathering speed

Then gently touching the shore.

Words can do this ...

A few simple words
Can reach out to touch hearts
Touch minds, touch souls ...

Such words have a purpose

In reaching out gently
They can cocoon your heart
To soften any blow,

And offer a shared understanding
Of another's deepest hurt,

And in time ... they'll point the way
And offer a brand new start

And these words?
These words are a gift

A gift of friendship
From me ... to you.

Before my flight back to the UK, I was invited to a special lunch in my honour and given a copy of the professor's book with the CD. At the lunch, I was asked by the producer if I would consider writing and recording a book of poetry for young children in China. Knowing that the poems I had were always 'given' to me, while out walking, driving, or most often while trying to sleep, I wasn't certain that I'd be able to do this. (I had never consciously sat down to write a poem. I had simply noted down words which I had *received*.) I agreed to think about it.

I had experienced a fascinating and exciting three weeks in China and was grateful to Gordon for the opportunities. I returned to the UK totally refreshed and ready to face whatever lay ahead.

Chapter 32
Patience: Not One of My Virtues!

Reading: 16 November 2004 - Janet

Following my return from China, I visited my mother in Kent and called to see Janet.

"Your father is saying, 'The tables are turning for you.' I would say that you have started something but you don't realise what the consequences are yet.

"You could be in China again soon. You were quite surprised at the greeting in China." [I was very surprised. I was met by Gordon and a customs official and was simply allowed through without having to walk the usual gauntlet of customs officials.]

"The cousin you saw, I feel he had a machine that was new to you?" [He had an apple peeler and corer and was anxious to show this off to everyone.]

"Your father is giving you a lot of love and is thanking you for what you are doing for your mother. I must give you a lot of love and a kiss on the cheek ... I am sorry he has gone."

Janet then took up Malcolm's photograph:

"You have also left something of yours behind in China?" [Yes, in error, a book.]

"The bed you slept on was very different, wasn't it? [A Japanese bed and not very comfortable; it was like sleeping on a park bench!]

"Do you have a fan that is black? [I have a Chinese fan with black edging.] *It is not a cheap one bought out of any old shop and it is not small.* [No, it was decorated by Kiam Hong, who is an artist, and is large]. *He is saying that you will be using it when you are abroad. So you must be going out into the heat.*

"I feel you were concerned when you were out there about a pair of shoes?" [Yes, they wanted to go mountain walking and I didn't have suitable shoes.]

"Malcolm is proving he was there when you discussed this. You were also very nervous while you were eating?" [I worried about spilling food down me as I used chopsticks the whole time.]

"The love from your father and your husband is so great. Tibet, I hear the word Tibet ..." [Sichuan is near Tibet.]

"I feel that you are going to be asked to write something at home to go back across the water ..." [I have begun to write the children's poetry requested by Jing.]

"Are you finding this difficult?" [No, I ask for help and the words come when I walk.]

"I have a roll of carpet and it is being laid out for you to walk on, you know, like they do for royalty. They are going to look upon you as somebody special in some way." [I was treated like royalty when in China, which was a little embarrassing. This was after they discovered my recording voice!]

"Malcolm is giving you the most beautiful bunch of freesias. [My wedding bouquet.] *He says don't worry, things will work out. He is saying your solicitor is a 'damn good man.'* [I agree.] *He is saying, 'Go on as you are because it is in the right direction. Don't give in and don't give way.'*

"I'm afraid I am losing him ... I'm sorry he has also gone."

Reading: 30 November - Dilys Guildford

Last night we had a very interesting evening. Dilys Guildford was working in Surrey and I invited her to stay with me. We were joined for supper at Mulberry Down by Pauline and Friday.

After breakfast, Dilys offered me a reading, which I accepted. Earlier we had been speaking about my father's recent death and I explained the story of how, while driving in France, I had *felt* the moment he had said his last goodbye to me. The following is a transcript of the tape.

"Tell me please about a condition that I felt, while meditating this morning; I had a tremendous amount of pain in my stomach." [I

confirmed that my father had died of a stomach aneurysm.]

"This person loves you and he is there for Malcolm, so you do not need to worry quite so much. He is saying, 'I want to prove that it is definitely me' ... He calls you by another name, Tricia, not Patricia. [My father always called me Tricia.] *He feels that what is taking place right now, this connection, is a miracle.*

"He is showing me a plant that has both green and red leaves [a poinsettia]. *Your mother really loves these plants. He is saying, 'Don't forget to get her one for Christmas, tell her that I sent it in a message.'*

"Your father came to you in France at the moment he died. Malcolm knew where you were. He is saying, 'Malcolm has taught me a great deal.'

"You've had something to do with the Constabulary in Kent? [The day before, I had telephoned the Kent Police regarding false house alarm calls.] *Your father was there, he heard you.*

"'I want to encourage you with the poetry because you underestimate the worth of it. But you need a good illustrator. To me, this is someone you really know well. You will provide a little library of books that people can collect.

"'The poetry is superb, because it is in everyday language that speaks volumes to people. It is exactly what is in their minds, their souls and their hearts. What you have done is create an androgynous work, one which appeals to both male and female.

"'The poetry will be solely yours and nobody can contrive anything from it. It is your copyright, they're your words and nobody can step in the way to take anything. We want to see you completely solvent, under your own steam, enjoying what you are doing. For you to have something that is completely yours. That is our dearest wish, something that nobody can touch.'

"The name Ian. He is saying, 'Ian can't touch you. Everything that you do will be yours. Don't look at this as if it is a chore. Everything you have will keep you solvent. If you had nothing from that man you will still have more than what he will ever have in his lifetime.' Your father is saying this to you in a very direct way. Malcolm takes the corners off but your father is direct." [This summarizes their characters well!]

"'You have got to establish yourself, get yourself in print.' These are your father's words but Malcolm is agreeing. 'Everything that you have done in supporting us all has been a most magnificent job, but this is your time now. Start to enjoy things. Remember the joy!'"

"Is the court case going to destroy us financially?" I asked.

"No! Malcolm says, 'You have made him realise that you won't be walked over and that is what Ian has always done. He did it as a boy, he has done it all his life and I can't thank you enough, from my very being, my soul, that you have taken this all the way. He needs cutting down. He is out of order and he knows it. He is running scared at the moment.'"

"I don't want to foul it up, I need guidance."

"'You will know immediately. If you can know when your father died, in that instance, surely you realise your dad and I are going to be in that room to help you? Please don't worry.'

"Malcolm and your father love you. Malcolm is saying that, 'You have been such an amazing woman.'"

Journal entry: 20 December - Kent

Christmas is on the horizon but I am very fed up for, although I submitted the children's verse weeks ago now, there has been no word from Jing. Has all my work been for nothing?

I was happy after my visit to China but I am now once more firmly back at rock bottom. Why does life have to be like this? I feel like a child that has been given a beautiful toy and then had it whipped away, put into a cupboard and told that I cannot play with it anymore.

It is difficult to concentrate on anything and I feel guilty that I cannot get into the Christmas spirit at all. These spiritual lessons in trust, acceptance and patience are hard and I am really not doing well. I was feeling so low that I opened the *Yellow Pages* and left my number for Terry Tasker, a medium from Hythe, asking him to call me back. I have never met him before but I felt so desperate.

On Saturday I received a call on my mobile. To my amazement (as it is so close to Christmas) Mr Tasker said he could see me at that afternoon. The following is a transcript of the tape:

Reading: Terry Tasker

"Your father is in the spirit world—he is here straight away. I don't know if your father wore a hat but I am being shown one." [We placed his favourite hat in his coffin at the time of his burial.]

"He is saying if he were here he would give you a good talking to! He would like to give you a 'one-to-one' to help you. Did your father have a problem with his heart?"

"No," I replied, "My husband had a heart aneurysm."

"Then he is here also. They are trying to help you to focus on what lies ahead. But you cannot at the moment, there are too many things going on in your mind and pulling you down. They want you to hold on until the end of January when changes will be made which bring you back up again. You are very spiritual and too open for your own good. Don't be afraid to say 'no' to people. Your father and husband want to help you. They are saying, 'If you look after yourself, it will pay dividends.'

"Are you seeing a solicitor for any reason? Your dad's brought in a briefcase full of papers and they are sorting them out and tearing up many that are not relevant in order to reduce the pile. I can see you signing something and then breathing a sigh of relief. There will be a conclusion regarding a legal situation. This will enable you to look ahead.

"Does the name Robin mean anything, or Andrew?" [Yes, both connected with the business.]

"Are you thinking of looking for another home? I am being shown a door key. There is a question mark over whether you are actually moving locally or far away. The deciding factor will be during the next two or three months." [I have been discussing my probable move with my sons.]

"You should be a teacher. I am being shown symbols of the cap and gown. You should pass on your knowledge to others. Do you do any spiritual healing?"

"I am told I will be healing with words."

"I don't know if you are aware or not, but at night when you sleep, you work in the spirit world. You work with those who have taken their own lives, you help in this respect. You also help children.

"You have natural healing abilities also. Your father and your husband want you to spread your wings. They want you to relax, meditate, and pray like you would on a retreat. [That is how I feel when I'm here in Kent.]

"They are both trying to help you get the best out of your life.

"Have you had any thoughts of writing a book? Or, perhaps, started one?"

I answered, "Yes."

"Your dad and husband both seem very interested in this book. I am afraid, my dear, once this book is published it looks as though you are going to have to write another one! Do you realise that you are being inspired?

"Does someone around you make marmalade?"

"I bought some about twenty minutes ago," I laughed.

"This is your husband wishing you to know that he is around you still. Forgive me, Patricia, but I have to ask you a very difficult question. Please do not be offended but I am being asked to ask this. When you eventually go to the spirit world, do you want to be with your husband?"

"Yes!"

"He still has a very strong link with you, you see.

"I can see you having the opportunity to do more travelling and not just in a holiday situation either ... they are symbolically packing your suitcase and pulling things together for you, saying that it is well deserved.

"Have you planned a journey to America, only I am seeing the Stars and Stripes? I get a strong Buddhist link with you, a very strong Buddhist aspect, and you have a monk around you. I also see a Native American with you.

"They want you to look forward. Next year is going to be a very busy year for you. Try and have a holiday. I am seeing China, you will be involved there. You will spend a lot of time in China and will be happy about it.

"You are very determined when you have a goal. Your father and husband are trying to push you forward—something will connect for you."

After returning home, checking for emails and finding none from China, I was still despondent even after this promising reading. The next day while walking along the beach a poem materialised.

Time to Fly

In icy wind I stand alone
A frozen pebble, on a deserted beach
A loan gull beats against the wind
Soaring high ...

The tide rolls endlessly to shore
Wings glint in the light of evening sun
Against a vast and glorious paintbox
Of sky ...

Our abilities are endless
Inside, our power lies sleeping
'Awake' there is nothing we cannot do
No aim too high ...

The light kindles hope within my heart
The ceaseless murmur of the tide confirms
Now the time is surely right
For me to fly ...

I have walked this way before
But, allowed life's lessons to slip away
I let all those careful teachings
Pass me by ...

But it's my turn now to ride the wind
To climb the banks of grey and purple cloud
And reach beyond the wild and silver linings
Of the sky ...

I gaze and watch the colours change
And in silence, wonder whose hand controls the brush strokes
Which, steeped in glory, fill these skies
For you ... and I

Monday dawned and I again walked along the beach, plugged into favourite music. It was taking so long to hear from China and the University. I reasoned that if they didn't want my work they should at least have the decency to let me know. The lack of communication about my future hopes and the loss of Malcolm became entwined and the words to 'Solitude' were noted. The joyous feeling I experienced while working in China seems so far away now. Did it really happen? Was it a dream? I feel like that child again, who has been given something wonderful only to have it snatched away. I am not sure if I am angrier at circumstances—or myself!

Solitude

A grey pencilled line marks the horizon
Aqua fades to china blue
Walking in solitude my crazy mind I cannot clear
All I do is think of you.

The fury of the tide is spent
Quiet now, it rolls gently to the shore
I think back to magic days
Knowing all I want is more ...

I walk in anger and with speed
To leave these thoughts behind
But pictures clear still fill my head
And words both soft and kind.

Two gulls I see upon the wind
Sharing the beauty of the skies
I wish with secret longing
Those birds were you and I.

Distance is so cruel
My thoughts and heart it binds
Did I only dream it?
Or was there a meeting of our minds?

Has fear become your master?
As it seems to now be mine
Will my prayers please be answered?
Will our angels soon be kind?

What happened to the music in my heart?
To the joy that made me shine
All I want is to reach out
Then feel your gentle hand in mine.

Chapter 33
Learning Tolerance, Acceptance and Faith

Journal entry: 10 January 2005

I am still confused as to why I have been asked, indeed *pressed*, to attempt writing poetry for children and then virtually ignored. The last personal contact I had from China was back in November and it was very positive. *'It is a great surprise to me, Patricia, that the poems you have sent are just what we want.'*

Since then I have sent out a further ten poems, along similar lines, and have not had a response. It is still normal to acknowledge receipt surely? I can't think of a suitable explanation.

Feeling 'at the bottom of the barrel' is not a place where I like to be. The view is not good, so I have decided to try and clamber up the side once more. This is not a game I enjoy, quite the opposite. I feel that, in the last nine years, I have had more than my fair share of this view. However, although I am tired of the game, I am not *too* tired and I will not let the negativity which has engulfed me win!

I believe that those weeks in China were meant to give me a glimpse of potential—my own! At the moment life is a puzzle but that does not mean I intend giving up on it. We cannot always see the reasons for the things which make us sad but that does not mean there are none. I guess it is true we do not always get what we *want* but usually what we *need* whether we understand the process or not.

If, as I suspect, I am being taught patience, tolerance, acceptance, faith, trust, belief and steadfastness all at once, then it is a very tough lesson and I don't much like it. But it doesn't mean I am giving up on my hopes, dreams and aspirations.

Nor will I ever give up on myself.

Journal entry: 13 January

I have decided to sell Mulberry Cottage and 'let go' of possessions that take up too much of my time and energy. Initially, I wanted to keep hold of our homes so that my sons and I did not have to cope with Malcolm's loss and the sale of his properties all at once. I wanted to retain the status quo so that my sons and I would not feel that our lives had been destroyed completely. Nor did I wish to have our standard of living frighteningly changed beyond recognition. I believed that holding onto our various homes and making them work simultaneously would help me to keep things a little more stable, for all our sakes. It did.

However, now that my sons are all over twenty-one and changes are happening to me emotionally I now know that I will not be happy living in Kent. I have never believed in going back and returning there on a long-term basis would certainly be that. It is only one door away from the nursing home that my father lived in. It is also where Malcolm and I spent many happy times when he could escape from the office. I don't particularly enjoy reliving these memories now that he is no longer able to share things with me. They make my loss more pertinent. I hope the sale is quick.

Journal entry: Wednesday, 13 January - 1.52 a.m. - Surrey

Finally, reassurance! I retired early to bed but spent the evening and the early hours of the night in turmoil. I could not drag my thoughts away from my current despondency about not hearing anything from China. Eventually, I went downstairs and found the Harry Edwards tape, *My Philosophy of Life*, and brought it upstairs. Thank goodness I did. Calmer after listening to it, I attempted sleep. I lay there listening to the electrical hum of the water boiler, the sounds of the house and foxes barking.

Then it came. The rushing began in my ears, my hands seemed to float and there was a rippling of energy through every cell in my body. I rode with the tide of energy, which I have so longed to feel but have not experienced for months. It was as though I was being cleansed. This always seems to happen when I am at my very lowest ebb. Oh! How I welcomed it.

As soon as I thought my thanks for the reassurance, as soon as I acknowledged it happening, it ended. But now I felt lighter in spirit, calmer and more centred. Maybe I have been yanked back onto my path, which had become increasingly more slippery of late? Perhaps I have been brought back to my 'soul' purpose? No matter the analysis, I was grateful.

I cannot explain this. I cannot summon or engineer these experiences. I have no control over instigating them. All I do know is that they cease when I begin thinking about them. I have longed for such reassurance for months. It always fills me with indescribable wonder. Certainly, I am not alone.

Reading: 13 January - Diana Summer

Arriving at her home, to my surprise, instead of channelling, Diana told me that, in this instance, she was being guided to use the Tarot cards. They were passed to me to hold and I then followed her instructions.

"It is now time to embrace and receive that which is your right. Allow yourself to regroup and recharge. You are moving through a transition at the moment. This is all about your period of adjustment. This can be quite emotional and this can also change everything. It can change your friends and your support.

"It is an extremely emotional time for all right now and this has a connection to the tsunami. Water indicates emotions and a huge tidal wave of emotion has journeyed around the world. Everyone is affected by it in some way. Do not get drawn into the fear and the sadness of it all. Stay centred and know that we are here to share light and knowledge.

"There is a lot of emotion around you. Know that when you are moved to express any emotion it is really powerful to let it go. It is important to release any righteous anger—let it happen! This will help, because releasing will enable clarity on a higher level of consciousness.

"You have this very powerful mother energy that is so protective and natural within you. You can ease up on that a little bit. You

are still guardian, protector and mother but easing up will give you much more energy. That is what this change is about; to give yourself permission and to give yourself that freedom. It is really important to begin changing your belief system about yourself. Stop judging yourself, you are too analytical. This is so you may move forward to embrace more truth.

"The future is opening up. But first of all you have to let go and set yourself free from all the negativity you feel about yourself. The more you open up the less negativity you can hold onto. You are very much the Goddess of the home. The home is your focal point; it has now become your sacred space. I can see you changing a lot of things at home."

I said, "I am doing so, right now."

"Aim high but don't take anything that is not appropriate for you. You are very good at knowing what is right for you. It is also about acknowledging your resistance to certain things. Resistance is also associated with fear when you are not quite sure what the result of certain actions will be. You decide to stay in the comfort zone because of fear. Sometimes we have to take a calculated risk.

"There is huge transformation here for you. The current turmoil you are feeling is because you are moving through this transition. What is happening is that all those thought forms, energies and emotions are being sorted out. You will start realising that you cannot keep hanging on to absolutely everything. You have to let things go."

"I have decided to sell my home in Kent, which is hard because it is like letting go of a broken dream."

"Major decisions are going to take you down a whole new path. You are going to blossom. Do you have any questions?"

I then explained about my confusion regarding the continued silence from China in connection with the poetry, especially after their initial encouragement.

"What you have put out will come back. Don't lose heart, just hold on. What you have sent out, you will get a response to. I can see that the energy is very busy around this. There will be a response that is going to bring you happiness. Have a little patience and trust. There is something that is buzzing out there to do with organisation

and arrangements. Stay focused and send positive feelings towards it. This is a challenge."

"I have had more than enough challenges in the last nine years. I am puzzled and hurting!"

"That is interesting—nine years—because the figure nine means completion so this could be the time that your karmic ride comes to a close. Think of this as a new beginning. The end of January/early February is the time for new beginnings. Make sure that you are open and willing to receive and it will come."

I then asked about the court case, which is to take place in October.

"Know how far you are prepared to go. There is something about decisions here."

I explained that, only days before, I had been shocked when my solicitors suggested that we employ a male QC to keep 'in step' with Ian's legal team. I was still reeling from this suggestion for I had utmost faith in the female barrister already chosen. I simply *knew* that she was the right person to cross-examine Ian. In fact, I had refused the suggestion of a QC entirely.

This decision of mine, against the advice of my solicitors, had added to my worries, but I was adamant that we retain the barrister chosen. I would not deny my 'gut feeling' that she was the perfect one for the job. I am not a sheep. I don't belong to any herd. If we were to be the only side without a QC, then so be it.

"This is all to do with your transformation," said Diana. *"Your change will bring you many blessings. Know that and believe it. Within you, know your heart's true desire. Be really honest with yourself and know how much you still want to put into this and go for it. Have patience because the process is still rolling on and spirit is saying, 'Do not give up, everything will come right.'*

"Patricia, because you know precisely what you want, you put across this really powerful presence. If you feel so confident about this barrister, then know that she is the one for you."

"I do know," I replied, "and the decision is made."

"She definitely has hidden qualities. She has a lot of strength and inner knowledge. She has a resonance with you also and understands what this battle is about. Once this court situation is out

of the way, you will find it is a huge weight off your back. Everything is occurring in perfect timing. There is nothing to worry about. Trust and relax. Let things flow as they should."

I asked about the recent power surge that I had received, explaining that it is something that simply happens to me—I can't make it happen.

"When the energy comes through, your soul has seen that you are ready to receive another wave of wisdom. As we become more open to higher consciousness we increase our knowledge of things. Those big surges are like the soul downloading, so it is really special and important when that happens. It is the divine love that is coming to you. When they see that the time is appropriate, they allow it.

"When we allow ourselves to go down and hit rock bottom— they cannot go down with us. Then, when we decide to rise again, they will step in and help you. It is all about not giving up, trusting, believing and being strong.

"Communication will be resumed. Take it step by step. This is one of your big challenges; what your life is about. When we feel disconnected it is the most powerful learning time because it is only then that we realise where we have been."

I am currently reading *Manual of the Warrior of Light* by Paulo Coelho and felt it apt to include the following here: '*The warrior of light is a believer. Because he believes in miracles, miracles begin to happen. Because he is sure that his thoughts can change his life, his life begins to change.*'

Chapter 34
The Year of the Rooster

Journal entry: 2 February 2005

I decided to surprise my mother with a visit. She has been very depressed since her first Christmas without my father. She also suffered a fall during the Christmas period, which shook her terribly but, fortunately, she didn't break any bones.

After a busy weekend, Mother was excessively tired and still very down. I felt I should attempt Reiki healing with her before returning home. I am a far from confident Reiki healer but I knew that I should try. If I can't make the effort for my own mother then it's a pretty poor show.

For twenty or so minutes, I *tuned in* to the silence and endeavoured to help her as she sat quietly in a comfortable chair. She fell asleep. I covered her with a blanket and crept silently out of the front door.

Much later, Mum telephoned and told me that she had slept soundly for several hours and felt much more relaxed than she had for many weeks. She also asked, "What do all the colours mean? Why did I see so much purple, pink, yellow and blue?"

I knew then that I had been able to channel the help that she needed in order for her to begin to feel better. Also, it gave me additional reassurance and confirmation, so necessary for me at that time.

*****

In late January, I was asked by Dorking Awareness Centre to read two of my poems at the onset of their meeting. I was a little concerned because the continued silence from China was keeping me dispirited and disheartened. It is so easy to lose heart. Still, I decided that this was an opportunity not to be missed, so I accepted the challenge and read 'Words of Friendship' and also:

Astral Travel

At night
I'd love to fly to mystery above rainbows in the sky
And as I travel view the stars
Like sparkling waters flowing by.

Then I'd sit among the crystal domes
Learning lessons to touch us all
Gentle guides would flock around as I'd gaze in silent awe.

The only tutor present
Would be the power of loving thought
Gently and with devotion my lessons I'd be taught.

And in the halls of learning
My fears they'd brush aside
With knowledge gleaned I'd then return
Armed with courage, but not pride.

As the silver thread to life on Earth
Would ease me back once more
I'd wake to face the precious day
My heart, stronger than before.

Both poems were well received and the organiser thanked me publicly and asked if I would consider reading on a regular basis. Delighted to be asked, I agreed to do so whenever I was in Surrey on a Friday evening.

There were two mediums present, neither of whom I had met before. Following my readings, Adam, the first medium, stood up to begin his work. But before doing so, he turned to thank me, complimenting me on the poetry. After he had delivered messages to people in the audience, he stood down in order for Betty, the second medium, to take over.

She also thanked me for the poetry readings and said, *"Do you realise, Patricia, that you will be writing a book?"*

I said that this had been suggested before.

Betty continued, *"I think you will then go on to write a second one because the first will be a real 'cracker'! Your grandmother and other guides are helping you. You are aware that you are inspired ... but they want you to realise that it is also you who are making all this possible.*

"You have a real gift and do not take enough credit for the work that you do. This work is important. They are saying that these books must be illustrated; they must not contain only writing."

Betty then moved to a gentleman sitting near me and began speaking about a male spirit present who had had many tools and worked a great deal with his hands. These tools he did not use professionally, just for family use and in his spare time. This meant nothing to the man.

She tried again, this time speaking about a woman spirit present who was very fond of cats and who had saucers of milk everywhere. This still meant nothing.

Betty said she would only try a third and last time and then if it still meant nothing to him she would cut the link. She spoke again, this time about the man having a recent out-patient visit to a hospital. Again it meant nothing.

I said, "I think you are still linked with me. I can take all of that. My father had lots of tools which he used a great deal. My grandmother loved cats and had saucers of milk everywhere. Also, last week I had to visit the hospital for an X-ray."

Betty apologised to the man and continued speaking to me, *"I am being taken to the month of November but this is not only November last year but also November in the future. I am being shown huge flowers like chrysanthemums, you know, the large pom-pom type but these are rather more unusual."*

My heart leapt! It was in October and November last year that I was in China and I took photographs of massive Chinese chrysanthemum heads at the exhibition in the park. Indeed, they were very unusual and I had not seen the type before.

I had never before met either of the mediums who were present that evening. And yet here one was restoring my faith with a few simple words. If this medium can be so accurate about the chrysanthemums I saw last November, then perhaps all the other mediums are also right about my future connections with China and the opportunity to record the book.

I was grateful for this small flame of hope, given when I felt lost in the dark!

Reading: 6 February -Terry Tasker

I am still waiting ... I travelled to Kent to be with my mother on her birthday, 4 February. I also telephoned Terry Tasker in the hope that he might be available to see me at short notice.

I arrived in good time and when we met, I immediately said that there were certain issues which were bothering me. Could I ask him specific questions?

His response to this was *"No!"* He would prefer to see what spirit had to say first and then, if necessary, we would deal with the questions at the end of the sitting. I accepted this.

"Would your father be in the spirit world? Only as I am looking at you I can see the movement of a figure behind you and he is coming in and telling me, 'Sit up and sit up straight!'"

Just seconds before Mr Tasker spoke I was thinking how annoyed my father would be at my slouching in the chair. I actually corrected my posture! It was *exactly* what my father would have said to me at that moment. *"Head up, shoulders back and sit up straight!"* was my father's mantra.

"I feel you using a solicitor. I cannot get away from legal documents at the moment. I don't want to go too far ahead but I am stuck with the month of May. I know it is a long time from now but life goes in cycles and I think by April/May time you will feel as though you are ready for a new start because one or two things will have lifted.

"Your dad and a grandmother figure are doing their best to help you here over the next two or three months. I see an easing of pressure. I am not saying things will be perfect, I wish I could, but things should be a lot better than they have been.

"Would there also be a connection with another country because I can see something to do with one? Could you be going abroad? Your dad's giving two aeroplane tickets here, which means a journey overseas.

"Is there a Peter living? Is he any help to you? Only Peter's name has come up in connection with the legal situation. [Peter Darby.]

"Your father is wishing your mother all the best. How old is your mother, if you don't mind me asking?"

"Eighty-one tomorrow."

"Your dad is there for her most days but he will be especially around tomorrow.

"Do you ever give talks to people yourself, Patricia?"

"I occasionally read inspired poetry."

"Good, because I can see you standing and reading to lots of people and that is wonderful because your dad, grandmother and other people are all inspiring you. This is the way they want to work with you, spiritually, which will help many other people. That will continue. Their advice is to keep copies of it all and hopefully at some point you will be able to get a book together. I can see you signing something in a book.

"Your father thinks that you would do well working for yourself. He is trying to bring ideas for you to look at regarding that. Your father is holding his hands over your back; he is giving you energy and pushing you forward to stop you falling back.

"I can see a Zulu warrior. Would this mean anything to you?"

"Zulu or Native American?"

"He has a spear and shield, I am sure he is a Zulu. He is standing very quietly listening to all that is said and I have a lovely energy from him, every so often he picks his shield up and puts it in front of you so, symbolically, he is protecting you.

"You are very good at speaking your mind but sometimes you ruffle people's feathers, this man is here to protect you. Please carry

on speaking your mind where it is necessary because that is the best way to be. I believe this Zulu gentleman is a guide. His name is Abraham.

"Is there one room in your home that you don't feel comfortable in?"

"The lounge where I work needs redecorating and it feels a bit drab and depressing. I intend having it decorated soon."

"Could you remember a gentleman belonging to your family who occasionally liked to smoke cigars?"

"My husband."

"Thank you, because I have cigar smoke and him coming through. You were very happy together. Patricia, they are all trying to help you, as you know your husband would. Have you got anything in a computer memory file to do with your husband?"

"Yes, poetry I have written since he died and a log of all that has happened to me 'spiritually' since then."

"He is showing me this, so he must have read them. He is one of the people who will inspire you, Patricia."

"Do you want to ask any questions now?"

"I have sent poetry to China as requested by them and I haven't heard from them since November. It is upsetting me."

"Leave it a little bit longer then telephone them. Your work is meant to go forward so another door will open. Your work is meant for many people."

"Am I likely to be returning to China?"

"Yes, by March there may be some communication again. I am going to end now, Patricia."

*****

Recently, Friday sent me a book. Oddly enough it was the same book that I had seen in a charity shop in Hythe, when I visited Terry Tasker. Because I was so fed up with all things Chinese at the time, I left it there. And now, here it was, received through the post a gift from Friday! I was born in 1950—the year of the tiger and this is an excerpt.

2005 The Year of the Rooster: '... *the tiger must resist the urge to be overanxious ... The seemingly immense and numerous problems that beset the tiger this year can be solved as help will come at the last moment from unexpected places or new-found friends. The tiger should refrain from pushing too hard to get his own way or else he could encounter even more resistance and more delays from the uncompromising chicken.*'

It could have been written with me in mind!

Journal entry: 9 February

I prayed earnestly and truthfully last night. No 'puppet' repetitions but from the heart, amidst a mixture of tears and determination, regarding all the things going on in my life.

My head and heart were both full and it simply poured out into the one main direction, in which I fully believe. By 1 a.m. I had not slept at all and went downstairs to make myself a drink, then returned to bed.

From 1.30 until 6.20 a.m., I was bathed in the gentle surges of the energy I now recognise. It continued throughout the early hours. I didn't sleep and gave thanks continually, yet, this time it did not cease when acknowledged by me. I rose in the morning with a new-found calmness and a feeling of having been *cleansed* once more. My heart feels balanced. My core feels centred. My mind feels calm and I feel reassured and refreshed. What an incredible effect this energy has upon me and what an enigma it is!

The words to 'The Power of Light' refused to be banished until I had written them down. Perhaps, after October the promised 'fresh start' will materialise. I hope so. I am honestly not sure how much strength I have left in me.

The Power of Light

Touch me with a finger of light
And wake me from my sleep
For the magic wand of love
Can rouse from slumbers deep.

Whisper, while I'm between two worlds
And remind me of my role
Fill me with the strength I need
To achieve my special goal.

Help me please, to understand
The meaning of my dreams
I know that there is more to life
Than perhaps, at times, it seems.

Speak in softened tones ...
Allow me, your voice to hear
Fill my heart with glorious hope
And chase away my fears.

Chapter 35
Courage Prevails

Journal entry: 6 March 2005

Some amazing things have happened. In late February, I received a telephone call from a distant nephew whom I have never met. Bill is a nephew of Gordon and lives in Hong Kong. He invited my sons and me to his wedding, which is to take place in Malaysia in April. Had he not taken the trouble to telephone me directly I would probably not have been quite so keen to go. However, he was an extremely pleasant young man and it seemed important to him that we consider it.

I spoke to my sons and we decided that Charlie and his fiancée Alice, Duncan and I will go. Alastair and his wife, Anne, will be abroad. It will be an adventure for us all and we are very excited. The groom seemed to be thrilled when we confirmed our plans and this was backed up by an email from him.

Two days later, I heard from Jing. She wrote that she likes the poetry and asked when I would be I returning to China to discuss royalties and to sign the contract? I was overjoyed!

What pleased me most were her comments, *"Generally speaking, I like most of the poems, especially those that deal with animals. The words are easy to understand while the images are so vivid that children will surely like them. What's more, they convey many moral meanings, which are regarded important in poetry for children in China. Still, what interests me most is that you write from the eye of a child, what she sees, hears, also what she thinks of the world ..."*

I decided that it would be sensible to try and tie up my visit to China to progress the book with the wedding in Malaysia. As I had always been told by Gordon that I was welcome to Chengdu any time, I emailed him to tell him of the good news. The reply I received was puzzling. He asked me if I could *"put my visit on ice"* as he had rather a lot of pressing commitments. He knew how long I had been waiting and I couldn't believe his reply.

As I would be in the right part of the world and we were both attending the wedding, it seemed ludicrous to me not to continue on to China. After waiting so long for a positive response I didn't want to waste the opportunity. I was a bit nervous of going on my own but after I had recovered from the shock of Gordon's reply, I decided to rise to the challenge and make plans to go anyway.

I was due to visit the Jonathan Atkinson Healing Centre for the first time that day with a friend. As I had only just received the somewhat shocking email from Gordon half an hour before, I was glad to be going there. I felt that I could use some healing.

When we arrived I was pleased to see Gilly Towers, a local medium there. She organises the Friday Awareness Group in Dorking, where I read my poetry. I asked if I could have a reading and arranged to visit her that same evening.

Reading: Gilly Towers (Trance)

Gilly barely knew my story at all. I kept quiet and simply listened to her channelling. Her voice, I noticed, had altered.

"We have watched your progress with interest and have much love and admiration for the courage that you have shown over the past years. This is all part of the evolvement of your soul, which you now understand. You have outshone all our expectations. You are truly a wonderful soul and you have a lot more work to do, which you already know about.

"Your poetry is just the beginning. You have a very sharp brain and you have to use it at all times. When you are low and feel very despondent, we cry with you.

"We like it when you are happy but when your dear, beloved husband departed, you lost your soul mate. He is still with you and is very close. He walks beside you and you feel him with you at all times. He did not want to leave you but it was his time to depart this

life.

"He is saying to you that you have handled the many problems that you have encountered along the way, maybe better than even he could have done, because you have inner courage, an inner strength.

"Sometimes you've scraped yourself off the ground. There have been many trials and tribulations. You have dealt with them in a most courageous way. Your husband is saying, 'It will be all right, even though you cannot see it now. You will reap the rewards in due course but you have to go on with your own life.'

"You have given your sons a very good start in life. They have had, apart from the loss of their father, a privileged background. They have been well nourished and nurtured and, really, they chose the ideal mother in you to send them on their way. They are special souls. Deep down there is a hidden strength and a spirituality, which will manifest itself in their more mature years. It is there now, you have seen a little of their light. They are very much on a growing path but they have to go through and experience heartache and upset as we all have to.

"We say to you, my dear, that they will be alright. They are a credit to you. Your husband is saying that without them with his loss, his passing, you wouldn't have known how to have carried on. They kept you on the straight and narrow. You were absolutely devastated at his passing but you now understand a lot more. Even though it is not easy and you still miss him, you understand more the pattern of things and why it had to be. It was the right time for that to occur in your life.

"Your father is in the spirit world; he is with me here. He comes to you with great love. He was very special and you were very close to him. He comes to you at this time because he knows how hurt and lost you are. 'You have had a sledgehammer blow,' he is saying. He is also saying that you will ride it. You will cope with it. At the moment you are in an emotional turmoil. He is saying, 'Sleep on this and ask your spirit guides to come to you. Ask them to show you the right path because this has to be approached in a logical way and you are not thinking logically at the moment, my dear.'

"He is saying, 'Think very carefully, but whatever, it is quite unjust.' You feel and know it is unjust but you have to think in a

*logical way before you tackle it, before you confront the parties.
You have a very logical, analytical brain even though you are very
sensitive and spiritual. That is the level you have to approach this
problem with. You will win. You will come out on top. It will come
about the way you want it to but it has to be done carefully."*

I was then asked, "Do you have any questions?"

*"Am I doing the right thing in going to China, alone, without
the assistance of my husband's cousin, who is too busy to help me
at that time?"*

*"We say proceed with caution. Be very careful. You will always
be protected but you have to go at the right time. Ask your guides for
help. You have to go with the right support."*

"They want to produce this book by 1 June so, as I will be in Asia,
I feel I should continue on as I do not want to miss this opportunity
just because Gordon is too busy."

*"Why is this person blocking it? Why is he stopping you? There
is no real reason for you not to go. Ask yourself these questions. We
say 'go' because we think you have enough connections there now.
You have to make a direct connection, bypass this man. Make sure
you are escorted and protected when you are there and if you can do
that then go. There is no further need of him. This is to do with his
ego. You have not yet been made aware of it until now.*

*"You must get the right people to be there to escort you when
you are there, to show you the right places. They are telling me that
you know enough about the area where you are going but you need
somebody who will help you with the business side of it. Get yourself
a chaperone. There is one lady in particular who will look after you,
she is younger than you, I think you know who [Jing!]. She will look
after you and she has seen this gentleman for who he is and this will
be revealed at some future point.*

*"You are going to publish this book. It is very important. It will
cause ripples. It will cause a stirring. You have earned this on a
spiritual level. Now it is your time to show your light through these
books. People already are coming to you for advice and you will
be teaching in some way. My guides are not saying how or what,
but you will be teaching. Please ask your guides to make you more
aware. You are very trusting but you must be more aware to protect*

yourself.

"*We have to go now; the energy levels are falling. We bring you blessings, my child, and we thank you for coming and giving us the opportunity to talk to you and share this information. God bless you, my child, God bless ...*"

Gilly seemed to shake herself out of her reverie and, after a few seconds, spoke normally.

"*I think you should stand firm; it is yours, this opportunity. You are your own person. You are on this spiritual path now. You have only just begun. Go to China anyway. Otherwise you will miss the opportunity and experience.*"

Why is life always so complicated?

Journal: 24 March

Some days after my meeting with Gilly, my address book fell open at Yvette Tamara's details. Still troubled by the momentous decision I had to make regarding going to China alone, I decided to call her.

Yvette said: "*You are going to be writing a book. This whole experience is all about you finding yourself. Your writing has great potential and will come together. Put all your energies into your writing.*"

After further thought, I decided that the opportunity in China was really too good to miss. I accepted that, perhaps, I was meant to do it on my own, proving to myself and others, that I do not need other people as 'props'. So I emailed Jing and told her that I would be in the Far East in early April and could travel on to Chengdu to discuss the book and record it after that if she wished. The reply was instant and positive. I asked her if she would organise my collection from the airport and reserve me a hotel in the city.

I prayed to my guides for their help and support with all the sincerity and honesty I had within me and I found that, as I began to get really stuck into making the travel arrangements, the poetry once again began to flow. I found that now I was focused on something else, during my daily walks or my nightly sleeping hours I began to produce more and more poetry and carried a notebook everywhere.

Once I had received confirmation from Jing, I rearranged my air tickets so that I could fly on to Chengdu from Singapore. Originally, the family and I were due to return home on Wednesday, 13 April. I knew there was a flight to Chengdu from Singapore each Wednesday and Saturday. I did not want to remain alone in Singapore, at great expense, without my family, so I decided to enquire about the Wednesday flights. There were only four seats left at the time so, regardless of the fact I had no visa, I took a chance and made the booking. I would be flying on to Chengdu and, on the same day, my sons would return to Heathrow.

I then looked into securing a business visa. There was no point entering the country under false pretences. I discovered that I would need an 'official' invitation from Jing. I swiftly emailed her explaining this then sat back to wait once more.

On the Friday at 3 a.m., the fax arrived and woke me. I decided that, now I had all the necessary paperwork to hand, the best thing I could do was not to trust the post, but go to London and try to collect the visa personally.

I arrived at Linda's house in Fulham at 7 a.m., parked, then jumped in a taxi. I was at the Chinese Consulate by 8 a.m. and had to wait an hour for it to open. It was freezing but, nonetheless, I was second in the queue. I learned a lot about visa applications while waiting in that queue with the various travel company couriers. At 9 a.m. we filed in.

My application form was scrutinised time and time again. In the 'occupation' box I had naively written 'writer/poet/photographer'. (I had written this rather proudly as it was the first time I could legitimately do so. It was also a rather *stupid* thing to have done!) My heart was in my mouth as I realised that all my hopes and dreams rested upon my application form and the faxed letter of invitation being accepted by the people behind the counter. I asked about multi-entry visas and the reply barked back was, "One entry only!" I smiled and thanked them and was then, finally, handed a precious 'pick up' receipt, with which to return later. Back out in the street, I saw the Langham hotel and decided to treat myself to breakfast and a thoroughly good warm up.

I returned to the consulate at 1 p.m. and this time was fourth in the queue. I learned yet more about the life of travel couriers. I was nervous that the precious piece of paper, from Jing, that I had handed over, would still not guarantee me the visa I required. I was fearful that it would be denied at the last moment.

At the magic hour of 2 p.m., and not a second before, the door was opened. After a few moments a smiling, young Chinese girl handed me my passport. Attached to my business visa was a piece of paper warning me that I must not act as a journalist while visiting the People's Republic of China! I was overjoyed that I could continue planning my trip in earnest, confident that my papers were in order. At home, I emailed Jing to tell her the good news.

Early the next morning I set off for Kent. My sister and I had arranged for her to take my mother on holiday to my home in Devon. Meantime, unbeknown to my mother, a friend and I would be tackling the 'renovation' of my mother's conservatory. We wanted her to be safe and able to enjoy the views of her garden upon her return.

My friend and I worked long and hard that week and achieved wonders in the time. When my mother returned to her home the following Saturday, she was overjoyed when she saw the result. It gives me great pleasure now to recall the joy that lit her face when she saw her transformed conservatory.

Heavily involved in my project for Mother, I forgot all about emails until Thursday of the following week. Jing had responded with her congratulations and saying that she was looking forward to my visit. She had found a hotel for me right next to her office, which was reassuring. It would be much more convenient being closer to the publishing house rather than a half-hour taxi-ride away. Courage had prevailed!

Chapter 36
Breaking Boundaries in Malaysia and China

Journal entry: 8 May 2005 - Malaysia and China

We arrived in Singapore and were met by Kiam Hong, who kindly took us to our hotel. The next morning, on the way to breakfast, I met an American woman, Doris, in the lift and she asked me if I was enjoying my trip. I replied that I had only just arrived. She told me that her own arrival had been the previous Thursday and that she had flown in from Los Angeles. She was teaching healing in the hotel. It became clear that we had much in common so we arranged to meet that evening.

We met by the pool and enjoyed a warm evening of shared conversation about our individual spiritual experiences. Doris asked why I had called my poetry *The Mulberry Collection*. I explained that our home is named 'Mulberry Down' and Malcolm's yacht 'Mulberry' and that the word is of great significance to our family. To my astonishment, she proceeded to tell me that she has three of the oldest Mulberry trees in her garden in her township in the USA and lives directly opposite 'The Mulberry Guesthouse'! We laughed at the synchronicities. It made us feel that we were in the right place at the right time.

The family and I travelled to Malaysia and another astonishing thing happened. There were about two hundred or so guests at the wedding and while we sat at the evening banquet, innumerable speeches were being read out, the majority in Chinese or Japanese. Into my head came the words *'read the poem!'* (I had written a poem in my card to the bride and groom.) I balked at this idea and said to myself flatly, *"No, I don't want to do that!"* Again the words came, more insistent this time, *'read the poem!'* I argued with myself once more, wanting nothing to do with the idea. I just wanted to relax.

I then received the instruction for a third time, loudly in my head, and was simultaneously reminded of the 'spiritual law of three', so I compromised by answering, *"If I have the opportunity to speak alone with the bride and groom in this vast ocean of people and they want me to do so, I will!"* Confident that this would prove impossible, I settled down again to enjoy the day.

Much later, I went out into the foyer to find the bathroom. When returning, to my absoluter horror, I found that I was entirely alone in the reception area with the bride and groom, Bill and Natalie. They were walking directly towards me, on their way to make one of the many changes of dress required by their traditional wedding customs. I could not believe my eyes! There were hundreds of people taking part in this event and, unbelievably, I found myself and the two of them, utterly alone in the hotel reception. I hesitated only for a moment; I knew that I had to keep my promise.

I spoke quietly to Bill, with whom my link was tenuous at best. It was the first time we had met and the first conversation we had ever had face to face. I said, "I've noticed that you have many Chinese and Japanese people making speeches, Bill, but no one from the UK as yet. As you are half English, would you like someone from England to speak on your behalf?" At the same time I was *praying* that as everything appeared to be so brilliantly and efficiently organised, he would say that it wouldn't be necessary and might complicate matters. But that was not to be!

"We would love it!" came their instant, joint reply. There was no turning back.

"Well, I can't really do a speech as such," I said, "but I could read the poem I wrote in your card." To my horror, we discovered that the card containing the poem was locked in their room and there was no time to fetch it. Bill and Natalie begged me to try and remember the words and I agreed.

They asked one of the reception staff to find me paper and a pencil. Then I took myself off somewhere quiet and tried desperately to retrieve the basics from my memory. Once I had exhausted my shocked brain cells, I returned to my table, gulped down some champagne for courage and waited for the signal from the best man that we had hurriedly arranged. I sat in absolute silence and didn't say a word to my family or anyone else. A few minutes later the best man walked over to me and whispered that it was time for me to make my way over to the stage. I made a point of walking around the furthest peripheries of the ballroom, leaving others at the table a little perplexed.

I was introduced and quietly stepped up onto the podium. There was a sea of expectant faces before me but, surprisingly, I wasn't at all nervous. This really surprised me. It was as though it was all simply *meant* to be. And more importantly, it *felt absolutely right.* I clearly and slowly said: "I promise this will not be a long speech. In fact, it will be a very short poem! The title is 'Unconditional Love'."

There is a love ...
Which is deeper than any ocean
And reaches far beyond the Universe.

It encompasses all that you are
And all you are certain to be

It will support you in every way
And touches the very core of you.

This love glories in your advancement
And lights your path.

Nothing can erase or daunt it
And it will surround you ...
Always.

Afterwards, to my great relief and absolute delight, a thunderous applause began instantly. The poem was very well received. I smiled at Bill and Natalie, very relieved that I had accomplished it without faltering. I had felt odd while speaking, it was as though someone else was actually doing the job and I was simply watching them perform. I felt as if I was flying. It was a truly memorable experience.

As I stepped off the stage the best man, a young Australian, came quickly after me again asking for the paper I had written the poem on. When I asked him why, he laughed and said good humouredly, "Thanks to you, I've now got to read it in Japanese—and Chinese!"

I walked slowly around the perimeter of the room again so as not to disturb those listening. On the way round I met Charlie, who had just returned from the washroom and had missed the main event. Somewhat shocked he whispered, "Hello, Mother, what the hell were *you* doing on stage?" (Charlie is wonderful—he is my true 'grounding'!) I kept walking.

We reached our seats seconds before the end of the Japanese version and my daughter-in-law, Alice, turned to me and whispered, "Patricia, that was brilliant! We didn't know you were going to do that!"

"Neither did I until a few minutes ago," I replied.

Duncan grinned broadly and said, "Well done, Mum."

There was an absolute uproar as the poem ended. Richard, Bill's father, looked directly at me with his hands clapping high above his head and everyone followed his example. Bill and Natalie came to the table together and kissed me. Inside I felt on fire. It was a marvellous experience.

That day, I clearly learned that a few well-chosen words can give so much joy. I felt very privileged to have taken part and thanked God for giving me courage when needed.

*****

On Wednesday, I travelled onto Chengdu and was met by Jing. I settled into the hotel directly opposite her office. It was a perfectly pleasant hotel but, after Jing and I had our first meeting and then ate dinner together, I felt very lonely in that room. Thursday, I was in the office by 9 a.m. and we had discussions with the illustrator and proceeded to choose, and work on, twenty of the poems for the children's book. We worked a full day, which was followed by another lonely evening in the hotel room. I had brought some cashew nuts and peanuts from the hotel in Malaysia and this was my supper. I was utterly miserable so used my mobile to call friends back home.

On Friday, we recorded all day and I spent that evening alone also but I did venture across the road to the supermarket and bought some fruit, water and other drinks. The work during the day was going very well but it was excruciatingly lonely in the evenings.

On Saturday I was free all day so I prised myself out into the street with my camera. Every step forward I took made me feel lighter in spirit. I enjoyed photographing unusual scenes. I met John (a complete stranger) from Colorado, who was a young mountaineer waiting in the street while having some maps printed. I then took myself into a fine-looking hotel for a coffee (and acceptable WCs!). I stopped to buy a notebook as I knew I would have writing to do later that day and ventured into a massive electrical department store where I was assisted by no less than five Chinese (including some passers-by who could speak a little English). It was rather a 'free for all' but great fun at the time. Eventually, I was the proud owner of an MP3 player, fancy headphones and microphone. My earnings from the previous day covered the cost and I could now listen to *Phonetics & Phonology,* the book I had helped to record on my previous visit. I was thrilled to see my name on its cover.

Back in the street, I visited the Bank of China where I changed some dollars for local currency and continued on to the local supermarket. I tried some bread and selected food for my evening meal. In another shop I bought some cheese, fruit and crisps so I feasted that night!

Jing rang me that afternoon, saying she wanted me to write a letter of introduction to the children for the book and one for each poem. We were to record these on the following Monday. I wrote solidly until just after 10.30 p.m., satisfied that I had done my best.

On Sunday I worked with Jing, going through each poem and adding footnotes, etc. Ironically, we realised that we were both using our father's dictionaries to aid us. Neither of us was hungry so we didn't stop for lunch and I finally arrived back in my room a little after five. Monday was, again, spent in the recording studio and it was a great relief when all the poems were successfully recorded.

My final full day in China was the Tuesday and Jing and I worked hard on the contract. I was due to meet friends of Gordon for lunch. After a quick shower, I hailed a taxi to take me to a previously favourite vegetarian restaurant at a temple. Afterwards, we returned to the roof garden and spent an idyllic afternoon and evening drinking tea, wine and Cointreau and sharing poached eggs on toast in the garden. It was a great way to end the trip.

The next day it was back to work on the final contract and Jing and I were both relieved when, in the late morning, the director of the university press office and I finally signed it.

Chapter 37
Spirit's Own Agenda

Reading: Terry Tasker

Following my visit to Chengdu, I visited my mother. She had been feeling under the weather and had fallen four times in one week. She asked me if I would consider taking her to see someone who might give her some insight into what was going on. I telephoned Terry, who agreed to meet with her the next day. It was her reading, not mine, but she was anxious that I accompany her, so a few of the messages crossed and were for me. These follow, although Terry was speaking directly to my mother:

"*Do you have any connections with Scotland at all?*"

"My daughter's husband."

"*I am being shown the Portsmouth/Southampton area. Are you considering selling a property there at all?*"

"That is for my daughter."

"*Have you ever thought of writing a book?*"

"That is also for Patricia."

"*Well, her father is saying that he is pleased. Things are going to be sorted out; materially, in her career and personal life.*"

Channelling: May 2005 - Adam

I delivered the professor's book to his old tutor at University College London. Upon my return that evening I had a message on my answerphone asking me if I could read poetry at Dorking the next day. The medium booked was ill and they were in a dilemma.

I phoned and agreed to read and then was told that another medium had 'stepped into the breach' at the last moment. The medium was Adam, whom I had seen once before.

That evening I read 'Unconditional Love' and 'Life's Lessons'.

Life's Lessons

None of us is perfect, not I and not you
We have much to learn and know that this is true
As we step along life's road, with heart and head held high
We're unaware of harsh lessons, gathering in the sky.

Sometimes we simply sail along and everything's just fine
Then a lesson trips us up and our hearts go in decline
Life is like an ocean wave, one moment we ride high
Next we spiral downward and luck seems to pass us by.

The lesson we must learn is, that in these highs and lows
Only *we* can find the strength to rise and onward go
When at times it seems there is no end to this dark night
Force your courage to return and balance dark with light.

And when you find you're in the darkness
Allow your light to shine.

For this will then encourage me
To do the same with mine.

Both poems were well received and I was relieved. Adam was the first medium to take the platform. Although I had seen him work once previously, we did not know each other. He was very complimentary about the poetry and said that poetry readings were one of the reasons why he and his colleague enjoyed coming to Dorking when invited. I was pleased to hear this. He spoke for several minutes about the poems and I took this as a huge compliment and an even greater reassurance.

He then said, *"Patricia, I now have to come to you as your father, who is in spirit, is anxious to speak to you. This man has a military bearing and he is saying that he ran his home in a military fashion. It was important to him that everyone had clean shoes and was well turned out. He was an authoritative person."* [All correct.]

"He says that you are too impatient! You are not to try and force things. Spirit wants the material things in your life settled first. He is saying you made a resolution at the onset of the year that this was going to be 'your year'.

"There is a brother-in-law who features somewhere who is trying to take more of something than is his fair share." [Adam knew nothing of my personal affairs.]

"There is something a bit underhand here and, at times, you feel as though the cards are stacked against you, but your father is saying, 'You haven't seen all the cards yet!'

"You are to have more time to yourself for peace and quiet so you can hear spirit. You wake a lot at night—especially between the hours of two and three and then cannot get back to sleep.

"There is a lady on the earth plane who is suffering with arthritis and who has recently had a bad back and she is feeling under the weather at the moment." [Yes, my mother.]

"Money is a bit of a worry for you at present." [The tremendous court costs.]

"There is another gentleman present who has stepped in briefly. He tells me that you go to a cottage in the country when you want to escape.

"There is a lady here who is showing me an apple pie and telling me she was a pastry cook." [Without doubt my paternal grandmother.]

"Your father could be quite brusque, he is telling me, and was often abrupt and outspoken but he didn't mean anything by it, it was just his way. [I know.] *Your father did not have a good education but he made up for it in later years by self-teaching methods and would read avidly when he had the chance."* [All correct!]

"Your father is saying that you are a lot like him. He has one final message for you; that you have always had his love but now you also have his respect. He knows that this will mean a great deal to you." [Absolutely right—it wasn't easy to gain my father's respect. This message was very dear to me.]

I waited and thanked Adam properly when the evening was over and he smiled and said, *"It was nothing to do with me, Patricia, spirit obviously has its own agenda where you are concerned!"*

Reading: 14 May 2005 - Terry Tasker

In mid-May, Sheila and I drove to north Kent to collect Gloria and then on to Hythe to have lunch. We each had a meeting with Terry later that day. We took our turns independently and while waiting enjoyed browsing in the little shops in Hythe. Sheila and Gloria had not previously met but everyone got on well and we had great fun.

The following is a transcript of my tape recorded by Terry that afternoon:

"Your dad is here straight away, Patricia.

"I can see something to do with a move or another property for you, and you getting rid of a lot of things and just taking what really you need to start elsewhere.

"Did your dad ever wear cardigans?"

"My husband did."

"He is here as well then and wants you to remember the good times." [I do, the trouble is they make me sad.]

"Do you do any painting, or do you have a painting in your home that has horses on?" [I later remembered that Kiam Hong recently sent me one of his 'seahorse' paintings.]

"At the moment are you near railway lines?" [My mother's home backs onto the Romney Hythe and Dymchuch Railway track.]

"Could you see yourself, Patricia, giving talks to groups of people? Spirit is trying to help with a book of your own and to get you more established.

"Apart from property, would there be any other reason why you need advice from solicitors? I see such a lot of documents here. Could you need advice from anyone higher up in the profession? Can you see a situation where you would wear a wig?" [No, but I can see a situation where a judge and barristers would be wearing wigs.]

"Your husband and dad are saying keep your chin up, they are backing you all the way. I can see some information might be looked

at again and be more in your favour.

"You are very spiritual and sensitive and should not be afraid of being strong. Your husband is passing you a warm and calming energy, he knows you are doing your best."

*****

After we had all received our readings, Sheila, Gloria and I travelled on to see my mother, who was looking surprisingly well. We enjoyed our time with her and left her looking rejuvenated. We then visited a pub for dinner. We were all getting on so well and laughing so much that I feared we might be thrown out. Sheila and I were drinking fruit juice and Gloria had only had one glass of wine. It was innocent merriment, what a refreshing change to be laughing! The party continued back at my home in Kent and we had a lovely light-hearted evening. We decided to form 'The Merry Widows Society'!

The court case is still looming, of course, so it is wonderful when other things fill my mind and especially to have some fun. But, no matter what else is going on, constantly, at the back of my mind, the fear is always there. The fear that I will lose the case and our way of life. I am afraid that I will lose my sons all that is rightfully theirs and in doing so, 'let down' my husband by forfeiting everything that he worked so hard to provide for us. Fear! It is always present. I am never quite able to shake it off.

Reading: Wednesday, 18 May - Pamela Wellsman

"You have a lot of healing here and this manifests in numerous ways; in your poetry and, certainly, in your care of others and your need to give them support. It could also be in a more 'hands-on' way. Your lifeline is long so there is ample opportunity for you to achieve your aims, even if you don't feel success is coming as quickly as you would like. Everything is happening for a reason and you may be leading up to a stage where you will find life is more fulfilling and worthwhile in areas you never thought of.

"I have the name 'Malcolm' predominantly here.

"Who is Peter? There are a lot of changes going on here regarding your links with him and a resolution soon. There is a backlog of things that should have been tied up and the last eight months have been particularly crucial.

"Who is Mary in all this? Has she been poorly? Spirit are watching over her very closely and, at times, you get really uptight about the fact that she might pass away, but they are not ready for her yet as she still has a job to do. She has to be there to support you.

"Your main concern is to know what your future holds when it comes to being settled and happy. Your calendar is full with people and issues to sort out but it is the innate feeling of not being with anybody that troubles you. You have always been a bit of an enigma really. You have always been rather lonely. It seems that you can only rely on yourself. You are alone with your thoughts a lot. Your mind is busy at night and you wake up frequently.

"You have had communication regarding work and success, in that you have achieved something. Ahead of you there is a work opportunity coming in which links you to a big building or big organisation. It is all connected.

"There is a link with a man who has, of late, treated you with two-facedness, which has put you in a quandary. It is in connection with a monetary issue and spirit is trying to organise closure to the problem.

"You are sorting out some money at the moment and there is a sale of a property and I have a Kent link with that though ... It is almost like you want to get your house in order so that you haven't got all these things to sort out later when you are very busy with other things. You have got money coming to you, a lump sum soon. You are winning. Financial security will remain.

"You will have final closure with a man who has been a male chauvinist. This man is condescending, domineering and old-fashioned, with an appalling attitude towards women. He thinks women are not worthy.

"You are angry at the moment about something. You are angry with your brother-in-law because of this. Hope and balance is going to be restored soon in an area where you have been pursuing

something for a while. Spirit are resolving issues and sorting out where you can finally let go of a problem, the closing of a door. So, it looks as though it is on the edge now.

"You need to resolve some issues where you have been feeling sad. There will be good news regarding something legal that also brings peace in your heart. Your ship is coming in and lately you should have seen some signs of that ...

"This problem was borne out of jealousy. Someone is jealous and does not think you are entitled. This is being resolved, the gift is here for you. October is in my head." [We finally go to court in October.]

"Jealousy, a money lump sum and anger, it's all here. Somebody is going to be jealous of your success. It ties in with a judge's ruling and it is in connection with a gift.

"Your husband gives you the thumbs up. It is a learning curve for you, so respect that. Spirit is working for you. Clouds in your sky are dissipating, new beginnings are here for you, luck is on your side and you are going to succeed. Money is tied in with that as well and this brings happiness! My God! These are unbelievable cards!

"This is all very positive. It is all good; in fact, it is perfect!"

*****

In early June, I attended the Dorking Awareness Centre with Sheila and we were both impressed greatly by Richard Peters and the evidence he gave to her during that evening. We had never met him before so I decided this was something I had to pursue. I made an appointment for the following week. It worked well as my mother was staying with me and I could take her to see Aunt Muriel in Sussex while I visited Richard.

Reading: 13 June 2005 - Richard Peters

"You are about to go away to somewhere you can have a complete rest and, more importantly, where you will find your energy will be recharged."

"Yes, to Devon."

"Have you considered writing? I am being told that you are very creative."

"I do write."

"There will be a lot of travelling for you in the future. I see the Asiatic, Pacific ring. Have you been to Australia? I am also being given the Stars and Stripes so it indicates America. This year will see a lot of fresh new starts for you, some are long overdue, in every aspect of your life. It is as though you have been shut off from the world somehow. There is a feeling of loss here and it is time for you to get back into the swing of life. You have built up barriers, which need to come down.

"I am being told that you are the mother of four children."

"I have three sons and a stepdaughter."

"I am told that you are her mother also, in a way ..."

"We are very close."

"I see something in connection with a university ..."

"She is studying for a degree."

"She will do very well indeed. She has strived for this and is quite driven. She will succeed. Your children are all very individual with their own particular strengths and gifts. Someone is getting married ..."

"Charlie, my middle son."

"Another will eat you out of house and home if you will let him!"

"Duncan is about to return home from university."

"One is the image of his father in looks and in manner ..."

"Alastair, my eldest son."

"You are the type of person who rushes around trying to do several things at once to fill the time and to avoid loneliness. Your husband always did several things at once and that was his mistake. You must learn to relax more! The holiday will help you to do this.

"Are you thinking of moving?"

"Only if I am forced to!"

"You won't have to but you may choose to, in order to allow other things to take off in your life. Have you any questions?"

"The court case in October?"

"Mmmm ... this is not really about the money; it is more to do with a principle and the making of a very important point. Your barrister is positive and you have a very good legal team around you. You are positive too. I do not feel anything negative at all regarding this. In fact, I think money will be coming from this situation.

"I see a lot of clearing towards the end of this year in every way as well as fresh starts regarding work, this situation and your relationships."

Journal entry: 22 June

Westfield was wonderful and I spent a great deal of time in the garden, which I find therapeutic. I also spent many hours with Gloria; she is excellent company. She had Pam Wellsman and her partner, James, staying for the weekend. We shared meals at Gloria's home on both Friday and Saturday evening.

I had no idea that James was a sceptic and we spent much of the time speaking of spiritual matters. I did notice that he asked me a lot of questions, which I answered as simply as I could. "Tell me, Patricia," he said, "what have you seen, heard and felt?"

So, I told him and followed it up by saying, "James, anyone can lie if they choose to. Anyone can lie to the world but not to his or herself! I *know* what has happened to me and this is what makes me strong. I am not trying to convince anyone else—that is not important to me. All that matters is my own knowledge and that I demonstrate that by the way I live my life. I was told a long time ago that I would be a catalyst. At the time I didn't even know what was meant by this but when I look back, I can see they were right! I seem to meet an enormous number of spiritual people and put them in touch with each other and others who seem to benefit from their knowledge."

Shortly afterwards, I received a text from Pam proving the above point. She wrote:

"It was so nice to see you and James really liked you. I was worried he would feel a bit lost with we three 'old souls' but he has truly opened his mind—a first! So, last weekend was a turning point for us. I owe it to you and Gloria, whom I would never have met

but for you. I feel so happy and know it is soon to return your way. Thank you!"

I felt as though I had been useful for once. It was reassuring too. It seems that I am walking the right path, which certainly seems to be that of a catalyst.

Reading: 29 June ~ Kelly

I visited Friday for help with a knee problem. While I was there he mentioned a medium he had spoken to and gave me her number. Her name was Kelly, from Essex.

Naturally, I followed the lead; after all, whenever I do this other people seem to benefit from these contacts too. It seems as though my role is to check things out and pass on information to others when they require it.

We spoke over the phone and Kelly followed up the reading with the tape sent through the post:

"You have felt emotionally upset recently or a bit run down? It seems as though you look strong and you are strong-minded but inside you are like jelly. What is the legal matter around you please?"

"A court case in October."

"We shall talk more about that later. Spirit is saying that you are going to be on a new path and you will see light at the end of the tunnel.

"I have a lady in spirit who wishes to be remembered to you, she is your mother's mother. She is saying that you look like your mother yet you are like your father. You have got to learn to calm down."

"True."

"Are you thinking about moving home, only this is on the cards? If you move it would serve a purpose, you would gain. You will find a property."

"I have one already."

"It is semi-rural, like a cottage, and you will be very happy. For the first time you will feel that you are doing the right thing.

"You have got to stop looking backwards and start looking forward. Your problem is feeling secure within yourself. You are

so open-hearted and generous; you are always looking at other people and seeing what you can give them. It is time for you to begin thinking what will someone give me? Do not be a doormat.

"The legal matter ... you know you are a winner and not a loser?"

"I pray so!"

"You don't have to pray, you are wasting your time, and your grandmother is saying, 'Don't be a fool, dear, you are going to win! You know they have told lies, big whopping lies, and they are going to trip themselves up.' Are you after compensation?"

"Yes."

"You will get that money. Whoever this person is, believe me they can afford to pay you but they don't want to. It is not the first time that they have done this type of thing and it won't be the last.

"Have you thought of living overseas?"

"No, but I spend time abroad."

"Your grandmother says that you are as British as they come and there is no place like home. You may holiday overseas but you will never consider it to be permanent.

"Did you not get to say goodbye to your husband?"

"No, he died suddenly without warning."

"He is saying he owes you an apology for that and wants to give it to you now, he is drawing near."

"An apology is unnecessary."

"Not to him, it isn't. He is saying he was often tired and moody because of pressure of work and he wants to get this off his chest. It is not always about you, Patricia, he needs to move on too.

"You need to write your husband a letter and get rid of all your feelings. He talks about you being deep; you keep a lot of things to yourself and you need to get these out of your system. Tell him everything, share it with him.

"You are very black and white and you have got to stop that. You come across as being rather abrupt. You have been holding on to heartache and grief for far too long and now you cannot see your way forward.

"They are saying you need to find you before you can move on. You are a really nice person but the shell needs to be broken for

people to see who you really are. You have very few close friends but hundreds of acquaintances and you need to sort them out. You know this and have begun to do this already."

"You are a winner, not a loser. When you go to court, they might say they want you to come back another day but don't worry, it is only because they want to dig further into it. Whatever it is you will come out on top so don't be negative. You have become so involved you cannot see your way forward but you are going to be totally fine.

"In work there is a new avenue that will be really good. It will be something where you have to learn new things but once you have started this work, you will never look behind again.

"Travel ... I see you somewhere hot and exotic, it will be a worldwide travel. Have you ever thought of travelling to the Far East or an Asian country? I can see you in Hong Kong! It is going to be good for you. [Kelly knew nothing about my life or China.] *There is an opportunity. It might be in China or Japan. It is all to do with your work; you are very creative. They are going to love you."*

Considering we had never spoken before, Kelly seemed to be pretty accurate!

*****

The pace was hotting-up with the court case. No matter how much these readings assisted at the time, in the small hours of the nights I was unable to sleep because fear was always so prevalent. I held the future of my family in my hands. All the hard work my husband had done to make our lives secure, I was fearful of wasting, by making wrong decisions and jeopardising it all. I prayed earnestly to guides, angels and, of course, The Source for help.

The poems are still flowing and I am beginning to believe in my work and myself. I have also had several emails from Jing in China, containing several of the illustrator, Mr Lio's drawings for me to check and respond to. I am delighted. At long last, I do believe this book is going to become a reality!

I am so grateful for this gift. I am totally enjoying it and all I want to do now is write and record this poetry. It is finally moving centre stage and I am grateful for this work that I love.

Reading: 4 July - Richard Peters

"You should be working for yourself; you have an inner drive. You are coming into a new time for yourself; your world is about to open up. It is as if you have had a six-/seven-year period of being in the shadow and now you are entering the sunshine.

"There is an end to a major event in your life and new beginnings for you—you will finally find yourself. Has anyone ever told you that you are a lady with a man's mind? You are; you know exactly what you want and will be driven to achieve it. You can hold your own in any situation.

"There is travel here for you, far travel, which will be good. Before the year is out there should be a trip to China and America is shown very strongly for you too.

"I see you, symbolically, being given a huge red bowl. This colour and symbol denotes wealth and good luck. I am being shown a red bowl with chopsticks and the bowl is flowing over with noodles. Energy, vibrancy and luck are being given to you. Your bowl is full and this is for you and you will make a living from writing.

"You will be healing using your voice, your creativity is strong and I see that you are coming off one very difficult road and are about to step onto one, which is much smoother. This will give you peace of mind.

"I see you with a job that gives you release and contentment. Look at this year as being beneficial to launch your career. America shows strongly here and is connected with legal paperwork; this could be in connection with your books. I see a quartet of books, poetry written about spring, summer, autumn and winter and these will be good for you. It is as though these are collections of books appertaining to the seasons.

"I can see you standing at a podium in front of an audience reciting what you have written. It is as though you have written coffee table books, which become 'must have' items. I see a series of books here. There is a lot more writing to be done and you must write when it flows. Don't try to write, do it when it flows.

"I do."

"With the court case, you should be positive; your solicitor is optimistic. This is a financial situation and I don't see you losing by it. Your husband was a very shrewd man. He thought he had tied everything up, he tried hard to do so and he did not expect this to happen.

"Who is Bill?"

"A nephew of my husband whose wedding I attended in Malaysia. He emailed me today."

"I think your husband is giving me this. There is a lawyer?"

"Bill is a lawyer."

"Your husband is around; he is telling you that he is present and trying to help you."

Chapter 38
Preparing for the Inevitable

Reading: 6 September 2005 - Richard Peters

*"You are coming into a time of change. New horizons are opening
for you. Travel plans are in your head at the moment and you are
trying to weave these into reality. I see far travel.*

*"Your husband was quiet in his own way, but behind this there
was strength and hidden depths. He held his own assurance.*

*"Are you having a book published? I think you will find there
is more than one book. I see cherry blossoms on a cover of a book
here. Definitely a spray of cherry blossoms and buds and I am being
told that the area where these are from is where your inspiration
comes from. I see you writing lyrics for music. It will all be very
soothing because you will enjoy the work and you will feel as if you
have really accomplished something.*

*"Are you considering moving to the coast, to Devon or Dorset?
If you do it will give you a lot of contentment. You like your own
company.* [Yes, but not all the time!] *"Your work will have a strong
impact and will be very healing. You are a good listener, you make
time for people and help to solve their problems. But you do cut to
the chase.*

*"Patricia, there is a whole band of indigenous people from
America and Canada who work with you. They are from numerous
tribes and nations—you also have something which is very rare, an
Eskimo guide. This is very special.*

*"On your spiritual side at present you are moving to a different
level of understanding. You have only tasted a fraction of what you
are capable of; you are just touching the tip. Your work will open up
and philosophy will form a large part of it all.*

"Why do you fear you will lose the court case? I see no loss here. I see you gaining in every way and it will make the whole of your life good once more. There is nothing to worry about and your own advocate is confident and optimistic."

Reading: Anita

I picked up a copy of the *Psychic News* and saw a number advertised for a lady called Anita who gives readings. I telephoned and it transpires that all the work she does is connected with a children's charity that she has set up: The International Child's Medical Aid. All her 'reading' money is channelled into this work. She is situated in South East London, close to Karen. The reading was given immediately. She only knew my first name and the fact that I was involved in a court case but no further details.

"The energies that are around you indicate that there is a situation that binds you in chains and you cannot escape. There is a lot of negativity around you, release it. Look after your own health then all will work out better for you.

"You are a giver and you have a lot to look forward to. After the dark cloud has shifted there will be brilliant new beginnings for you and success is near but just out of your grasp at present. Any judgement will be in your favour.

"Your father is here and he is surrounding you with shoes and saying, 'These shoes are made for walking.' Indeed, Patricia, you have a lot of travelling to do.

"You have three children and they are all very spiritual and will do well. You are to stop worrying about everyone and make more time for yourself.

"Your husband is here, he is a very smart man and very gentle. Much healing is being passed to you from him and this will give you the energy and security you need at this time.

"You need patience. Learn, study and gather information because all knowledge will eventually be put into words. You are a great healer with fantastic abilities.

"Your work will accelerate; success and prosperity will be there for you. Things will go forward. At the moment you feel as if your

hands are tied and you have a blindfold on. Trust in yourself more."

After the telephone reading, we had a long chat and I feel that I am meant to introduce Karen to Anita for some reason. We have agreed that, when it is easier for me, we will meet for lunch, together with Karen.

Journal entry: 9 September

Recently life has been extremely difficult. I have had to give up my three weeks in Devon because my poor, sweet mother has been in hospital. I don't begrudge her this time but I missed being at Westfield. I have had to fight a battle with the NHS and I have been travelling backwards and forwards between Kent and Surrey. My mother is now suffering with depression and it has been emotionally and physically exhausting for all of us.

Reading: Pamela Wellsman

"You have a very long lifeline. Spirit obviously has a purpose for you. They are encouraging you to think deeply and produce good works of art.

"Most creative people are traumatised and emotionally disturbed from time to time because of events which involve them and the problems of other people. Things come out when you are deep in thought. It happens when you get very low. All sorts of information will come into your head. It is spirit's trick to get you to produce something that will be of advantage to other people and get you well known in order to help others, in the world generally.

"Your emotional status is high at the moment; your heart line is heightened more than any other area of your life. You are uncertain about a lot of things that have not come to fruition. Success is going to happen for you, you will achieve your aims.

"Spirit is saying that there is a Peter who is linked to your opportunity to feel more secure and his comments will be instrumental in this. You have many fears which are ungrounded. Success is here in connection with your feelings, plans and actions. You are going to achieve your aims. It is not far off.

"You are learning about grief, about life and understanding of men. You are getting your head around a lot of things. You are financially secure even though you are worried about money.

"Your brother-in-law is trying his hardest to achieve something here and he is interfering to some extent. Spirit is doubly taking an interest in his influences over you and there is nothing here to show he has success at all.

"From closure comes fortune for you in every way, not just money but peace of mind also. This is about timing and it's nearly over. You have felt robbed of late but there is good news coming in the form of an official document, which is favourable.

"Hope is being restored in the area where you have constantly been pursuing something with a principle if nothing else. It is certainly where you have been pursuing something of a spiritual nature.

"Hope is being restored where men have been a problem to you. The constancy card here shows the spirits are supporting you ... it is very important ... dreams will be realised."

Reading: Melissa

Because of the enormity of the pressure, I eventually managed to escape to Devon to study the court papers. It was a huge relief and I took my studies seriously. I cut myself off from everything and everyone and applied myself to reading the disclosure files. It was an enormous task as there were many but I was determined to do the best job I possibly could. Our family's future was at stake.

I arranged to see a local medium whom I had never met before. There was no discussion and all Melissa knew about me was my Christian name.

"There are forces at work that are trying to break you, forces that need to be controlled by you. Once October has passed you will certainly be able to move on, but the way you move on will be important.

"Whatever you feel in your heart, you must do. This advice comes from a person in spirit. You will achieve what you want from your own strength and determination. The strength you have within

will be boosted when you really need it.

"*I am assured by your husband in spirit that he will be with you on the days you attend court. Your peace and good health is paramount to him.*

"*You have a brother-in-law who is a stubborn man, hardened by his career. He sees you as a woman who will never be able to achieve victory alone. With him it seems to be a question of male superiority.*

"*You are coming to an end of something now. Your family understand fully that you must see this through to the end. Ignore anyone else's opinion; your energies must be concentrated on yourself.*

"*These next few weeks will be crucial; you need to build yourself up. Reiki would be beneficial, see if you can find someone who can do this. Your grief is still raw, only you can heal this by turning it around to a warm feeling of 'remembrance'. Tears are beneficial for releasing but too many of them become damaging. Your problems are numerous. I would go as far as to say they are too much for one person to carry but you will overcome all that is happening.*

"*You feel alone in all of this, in fact, you have felt alone for a very long time but there are those with you who have kept you going and they will not fail you. I am obviously talking about spirit; those you cannot see, but they are there, and you will get through this.*

"*You also concentrate a lot of your energy on other people. For a while this must stop until you can afford to give your own energies out again, but that time is not now. It is easy to say that we all go through problems in life, some more horrific than others. There is always a reason for our challenges. The harder the lessons, the more important is the work that we must do.*

"*You will move to Devon and your whole life will change. There is work for you to do. You will meet the right people who will help you along. The benefits you have will make you comfortable and happy. You will not have to worry about working and you will be able to follow whatever work is laid down in front of you.*

"*Your brother-in-law situation can only be resolved by you. Show the strength that you have within you but, firstly, believe in yourself. Believe you can live the way that you choose and then nothing will stop you.*

"Remember, spirit is more powerful than any earthly power and they are on your side. Use them and their advice."

*****

When I was satisfied with my revision of the court papers I invited a couple from the Dorking Awareness Centre to join me for dinner at Westfield. They had recently returned to live in Devon. It was pleasurable and enormously helpful as they had both had experience of attending courts at different times. They seemed optimistic on my behalf and I felt reassured.

As suggested, I organised Reiki with Pauline the week before court and found it calming. I travelled to Kent to see my dear mother who, despite being unwell, was always welcoming. I felt treasured, enveloped in love, in her company. I shall never forget that feeling. Whenever I walked into a room where she was, her eyes lit up, making me feel so special. I feel privileged to have had two such wonderful parents.

My mother had also organised Reiki for me for that Saturday afternoon, with Lisa, a healer who had previously helped my mother. Her healing was strong and I instantly felt the benefit. I asked her who her contacts were in Kent, as I have so few but am interested in meeting more like-minded people. She said that the first person she met was Terry Tasker. I replied, "That's amazing; I am having a reading from him later this evening!"

I had telephoned Terry earlier that same day and he could obviously hear how anxious I was as he kindly agreed to do an urgent reading for me that evening.

Reading: Terry Tasker

"I am being shown a briefcase full of documents and told that your barrister has very good vibes about this. Someone in this situation is trying to get as much out of you as he can. If he had been more flexible and come to a mutual agreement earlier, then this would

have been over long ago.

"Your father in spirit is showing me some plans; tell me, Patricia, if it went your way are you considering doing an extension?"

"Yes, I hope to."

"Your father is viewing the plans and he is giving them a large 'tick'. You will be able to.

"Your husband is confused and perplexed with his brother and he is saying he is sorry there is no formal document that states a proper agreement. He is trying to help you to keep calm and will be there on the day to help you with clear thoughts.

"I am being told this is going to take place in London. There is a solid case on your behalf. There is somebody in this situation who is not telling the truth. I think the untruths will be discovered and this will upset the judge.

"I hope so!"

"Would you know a Fred?"

"My late father."

"He wants you to know that he is helping. Your father is showing me a safe with documents inside it, which are appropriate for use in the court case." [Just that morning I had placed some original documents in our safe to take to the solicitor on Monday next.]

"I feel that the opposition has an unpleasant personality and when these proceedings are taking place he will have a job to control himself. It will not be good for him." [I have insisted upon a lady barrister!]

"Patricia, spirit is proving to you that they know what is going on in your life at this time.

"Remember to wear your wedding ring—much support and healing is passed through this to you from your husband."

"I always do," I said.

*****

I returned to Surrey late Sunday morning. I worked most of the day in the solicitors on Monday, 3 October, but we learned, during the course of the day, that I would not be required in London until later that week. The judge who had been appointed, naturally, needed time to 'read in'.

I delayed setting off for another day. On Tuesday I packed and arrived in London, where I had arranged to stay with Linda for the duration of the hearing.

Journal: Wednesday, 5 October

To my amazement, I received a call on my mobile from Anita with whom I'd had a telephone reading only a few weeks earlier. We have never actually met! I was delighted to hear from her.

She said, *"Patricia, I have an urgent message from the spirit world, which they have asked me to pass on to you. 'All will be well. Do not keep deep thinking about the situation. The universe is aware of the work that you do in its name. It will not let you down!'"*

Anita went on to say that she has lit candles in her shop for us and our situation. She has placed me and my situation in every healing book that she knows of and has asked all the healers she knows to pray for me for the duration.

I was overjoyed that a woman whom I have not even met could be so kind and offer such reassurance and comfort to me. Clearly, this shows the mysterious way that spirit works!

I spent the entire day alone at Linda's, working on papers, studying hard, but greatly heartened. During the evening, I had a call from Karen, which cheered me enormously.

She said, *"Remember, as soon as you have Ian in court, as soon as you have stepped through the door, you have completed the journey that you were required to take. No matter what happens when you are in there, you have taken the steps you needed to take and brought the journey to its conclusion."*

Chapter 39
Irvine v Irvine (2006)

Court: Thursday, 6 October 2005

Thursday morning dawned. Surprisingly, I had slept well. Normally, I find London too light and far too noisy but I believe I was being helped by the good company I had in Linda and a power far greater than my own understanding. I badly needed to be refreshed and capable of facing whatever lay ahead.

I left early and took a taxi to the court. I walked to the Thames and made a few calls. Returning through Temple Gardens I stepped inside the RAF church of St. Clément Danes in The Strand. I noticed an old building with a stone-carved sign advertising 'cigars'. (Malcolm enjoyed a cigar!)

The courier who delivered the court documents was called 'Malcolm'!

Spirit was certainly trying to reassure me.

Court: Thursday, 6 October 2005

The judge arrived and various papers were distributed. My team consisted of the barrister, the main litigator, his excellent assistant and a solicitor's clerk from the dispute department of a Surrey firm of solicitors. I had learned much earlier that they were delighted with the choice of judge, who is reputed to be an experienced and fair-minded man who takes his job very seriously.

He had read the skeletal arguments previously but chose to be guided through the chronology of documents which were prepared. This was good news but an anticipated lengthy exercise.

I preferred to sit beside the solicitors. After all, I had worked long and hard on this case and I wanted to do anything possible to assist. All day the chronology was explored and there was virtual silence from the defence. There was little to dispute, the papers are factual. The costs I knew would escalate and this frightened me. I ignored my brother-in-law and simply concentrated on the task.

At the end of the day we returned to chambers to take stock and regroup. Exhausted, I returned to Linda's Fulham home.

Court: Friday, 7 October

I caught a taxi from Wandsworth Bridge Road. I asked the driver where he came from. "Crawley," he replied. He passed through Betchworth daily and had noticed our house with the red telephone box outside.

Earlier, I had spoken with my friend, Carol O. I'd felt wretched with anticipation at the time. As I stepped out of the taxi she called me back with the following message from her astrologer friend.

'She'll fret because her Mars in Virgo is the material, worrying kind. It doesn't ultimately rule her or she'd never have entered this fray. The fight was heroic, typically Arian. Her sun will serve her now. No other sign has such recuperative, regenerative powers as Aries. Tell her she will be able to cope. She has immense mental and emotional resources to use to recover from this. She is strong, even if defeated she, personally, is essentially undefeatable.

Losing only really happens when she fails to cope with the consequences of the fight. She must cope, as that's what her husband would want most of all. She should not let this bring her down, her self-respect will not allow this in the long run, however vulnerable she feels right now. Considerable courage, that has taken her this far, will help her to recover her balance and spirit. They won't rob her of those.'

I was grateful for this message of encouragement.

I walked from the Thames towards court and drank a coffee standing in the street like other city suits. I entered the RAF church and sat, giving thanks for the message received and to collect my thoughts. I noticed that the pew behind me was named after the family 'Slessor'. My house at school had been 'Mary Slessor' house. Opposite was a pew, named 'Newall', the surname of my sister's partner and son. All these synchronicities helped. I accepted them gladly as signs from spirit. They were with me and pointing out such synchronicities to strengthen my resolve. I acknowledged the help.

Once more the day was dedicated to the prepared chronological document presentation and again the defence rarely raised a point. Many issues about minutes and incorrect company procedure were mentioned.

These days spent going through the documentation were enormously helpful to me as a form of further revision of the facts, and dissipated much of the confusion which can arise from so many papers. I am glad that I have resolved to be so 'hands on'. My husband and father would expect no more, and absolutely no less, of me!

Journal entry: Saturday, 8 October

I returned to Surrey for the weekend. Malcolm's youngest brother was living with us following his return from abroad. He was job hunting at that time and using Mulberry Down as his base. It was telling that he had chosen to return to Malcolm's home, not Ian's. A friend joined us for a meal in Reigate. I kept the mobile with me and halfway through I went outside and telephoned Dilys Guildford, desperate for encouragement.

She said, *"You will not lose Westfield, so stop worrying."*

This gave me heart to carry on.

I also spoke briefly with Richard Peters. He told me the following:

"Be confident and do not look on the negative side. You should already have noticed all the things that have been put in place to help it to go your way. Just believe in yourself."

I was comforted because Richard had voiced what I felt in my heart to be true. I know that I chase too much for reassurance but I need it. I am permanently frightened. It's not only my future at stake but that of my sons.

Court: Monday, 10 October

The opening submissions continued but the lengthy process was worthwhile as far as I was concerned. I was determined to be present in court daily and to listen to every word spoken.

The three main points in *Irvine v Irvine* were the issue of excessive and unreasonable remuneration paid to Ian; his failure to pay adequate dividends, honouring the historical three-sevenths, four-sevenths split of the profits to Malcolm's beneficiaries; and the procedural irregularities of the company.

I could not accept that the remuneration paid to my brother-in-law since the death of Malcolm, and the lack of dividends paid to us, was fair and reasonable. On the contrary, I considered it to be excessive, unjustified and unfair.

I considered that the amount of money my sons and I had received since Malcolm's death, for his forty-nine per cent of the thriving family business, to be inadequate, bearing in mind the excessive remuneration Ian had paid to himself. The one 'golden' share was left by Malcolm to his brother in his Will, so that Ian could continue to run the business unfettered, for the benefit of all, not to use as a weapon against his brother's family.

My team's opinion was that he should have taken a just and fair salary for the heavy workload he carried, and then correctly and fairly divide the balance of profits between the shareholders in the historical way of three-sevenths to Malcolm's family and four-sevenths to Ian. However, Ian alone decided the amount of remuneration he would pay to the trust and me, then proceeded to take the majority of the profits of the company for himself. This act failed to acknowledge, in any way at all, the tremendous contribution my husband had made to the building of the highly successful company.

I had been jet-propelled from being a wife and mother, caring for children and the family homes, into a role whereby I was required to cope with being both the mother and a father figure to my three young sons. I had also to try and understand the complicated family finances, previously always dealt with by Malcolm. I tried hard to find out what my duties were regarding the company and the children's trust but was greatly disadvantaged.

I struggled to receive clear direction from those placed by Malcolm to protect us in the event of his death. Malcolm had been confident that we would be looked after fairly, but this did not prove to be the case.

By my own failure to understand, and by my not having received copies of detailed profit and loss accounts, I was denied the opportunity to discover how the company profit and loss worked. I did not know the expenses, how they were incurred, or how they were broken down. I lost the opportunity, even with the help of enlisted loyal and concerned friends, to raise queries and concerns on the accounts.

My position as a director of, and representative of, just under fifty per cent of the shares of the company was not acknowledged. My initial confidence in those I should have been able to trust (and who Malcolm had instructed to care for his wife and sons) was entirely destroyed. It was clear that the only one holding the reins was my brother-in-law. Any reasonable enquiries made of Ian, regarding perceived discrepancies, produced a frighteningly furious response from him.

He was a man's man, then a colonel in the TA, and I admit, shamefacedly, to becoming increasingly more frightened of him. I knew that he was a man who did not like to be crossed and I was acutely aware that he held our future in his hands. It was with reluctance that we deemed it necessary to bring the matter to court in an attempt to find justice and resolution.

Malcolm and his brother were opposites, rarely meeting socially but their combined personalities and work contributions produced a successful family company. When Malcolm was alive to protect us, life was a joy. Similarly, for all those who knew him, for he touched many lives. But everything changed on the day that he passed.

Court: Monday, 17 October

I was the first witness to be called. There was, at one point, a discussion regarding the 'waiver of privilege', which outraged my barrister at the time and caused quite a lot of consternation. I wouldn't pretend to understand the technical legalities but I noted my barrister's opinion. She clearly felt that it was an outrageous thing to do while I was in the witness box. After days of everyone reading through the documents, for this point to be sprung at such a late hour she felt was not at all in the spirit of procedural rules.

Time marched on and at 4.15 p.m. the judge rose. Before doing so he spoke directly to me: "Mrs Irvine, I give you the warning or advice that I give to all witnesses when in the witness box which is that, until you finish your evidence, you are not to discuss it with anyone."

I replied that I fully understood as this had been explained to me.

Court: Wednesday, 19 October

My next day in the witness box was confusing to say the least. Questions were asked about events which took place long ago and, although I had done my homework as thoroughly as I could, I still felt very lacking when questioned. I was conscious that I was under oath and terrified of making a mistake.

I realised, of course, that it was the job of the QC for the defendant, to wear me down and confuse me. As the questions continued I felt very silly when I had to keep repeating that I couldn't recall various intricacies of meetings. I emphasised that this did not mean they had not occurred, it simply meant that I couldn't recall them. As the day progressed I felt increasingly more vulnerable, foolish and angry with myself.

As I listened to the questions, I realised that I should have personally taken more responsibility much earlier on when it came to my children's trust and my own shares. I had allowed grief and fear to dominate me and had wrongly relied upon being 'looked after' by those trusted by Malcolm, but virtually unknown to me. I felt an ignorant, foolish woman who should have taken a great deal more notice than she had done. My confidence plummeted.

At one time, exasperated, I remember responding, "I do not have a legal mind or an accountant's mind but I do have one. I could, had

I been encouraged to, have become involved [in the family business] without question!"

There was another moment when the QC had the audacity to suggest that I had been frightened by my husband. My response was to look directly at the judge and reply, "My Lord, it is clear that this gentleman has never had the honour of meeting my husband."

At the end, we retired to chambers to discuss the day and prepare for the next. That evening, I was relieved to climb into a taxi and return to Fulham where, although I was unable to discuss any of the details, I could relax and enjoy a meal in Linda's company, in the comfort and safety of her home.

Court: Thursday, 20 October

It was another long, hard day. The defence was trying to establish how much of my witness statement was from my own recollection and how much had been reconstructed from papers. This was very difficult and arduous; after all, I had worked long and hard with the solicitors on the paperwork at every opportunity. Not understanding the difference between 'submissions' and a witness statement, it was all very confusing. I assumed that the truth was simply that, *the truth,* whether written or spoken, read or heard.

Worse was the feeling that I had willingly worked very hard to assist with the case but now, in the witness box, I was beginning to feel as if I had done something wrong. For example, luckily I was one of those 'sentimental' women who kept hold of her husband's diaries, when most might consider it pointless.

With Linda's help (she had worked for Malcolm for twenty-five years), I had taken my laptop into the solicitor's office where together we worked on these. We were able to glean useful details of the innumerable meetings Malcolm had attended through the years. This exercise helped me to easily prove what I already knew, Malcolm's major role as 'Mr Travel' of CIL, as he was known by many at Lloyds of London at the time. This was an important fact which his brother was disputing in his argument.

On another occasion, my solicitors and I had travelled to the company accountants in Oxfordshire, to study CIL's company files there. At the time I was still a director and had every right to see the files, read them and glean any useful information required to establish and confirm my husband's major input into the success of the company. The date was 30 October, a fact I remember well, for it was Malcolm's birthday. All was arranged, the defendant's solicitors were also informed. They decided to do the same exercise later that afternoon.

We arrived and began work in earnest, requesting copies of numerous papers. At one point the accountant came into the office we had been allocated, telling us that the other 'side' were arriving shortly and he looked askance at the number of documents we had copied and mumbled something about 'the others may not agree'.

My intuition is strong. Knowing that I had a perfect right to the papers, I quickly decided to place all the documents we had copied thus far into my briefcase and take them to my car before anyone could interfere. I had an uncanny feeling that we were going to be stopped. I had no wish to find that my solicitors and I had travelled to Oxford at my great expense, spent hours doing this work, only to be stopped at the last minute.

I asked my solicitors to continue their work and left the office. I had no qualms at all about calmly gathering up my briefcase and walking out of the premises to my car. I emptied the papers from my briefcase, placing them beneath the driver's floor mat out of sight, and then returned to continue the task.

While I was gone, my intuition had become a reality. A call had been made to Ian as the company chairman, to inform him of the wealth of copies we were taking. Ian was out so the accountants had left a message with his office. Clearly, they were concerned that Ian might be uncomfortable with the number of papers being copied. They were still waiting for his direction and were expecting a refusal of cooperation imminently.

As a legitimate director and entitled to do so, I asked my solicitors to hand to me all further copies taken and I placed them in my briefcase. All originals were returned. The accountants were still awaiting Ian's call. As chairman, he would have the final say. I guessed that a forewarned Ian would refuse continued cooperation and we expected someone to enter the room at any time demanding the papers to be returned. I decided to beat them to it and suggested to my team that we leave immediately, with all copies safely inside my briefcase. I carried the papers. I was entitled to them. We collected our belongings, handed in our visitors' badges, said goodbye to those present and walked out of the door, with me leading the way.

Earlier, on my first trip to my car, I had noticed an Italian restaurant nearby. Realising that we all needed lunch, I asked the solicitors to follow me and walked swiftly in the direction of the restaurant. When we were all seated, I said, "You are not aware of this but today is most definitely a call for celebration. Finding all those useful papers, clearly it is our day. It is also Malcolm's birthday and *he* would like to buy you lunch!"

That was a good day.

*****

Back in the witness box it was less so and, at times, I was struggling.

At one point the judge explained that, in the old days, a witness would go into the witness box and speak from his or her own recollection. The court's task now was to try to ascertain to what extent the reading of the disclosure files was genuinely the recollection of the witness and to what extent it had come from reconstruction. He would then decide how much weight to put upon a remark about something. I found it very difficult to understand why it actually mattered.

So I said, "My Lord, may I ask a question? I have never been in a court before but I have worked hard on this case. What I do not understand is just because I have found useful papers it does not stop what I say from being a fact. I am not lying in my witness statement."

The judge responded kindly, explaining that nobody was blaming me but that they needed to know which parts of my witness statement were my own definite recollection and which parts derived from the reading of documents; what parts I had witnessed and what parts I knew because somebody had told me.

I replied, "Yes, my Lord. But if I have read things, it does not necessarily make them untrue. If I have read a letter from my husband to the accountant and included that in my statement, it does not make it untrue because he did not discuss it with me at the time."

He replied that it didn't make it true either, which flummoxed me. I pointed out that the letter was surely a tangible fact? But I didn't want to push the point further. I began to feel even more ignorant than before. The judge emphasised that I should not worry any more about it but simply answer counsel's questions as to whether the points made were my own recollection or reconstruction.

And so it ground on, with me feeling grateful for the explanations but still concerned that I had committed some awful error.

We returned to chambers. I felt as though I had let the team down, although they gave no indication of this. I guess I was simply beginning to feel the strain.

That night in the taxi I realised that tears were pouring from my eyes. I felt totally drained and was grateful to be returning to Linda's home. My sanctuary!

Court: Friday, 21 October

I was in the routine of catching a taxi near Wandsworth Bridge Road and asking the drivers to go along the Embankment before spurring off towards The Strand. Being near the water, the space of the Thames and the large sky comforted me. It became a habit, after my morning coffee, to go and sit in St. Clément Danes in The Strand to pray for help and guidance.

It was another gruelling day in the witness box. Question after question, repeated and represented in different guises and, behind it all, the knowledge that the QC opposing me simply wanted to make me look a complete fool so that my evidence would be rendered useless. Asked why I was fearful at one point in time my reply was, "Because it was yet another area that I was being rocketed into, that I did not understand and, frankly, since 1996 I had had plenty of that!"

I believe my voice may have broken, for the judge asked me if I'd like him to rise for a moment or two.

I replied hastily, "I am sorry, no, I am fine. Thank you." I did not wish to appear both foolish and weak. So we ploughed onward.

There was then another drawn-out discussion in respect of waiver of privilege, regarding certain documents which had been raised previously. This recent, late 'ambush' had caused a feeling of consternation at the time and had involved a great deal of additional work for my team. I won't pretend to understand quite what this entailed but the extra work, I knew, would be an uphill struggle. Fortunately, the judge was not sitting with our case on the Tuesday, which allowed a day's grace for my barrister to attend to this.

At the end of another very long day and a session at chambers, I hailed a taxi and sped back along the Embankment to Fulham. I was relieved to shut Linda's door behind me, closing out the world. I collapsed into a heap.

As the cross-examination had not finished and my time in the witness box was to be extended, despite an earlier indication by the judge that I had been in there far too long, I still couldn't discuss the case with anyone, including Linda and my mother.

It was going to be a long, lonely weekend. We took refuge at my mother's home, but I kept my word to the judge. In fact, it was a relief to think about other things.

Court: Monday, 24 October

It was another arduous morning in the witness box and I was relieved to finally hear the words, "Thank you, Mrs Irvine, you have been quite long enough in the witness box and I am not going to put any questions to you. Thank you very much for your evidence."

During the next two days other witnesses were called, including Alastair and Duncan. The cross-examination was shorter than expected, so the judge rose early at 3.30 p.m. on the Tuesday. While arguments regarding reducing the need for specific witnesses continued behind the scenes, I was pleased to be able to take an earlier taxi to my refuge that day.

Charlie was a very short time in the witness box the next day because some of the argument had been withdrawn from both sides. I was pleased for him. I had not enjoyed seeing my sons in the position of being questioned in court at all.

I was pleased, however, when it was the turn of the professionals to be called. Because I was so aware of my own ignorance and shortcomings, I was relieved to see how they could reply calmly, truthfully, emphatically and more importantly, *knowledgeably,* when pressured.

Court: Thursday, 27 October

Peter Darby's evidence began yesterday and continued this day. He was a fabulous example of a true and competent friend. The amount of work he has expended over the years in the direction of this case, without any request for payment whatsoever, is exemplary.

While in the witness box, in his calm quiet manner, the replies he gave pretty much summed up the position my sons and I had found ourselves in. In reply to one question he intimated that whenever Ian does not get what he wants, he tends to be incensed. He further explained he had personally experienced, on two occasions, Ian's reaction to somebody who did not do what he wanted.

Peter's experience was that, as our previous attempts at conversation with Ian had not produced any kind of sensible response other than, 'This is what I want and this is what I am going to have,' if there was going to be any accommodation, it was going to be once we had drawn Ian's attention to the seriousness of the problem, by means of a solicitor's letter. He felt that, if people are absolutely adamant that they are right and not listening to anybody else's point of view, "One has to put a shot across their bows to make them listen."

He explained that the trust and I were not prepared to be bullied any further. Bully-boy tactics had been deployed previously, with Ian stating, "Either you accept seventy/thirty or it is eighty/twenty—or nothing!" There was a fair amount of pressure being applied to cave in and do as Ian wished, which had needed to be addressed.

Various witnesses were called, but it wasn't until later on the Thursday that Ian finally took the stand. From my position on the bench, alongside the solicitors immediately behind my barrister, I listened intently to every word spoken.

For me this was an emotional roller coaster but I was absolutely determined that I would remain calm and as 'professional' as I was capable of being. I was grateful that I was allowed to sit with the solicitors rather than alone. We sat, collectively, behind the bank of disclosed document bundles and I found that I could, in fact, be of use even if it was only to locate and pass selected bundles to them when required.

If, occasionally, my eyes began to well with frustration or nostalgia, I simply looked away until it had subsided. At all other times my focus remained on the judge. I did not wish to look into the eyes of my brother-in-law.

I also had a notebook and pen active so that when I heard something which I felt needed to be contested, I noted it down. However, my solicitors and barrister were all 'red hot' when it came to documentation and recall but it made me feel better. It made me feel useful. Ever conscious that it was my ignorance which was partially to blame for this situation, I wanted to be occupied and involved.

It was an afternoon of brilliant cross-examination by my barrister and it was a real education to listen and watch my team of solicitors working as one with her. There were also many lengthy answers from Ian, which were an education of an entirely different kind!

*****

The following day, Friday, my barrister's cross-examination continued. Her words were ringing around the courtroom, indicating that if I towed the line, did as I was told and fell into line regarding plans that Ian had for the company—it was clear that only then was he prepared to pay me a bonus.

In connection with a letter sent to him by my solicitors, notice was drawn to the fact that, because he was livid and incensed, he allowed that to influence how he would distribute the profit from the company. She pointed out that I had been punished for having the temerity for taking him on which influenced his decision to pay no company bonus to me in 1999.

I remember thinking, *Spot on! Spot on!* This was my experience of the man exactly ... just as my mother-in-law had once said to me, "Be warned, Patricia, it's always Ian first, Ian second and Ian last of all."

My barrister was clear, calm, concise and in total control. How glad I was to have insisted upon retaining this particular female barrister and not been persuaded to use a male QC! She was, quite frankly, magnificent. It was electrifying.

The usual debriefing and discussion in chambers followed before a taxi was called. The solicitors and I shared it as far as their station. During the journey I was surprised but relieved when the main litigator said to me, "Patricia, I owe you an apology. I was wrong when I suggested that we might need to find a QC, so that we were in step with Ian's team. I know this unsettled you. We even offered you details of three male QC's who were available. But you would not move, would you? You remained adamant that, unless it was a lady QC, you were not interested and that you would prefer to stay with the chosen barrister anyway. You ignored our advice on this occasion. Well, you were right. I have never seen anyone more committed to a case than this particular lady is to this one. I apologise for putting you through that."

"Thank you," I replied, "I was concerned at the time. Going against your advice was not something I wished to do—but my intuition was very strong and I decided to listen to it."

He smiled, "I think we both know, Patricia, that we are having a great deal of 'help' from an unknown source and have done so for some considerable time now."

They left the taxi at their station and, unlike too many other nights, no silent tears coursed down my face while I travelled back to Fulham. Instead, I felt elated.

Chapter 40
Malcolm Campbell Irvine: The Last Word

Court: Tuesday, 1 November 2005

We had a shock this morning. When we arrived in court we were met with the news that Ian (although present) was unwell and they were hoping for an adjournment. It had been made clear earlier in the proceedings that he had a bad back and, on one occasion, he asked the judge if he could stand while giving evidence.

We were now told that a knee operation, which had initially been scheduled for this day, had been rescheduled for 29 November to avoid him having to give evidence while under the effects of anaesthetic. His knee was now troubling him as well as his back and so his QC was requesting an adjournment.

There was further discussion, explanation and apologies, of course. Then the judge spoke directly to Ian, asking about his condition. Ian explained that he had been using strong painkillers and anti-inflammatory tablets—perhaps unwisely—and that during cross-examination the previous afternoon he was totally confused and had lost his concentration.

The judge accepted that if Ian was not feeling well it would not be right to continue, but said that he wished Ian's evidence to be completed as soon as possible, as it was in everyone's interest to do so. The judge asked if Ian intended seeing his doctor and Ian said that he would. He said that Ian should make it clear to his doctor that it is the judge's very firm wish to continue if possible and he should prescribe accordingly. The judge also required something from the doctor to explain the position, saying that he would like it in some detail rather than just a scrawled sentence or two, in the way some doctors tend to do.

My barrister spoke to the judge indicating that she was concerned that she would be required to revisit all the previous afternoon's cross-examination. But the judge made it clear that he had his own impression of the evidence and the firmness with which it was given. He said that, even though there were one or two places where Ian had seemed confused, particularly about the letter of June 1999 and a specific meeting, the judge did not suggest that it would be necessary to go over it all again.

I believe we all had our own opinions of the events of that morning. I certainly did.

Court: Wednesday, 2 November

Apologies were made for Ian's absence. I confess to having a vision of my brother-in-law, 'swotting' franticly over the disclosure files which he had undoubtedly been given previously but perhaps not studied quite so well as he might have done. This could, of course, possibly have accounted for some of his 'confusion'.

Cross-examination continued all day of other witnesses. It was a gruelling time but important points were made and noted. It was hard for me, listening to all this. My emotions were in turmoil. The one person I wanted to discuss it all with, Malcolm, was no longer directly able to do so.

In the taxi that night I had several calls from spiritual friends; some with messages; others simply offering me their support. Once again tears rolled silently down my face and I am thankful that it was a different taxi driver each night. All I wanted to do was collapse in Linda's lounge, have a decent meal, a glass of wine and some friendly company.

Court: Thursday, 3 November

I felt particularly bleak this morning, whether it was because Ian was expected in the witness box again, I don't know, but I felt desolate. Once through security, I sat waiting for the others to arrive and, while I did so, the following words came to me, which I hastily wrote down:

In the Royal Courts of Justice

Black city suits and sombre faces
Are putting clients through their paces
Stained glass and grey stone set the stage
Absorbing pain from every age
Mosaic tiles and ancient splendour
Greet those, whose paths now bid them enter
Cold marble, stone and coloured glass
Record poignant times, present and past
And here sit I ... silent and alone
My back pressed against the cold, grey stone
Prayers nestle deep within my heart
While waiting for the day to start
"Lord, hold fast my hand and comfort me
Please, help me be the finest I can be."

Ian resumed his position in the witness box after lunch. There were a lot of questions. In particular, clarifications about a meeting I had attended and a letter I was supposed to have received yet had not. Also, the fact that profits had always been split four-sevenths, three-sevenths between Malcolm and his brother's shareholdings respectively but, after Malcolm died, this had been abandoned.

At one stage it was pointed out to Ian that he was giving a different account from that of the previous Monday's evidence. A little later, my barrister said that she would be inviting 'his Lordship' to find that my recollection of a specific meeting was the correct one and that Ian's was flawed. Equally, that Ian's recollection of his failing to give me an important letter, resulting in my not being able to see what profits he had taken from the company and further, a suggestion by the accountant of a future fairer division of such profits.

My barrister pointed out that Ian's method of running CIL was to keep everyone in the dark, say nothing, and decide at his own exclusive discretion what he personally would take out by way of a bonus. She continued that it appeared Ian had decided such things without any proper exercise of his fiduciary duty and, once he was locked in a dispute with me, he had clearly decided not to give any profit to the trust or me at all.

My barrister continued, pointing out that there was no 'special formula' as intimated by Ian, but that the company accountant was simply doing his bidding and that all the money, except what was required to stay in the company for financial services, was paid out substantially to him as a bonus. She offered to go through the accounts one by one if he thought it necessary.

Court: Friday, 4 November

Ian returned to the witness box. My barrister continued in her own inimitable way ... pointing to fact after fact and suggesting that Ian had his wires crossed when it came to the facts and figures, in particular the four-sevenths, three-sevenths agreement between the two brothers. This had clearly died with Malcolm, even though Malcolm's family were entitled for it to continue as forty-nine per cent shareholders. Ian simply made payments at his own discretion.

One year a figure was paid to my sons and me in respect of the company profits and simultaneously Ian paid himself the same amount multiplied by 9.37. That year the 'golden share' left to him by Malcolm enabled him to pay himself a dividend in excess of £900,000.00. (I have the exact figures, they are undisputed.) It was pointed out to Ian that it appeared from the paperwork that he was only 'happy to pay dividends' to us, if they were of a token nature, as he stripped out the majority of the profit by way of his bonus.

My barrister explained to Ian that he was not entitled to simply withdraw the entirety of the profit for himself. She condemned him for not heeding his position within the company and for abusing it instead. She made it clear that dominating and controlling the company with no opportunity for directors to question his judgement on financial issues was the very reason we were in the courtroom that day.

The argument ground on and it resulted in Ian being required to remain under oath for another weekend and to return to the witness box the following Monday.

I was very happy that the weekend had arrived and took solace in the fact that I could return to my mother's home. Now that I was no longer in the box, I could discuss the case with her as much as I desired. What a huge relief that was!

Court: Monday, 7 November

Ian was back in the witness box and, again, my barrister was thorough in her cross-examination. Her own and the solicitor's joint knowledge of the minutia contained in the bank of files before us was exemplary. Point after point was made and driven home, though always politely, always precisely and always effectively, it seemed to me. I was very relieved that my intuition about choosing this lady was proving to be so sound.

There was much argument about a potential sale of the company and the fact that details were kept from both me and my advisors. My barrister pointed out, again, that Ian was hopelessly confused when arguing the point about a particular telephone call, the details of which he had changed in his second witness statement. He had intimated that a telephone call had taken place between him, Peter and myself insisting that we had agreed certain details which neither Peter Darby nor I could recall.

My barrister also made clear to Ian that, should he wish to sell CIL, he would need the consent of both me and the trust and that he could not simply railroad us into a deal if we did not agree. This continued until the end of the day.

As the taxi finally trundled along the Embankment, I gazed out of the window, lost in the day's proceedings. My phone rang and it was Dilys offering support. I was exhausted. I had no idea that I would feel so drained at the end of each day.

I reached Linda's home and stepped inside, grateful to be somewhere which felt 'safe'. We had a glass of wine and another of her exemplary meals and we sat and mused over the day. At least I could now discuss the case.

Each night I spoke to my beloved mother and, occasionally, to my sons who were back at home. I didn't want to burden them too much. Often a friend would ring with messages of encouragement and reassurance. I counted myself lucky to have all this support. It kept me calm, balanced and centred, ready to begin again the next day.

Court: Tuesday, 8 November

My barrister was on form again, pointing out to my brother-in-law that Peter Darby's and my witness statements are thorough and detailed, making it clear that Ian's second attempt was still confused. He had overlooked the fact that Peter received a document from the company accountants, which Ian had failed to disclose to me much earlier when he should have. Then, pointing out his confusion over another telephone call between him and Peter, she explained that Ian remembers that call, and so does Mr Darby, because Ian was 'especially rude to Mr Darby at the time'.

Ian was in the witness box for most of the day. His cross-examination continued and after that there was re-examination by his own QC before he was eventually invited to stand down. There was then a long, complicated discussion about timetabling, and other facets of court business, which the judge was required to attend to. It seemed to the layman that it was an intricate type of juggling act but with no humour attached, just the poignancy and pain attributed to such events. I remember being terrified when we were listening to the proposed timetable that this would be hanging over my head for weeks and weeks. It did not bode well.

There was one light moment, when the judge and my barrister were trying to find a way through, which would be agreed by everyone involved.

After many minutes of reasoning and timetable juggling, my barrister said, "Your Lordship's patience is ..."

"Infinite," interjected the judge.

"Indeed," came the reply.

We were going to have to try and conclude the evidence and then wait to return to court when submissions would be given by either side. The extra cost of this worried me deeply as I already knew that my sons and I would lose our homes and every penny we possessed if we lost this case.

It was already a major tragedy for us to have lost such a wonderful husband, father, and protector but at least, so far, our lives had continued along similar lines to that when Malcolm was alive. Our lives would change dramatically if we had to pay the court costs. It was clear that my decision to stand up for the trust, and to oppose my brother-in-law's dictatorial and greedy behaviour, could ruin our financial security completely.

But I was encouraged by the consistent spiral of reassurances I continued to receive from 'spiritual' avenues. Nonetheless, I was pleased to head for solace in Fulham again that evening.

Court: Wednesday, 9 November

Taxi, coffee, church, this was my start every day. I found entering St. Clement Danes each morning helped to calm and steady me. It was therapeutic. I was used now to the routine of going to court. I found it interesting and absorbing but there was no enjoyment, as the fear was so great.

Expert witnesses were called and much of it went completely over my head. Largely, it was about the three-sevenths/four-sevenths split agreed by the Malcolm and his brother, which Ian had virtually ignored in the recent years when it came to paying profits to the trust and me.

And so it went on, as the experts' reports were picked apart and reassembled for the duration of the day.

Court: Thursday, 10 November

The expert witness's evidence continued. At one point there was reference made to a document Malcolm had prepared for me, in the event of his death. I had brought his attention to the fact that if anything were to happen to him then I would not know where to begin looking when it came to our financial position, insurance policies, etc.

For my protection, Malcolm immediately put his affairs in order and listed all financial details for my use in the future should it be necessary. As, sadly, it was. The document was No. 776 in File C.

It was an aide memoire by Malcolm for me; the action of a very solicitous husband saying, "If I go under a bus, you will know where everything is."

It also recorded how the profit was taken out of the business and confirmed that, at that time, the brothers were equal shareholders. My barrister also pointed out that the four-sevenths/three-sevenths division of profits operated even before Malcolm got fifty per cent of the shares and that, until his death, it was Malcolm who was the main link between the company and the accountants.

Following these points, my barrister began to delve deeper, showing examples of the recent disproportionate fiscal history ... reading out figures which clearly proved that Ian received a figure, representing a bonus to himself of 2,770 per cent. And when the expert witness, on behalf of the defence, agreed that this was 'far greater' than the organisations he had used as examples, my barrister's response was immediate saying that it was 'off the scale' and a totally disproportionate remuneration.

She pointed out that the position within CIL, when it came to operating in general, documents prove that Ian would seem to have a conversation with his shaving mirror alone when inviting himself to decide upon the division of profits.

The judge rose and we regrouped in chambers at the end of the day, as usual, and then went on our various ways home. All except the barrister, of course, who would no doubt have to burn the midnight oil for the duration.

A taxi to Fulham and refuge were my aims, as soon as humanly possible. This had been a fraught and frustrating day for me and, although my barrister's performance was valiant and unrelenting, I was still fearful of the outcome.

Court: Friday, 11 November

The judge arrived in court at 10 a.m. and announced that the court would observe the two minutes Remembrance Day silence an hour later.

My barrister continued with her cross-examination of the final defence expert witness. The argument continued, regarding whether or not I had been correct in refusing to accept unsecured loan notes in regard to one of the proposals put to me in respect of the proposed sale of the company. Ever fearful, I had refused.

At one point, the witness pointed out that 'someone else would have been prepared to accept unsecured loan notes', to which my barrister replied like a bullet out of a gun, "So what? There is no point, if I can put it like this, in the herd mentality. Just because somebody else has accepted it, it doesn't mean that it is good for Patricia." (Bravo!)

And so it ground on ... with words reverberating around the room like missiles, terribly polite missiles, of course, but very intense nonetheless. I listened to each and every one. At last both petitioner's and defendant's barristers had made it clear that they had no more questions for the final witness.

The judge, satisfied that they had finished, proceeded to ask the witness a few questions himself. He asked him to look at a specific file and page which contained a sheet of Malcolm's own jottings made in 1992. The judge pointed out a series of figures and asked the witness to verify them at each point. He spoke aloud the details shown on the paper in evidence. There was my own salary, Malcolm's and Ian's, their drawings, dividends paid out, all of which were grossed up to a particular figure, including one allowed for tax.

The judge then pointed out where, in his own jottings, Malcolm had clearly divided the grossed-up figure into "three-sevenths Malcolm, four-sevenths Ian." The judge asked the witness to verify that he could understand the figures and clearly see that this was Malcolm's own record of how the brother's agreement was historically worked out?

The witness agreed.

The judge pointed out once more that the total figure included the grossed-up dividend and he asked the witness if he could see that.

The witness agreed once more.

This single piece of paper clearly proved the way that Malcolm and Ian had agreed to deal with profits in the past. The final split would take the dividends into account along with the salaries and bonuses and then be divided.

The judge was referring to a sheet of paper upon which were Malcolm's own handwritten notes, clearly demonstrating the way in which he had annually worked out the agreed three-sevenths/four-sevenths split of profits, that I had found quite by chance after his death. It was tucked in an old envelope, which he had placed upside down, in the bottom of one of his desk drawers. It fitted closely and looked like a drawer lining.

The judge then asked both prosecution and defence if there were any further questions arising from the final document presented.

There were none.

He then thanked the court saying, "I think that concludes the evidence."

The witness withdrew.

My barrister turned to face us smiling discreetly and whispered, "It seems, Patricia, that Malcolm has been allowed the final word on this matter!"

My heart leapt. This handwritten note had been discovered by me. Ian had visited our home, the weekend following Malcolm's death, and he had stripped it of all contents to do with the company. But in his haste, Ian had missed this! Years later, while searching for as much proof as I could muster to help us fight this case, I discovered it. Now, it had allowed my husband to have the final word.

What a magnificent end to the proceedings!

Epilogue

The judgement found in our favour and was dated 10 March 2006. Ian was ordered to buy our shares in the company and the price had to reflect the excessive remuneration he had paid to himself in the past. This resulted in my sons and I retaining the lifestyle that Malcolm had so carefully crafted for us.

Karen trained to be a teacher for children with special needs but has since decided that nursing is her forte and so has changed to that sphere.

Clare is now running a successful health and life coaching business in Surrey, (www.coachingforaspirations.com), helping others on their 'journey'.

As for me, the writing continues. There are over three hundred poems on file, some for adults and some for children, and I am in the process of launching these under the umbrella title of 'The Mulberry Collection'. I am often asked to read my work at weddings, funerals and similar occasions.

*****

There are several reasons why I have decided to tell my story:

One, I made an unwritten promise to record all that was happening to me, with whoever or whatever was orchestrating the experiences. I now believe that it was so that these notes could be of use to others, who might be undergoing similar spiritual experiences, to reassure them and make the process less fearful.

Two, it is also a David and Goliath story and thought-provoking for all misogynists and bullies who think they are entitled to force their own views upon others, no matter the shame it brings to them, or at what consequence to their vulnerable adversaries.

Finally, it is an important lesson in truth, faith, trust and integrity. For if these are lost, what is one but an empty shell? How could one ever hope to flourish ...

'In Light and in Shade'?

About the Author

Patricia Irvine has always written for pleasure. Prior to being widowed in 1996, while raising her three young sons, Patricia studied photography to LRPS level. Encouraged and facilitated by her generous-hearted husband, she travelled widely and has previously had travel articles published in magazines accompanied by her own photography. Now that she has more time, Patricia hopes, once again, to focus on combining her written work with her photography.

Following the spiritual 'wake up' call prompted by the untimely death of her husband in 1996, Patricia had a break from writing. However, poetry unexpectedly became a new factor in her life, resulting in a substantial body of work, spanning many years. Her work includes poetry with a spiritual theme and, as a confident public speaker; she has been invited to read her poems at spiritual gatherings, funerals, weddings, and other occasions. One of Patricia's poems 'A Gift for Betty Shine' was published in *Shine On-Visions of Life*, ed. Janet Shine, published by HarperCollins UK, 2003.

In 2005, Patricia was commissioned to write and record a book of children's poetry by the Sichuan University Press (China) and, around that time, was also asked to record a CD version of a phonetics and phonology book for them. She was also commissioned to write poems, for artist Tay Kiam Hong's exhibitions 'Sea Creatures 11' and 'Ocean Heartbeats' used in his brochures (8–19 November 2008) and displayed at the Muse House, Katong, Singapore. She has been asked to write for his next exhibition in 2020.

In addition, Patricia has penned three books of poetry; two of children's rhymes and a series of 14 books for her young grandchildren, under the umbrella title of, *The Naughty Magic Parrot*, (for which she is seeking a publisher).

Since her spiritual awakening, Patricia has spent a number of years turning her journals of that very difficult period into this book, *In Light and In Shade*. In June 2018, she was interviewed by *Spirit & Destiny* magazine in the UK, resulting in a three page article about her story. Westfield, Patricia's home which features prominently in the book, also appeared in articles by *The Sunday Times* in 2014 and *Devon Life*, in November 2012.

Patricia lives in Devon, Surrey and Kent in the UK, travelling frequently between the three counties. She has three grown-up sons and five grandsons (aged 7–10).

As a member of the Society for Authors in the UK, a website, to promote Patricia's work, is currently under development and will be up and running shortly. In the meantime, she is a committed correspondent, and readers are welcome to submit any queries regarding the book, via email to patricia@themulberrycollection. co.uk who will respond as swiftly as time and existing commitments allow.

Patricia wishes you enjoyment, encouragement, light and a healing benefit from the words within this book... In Light and In Shade.

If you liked this book, you might also like:

Payment for Passage
by Janie Wells
Embracing the Human Journey
by Janie Wells
The Anne Dialogues
by Guy Needler
Baby It's You
by Maureen McGill
Live From The Other Side
by Maureen McGill & Nola Davis

For more information about any of the above titles, soon to be released titles, or other items in our catalog, write, phone or visit our website:
Ozark Mountain Publishing, Inc.
PO Box 754, Huntsville, AR 72740
479-738-2348
www.ozarkmt.com

For more information about any of the titles published by Ozark Mountain Publishing, Inc., soon to be released titles, or other items in our catalog, write, phone or visit our website:

Ozark Mountain Publishing, Inc.

PO Box 754

Huntsville, AR 72740

479-738-2348/800-935-0045

www.ozarkmt.com

Other Books by Ozark Mountain Publishing, Inc.

Dolores Cannon
A Soul Remembers Hiroshima
Between Death and Life
Conversations with Nostradamus,
    Volume I, II, III
The Convoluted Universe -Book One,
    Two, Three, Four, Five
The Custodians
Five Lives Remembered
Jesus and the Essenes
Keepers of the Garden
Legacy from the Stars
The Legend of Starcrash
The Search for Hidden Sacred Knowledge
They Walked with Jesus
The Three Waves of Volunteers and the
    New Earth
Aron Abrahamsen
Holiday in Heaven
Out of the Archives – Earth Changes
Justine Alessi & M. E. McMillan
Rebirth of the Oracle
Kathryn/Patrick Andries
Naked in Public
Kathryn Andries
The Big Desire
Dream Doctor
Soul Choices: Six Paths to Find Your Life
    Purpose
Soul Choices: Six Paths to Fulfilling
    Relationships
Patrick Andries
Owners Manual for the Mind
Dan Bird
Finding Your Way in the Spiritual Age
Waking Up in the Spiritual Age
Julia Cannon
Soul Speak – The Language of Your Body
Ronald Chapman
Seeing True
Albert Cheung
The Emperor's Stargate
Jack Churchward
Lifting the Veil on the Lost Continent of
    Mu
The Stone Tablets of Mu
Sherri Cortland
Guide Group Fridays
Raising Our Vibrations for the New Age

Spiritual Tool Box
Windows of Opportunity
Patrick De Haan
The Alien Handbook
Paulinne Delcour-Min
Spiritual Gold
Michael Dennis
Morning Coffee with God
God's Many Mansions
Carolyn Greer Daly
Opening to Fullness of Spirit
Anita Holmes
Twidders
Aaron Hoopes
Reconnecting to the Earth
Victoria Hunt
Kiss the Wind
Patricia Irvine
In Light and In Shade
Kevin Killen
Ghosts and Me
Diane Lewis
From Psychic to Soul
Donna Lynn
From Fear to Love
Maureen McGill
Baby It's You
Maureen McGill & Nola Davis
Live from the Other Side
Curt Melliger
Heaven Here on Earth
Henry Michaelson
And Jesus Said – A Conversation
Dennis Milner
Kosmos
Andy Myers
Not Your Average Angel Book
Guy Needler
Avoiding Karma
Beyond the Source – Book 1, Book 2
The Anne Dialogues
The Curators
The History of God
The Origin Speaks
James Nussbaumer
And Then I Knew My Abundance
The Master of Everything
Mastering Your Own Spiritual Freedom

For more information about any of the above titles, soon to be released titles,
or other items in our catalog, write, phone or visit our website:
PO Box 754, Huntsville, AR 72740
479-738-2348/800-935-0045
www.ozarkmt.com

Other Books by Ozark Mountain Publishing, Inc.

Sherry O'Brian
Peaks and Valleys
Riet Okken
The Liberating Power of Emotions
Gabrielle Orr
Akashic Records: One True Love
Let Miracles Happen
Victor Parachin
Sit a Bit
Nikki Pattillo
A Spiritual Evolution
Children of the Stars
Rev. Grant H. Pealer
A Funny Thing Happened on the
    Way to Heaven
Worlds Beyond Death
Victoria Pendragon
Born Healers
Feng Shui from the Inside, Out
Sleep Magic
The Sleeping Phoenix
Michael Perlin
Fantastic Adventures in Metaphysics
Walter Pullen
Evolution of the Spirit
Debra Rayburn
Let's Get Natural with Herbs
Charmian Redwood
A New Earth Rising
Coming Home to Lemuria
David Rivinus
Always Dreaming
Richard Rowe
Imagining the Unimaginable
M. Don Schorn
Elder Gods of Antiquity
Legacy of the Elder Gods
Gardens of the Elder Gods
Reincarnation...Stepping Stones of Life
Garnet Schulhauser
Dance of Eternal Rapture
Dance of Heavenly Bliss

Dancing Forever with Spirit
Dancing on a Stamp
Manuella Stoerzer
Headless Chicken
Annie Stillwater Gray
Education of a Guardian Angel
The Dawn Book
Work of a Guardian Angel
Blair Styra
Don't Change the Channel
Who Catharted
Natalie Sudman
Application of Impossible Things
L.R. Sumpter
Judy's Story
The Old is New
We Are the Creators
Jim Thomas
Tales from the Trance
Nicholas Vesey
Living the Life-Force
Janie Wells
Embracing the Human Journey
Payment for Passage
Dennis Wheatley/ Maria Wheatley
The Essential Dowsing Guide
Maria Wheatley
Druidic Soul Star Astrology
Jacquelyn Wiersma
The Zodiac Recipe
Sherry Wilde
The Forgotten Promise
Lyn Willmoth
A Small Book of Comfort
Stuart Wilson & Joanna Prentis
Atlantis and the New Consciousness
Beyond Limitations
The Essenes -Children of the Light
The Magdalene Version
Power of the Magdalene
Robert Winterhalter
The Healing Christ

For more information about any of the above titles, soon to be released titles,
or other items in our catalog, write, phone or visit our website:
PO Box 754, Huntsville, AR 72740
479-738-2348/800-935-0045
www.ozarkmt.com